The Spirit of the School

Also available from Continuum

Education and Community, Dianne Gereluk

Is Religious Education Possible?, Michael Hand

Key Ideas in Educational Research, David Scott and Marlene Morrison

Philosophy of Education, Richard Pring

Schools and Religions, Julian Stern

Theory of Education, David Turner

The Spirit
of the School

JULIAN STERN

continuum

Continuum International Publishing Group
The Tower Building, 11 York Road, London SE1 7NX
80 Maiden Lane, Suite 704, New York NY 10038

www.continuumbooks.com

British Library Cataloguing-in-Publication Data
A catalogue record for this book is available from the British Library.

ISBN: 978-1-8470-6109-6 (hardcover)

Library of Congress Cataloging-in-Publication Data
A catalog record for this book is available from the Library of Congress.

Typeset by Kenneth Burnley, Wirral, Cheshire
Printed by the MPG Books Group in the UK

Contents

Acknowledgements   ix
Preface   xiii

Chapter 1: Introduction: exploring humanity, spirituality and
                        religions in school   1
   The project   1
   Spirituality to and into dualism   2
   After dualism   5
   Spirituality overcoming dualism   7
   Defining spirituality again   11
   Policy on the spiritual   12
   Spirituality, religion and ethos   15
   Researching humanity: community, learning, and dialogue   18
   The structure of the book   21

Chapter 2: School communities and the possibility of friendship   23
   Introduction   23
   Community   24
   Friendship   28
      Friendship, freedom and fear   30
      Friendship and irreplaceability   32
      Friendship and difference and inequality 33
   The spirit of the schools   36
      Close to me   36
      Working together: friends in deed   40
   Conclusion   45

Chapter 3: Learning together in the creative school   **47**

     Introduction: inclusion and creativity   47
         The meaning of inclusion   47
         The meaning of creativity   50
     Inclusive learning   51
         Weak inclusion   51
         Strong inclusion   52
         Inclusion of the curriculum and of people   54
     Making sense: the spirit of creativity   56
         Agency, originality and value   57
         Creativity, discipline and authenticity   59
     The spirit of the schools   63
         Inclusion in and out of groups   65
         Made up   70
     Conclusion   72

Chapter 4: Monologue or dialogue? Stepping away from the abyss   **75**

     Introduction   75
     Dialogue and duellism   78
     Existential vocationalism and abysmal dialogue   82
     Lessons in dialogue   85
     Dialogue within and beyond schools   88
     The spirit of the schools   91
         Dialogue within the school: silence and being there   92
         Dialogue beyond the school: dead hamsters   96
     Conclusion for persons   100

Chapter 5: 'Great-souled' schooling and the spirit of the leader   **101**

     Introduction   101
     Avoiding loneliness   104
     Solitude and privacy for school leaders   113
     Crafty leadership   117
     From virtuosity to virtue: magnanimity and humility   125
     Conclusion   133

Chapter 6: Conclusion: understanding and promoting the spirit of the school **135**

Introduction 135

The virtue and value of research 136

Vicious research, stealing or ignoring souls 137

Bad poetry 144

Virtuous research 147

    The virtue of sincerity 147

    The virtues of humility, modesty and openness to criticism 150

    The virtues of respect, courage and trust 152

    The virtues of kindness and truthfulness 155

Valuable research 156

Hoping for the spirit of the school 160

    Defining the spirit of the school 160

    What more is needed to promote the spirit of the school? 161

Appendix: The *Spirit of the School* methodology and toolkit **165**

Introduction 165

Guidance to participants 165

    The Salmon Line 167

    What is typically said? 168

    Friendship, membership and thought circles 170

    Interview questions 171

    Additional information for adult participants 174

    Additional information for pupils 176

    Information about you: staff 177

    Information about you: pupils 177

    Consent form for institutions/organisations 178

    Consent form for individual adults 179

    Consent form for the parents/carers of individual young people 180

    Consent form for individual young people 181

Research schedule: questions and activities 182

Bibliography **191**

Index **201**

Acknowledgements

First acknowledgements must go to the researchers and researched. The team of people involved in various ways in the research reported here included co-researchers with whom all aspects of the project were discussed and clarified: Marie Stern and Sarah James (of the University of Hull), Sue Holmes (of the East Riding of Yorkshire and the York Diocesan Board of Education), Yu Huen, Pang I Wah and Timothy Yuen Wai Wa (from the Hong Kong Institute of Education). Brenda Wilson organised most of the visits to schools, and Kaylash Gooljar completed most of the transcriptions (both working for the University of Hull). A total of 144 school staff and pupils in 13 schools consented to and participated in the research, in the UK and in Hong Kong, and I am indebted to them all. Although these participants cannot, for reasons of research ethics, be named in the book (the names of people and their schools are replaced by pseudonyms), it is hoped that they may recognise themselves in the research – either through quotations or through their influence on the arguments as presented here. Participating schools will receive individual reports on their schools, which will be additional thanks to people in those schools.

Many colleagues and friends from outside the small research team discussed the issues reported in the book. At the University of Hull, these included Mike Bottery (who inspired Chapters 5 and 6), Paul Dearey (influential on Chapter 1), Margaret Holloway (especially on bereavement), Chris Botton (on music) and Wilf McSherry (who has since moved to Staffordshire University, on health), along with other members of the Centre for Spirituality Studies, and David Glenister and colleagues in mental health nursing (on Buber and dialogue). Nick Owen and Michele Crichton both completed doctorates at Hull, on creativity and inclusion respectively, and their work contributed significantly to Chapter 3. In the Hong Kong Institute of Education, there was Wong Ping Ho (of the Centre for Religious and Spirituality Education, on 'mundane' spirituality), Wong Ping Man (on policy), Samuel Leong (on creativity), and a number of other colleagues who participated in policy research conferences and colloquia in Hull and Hong Kong. Janet Orchard and Terence Copley of the University of Oxford discussed the project from its earliest stages. Members of the East Riding of Yorkshire SACRE (Standing Advisory Council on Religious Education), and the Christian Education Research Committee, helped clarify the research. Participants in several academic conferences challenged and encouraged in a number of ways. These conferences included BERA (the British Educational Research Association, London 2007, Edinburgh 2008), EERA (the European Educational Research Association, Gothenburg 2008), and ISREV (the International Seminar on Religious Education and Values, Ankara 2008, with particularly helpful comments from Jeff Astley, Sherry Blumberg, Mario D'Souza and Reinhold Boschki).

There have also been discussions about various elements of this research in Old Saybrook, Connecticut (2008), at the John Macmurray Fellowship (2005), in EFTRE (the European Forum for Teachers of Religious Education, Helsinki 2004), during various Westhill Trust Seminars (2004 onwards), and at a number of meetings in Hull, the East Riding of Yorkshire, and North Lincolnshire. Others who have influenced the research include John Hull (The Queen's Foundation, Birmingham), Peter Schreiner (the Comenius-Institut, Münster), Chris Sink (Seattle Pacific University), Jonathan Smith (Anglia Ruskin University), Jeremy Taylor (Chichester Diocesan Director of Education), Chris Hay (University of Lincoln, on architecture). Pam Rauchwerger discussed and proofread almost everything.

David Hay (University of Aberdeen) inspired through his books on relational spirituality. It was the title of his influential book with Rebecca Nye, *The Spirit of the Child*, that led to the title of this book (i.e. *The Spirit of the School*). Unusually, this is a book generated almost entirely from the curiosity surrounding the words making up its title, so the influence of Hay's earlier title is that much more significant.

Although the book began while I worked for the University of Hull, I recently moved to York St John University. The stimulation and excitement generated by staff and students at both universities have driven this project, and will continue to drive this project in the future.

Marie Stern is a co-researcher on the project, and has had to live not only with the project but also with the book's author for years. Over six centuries ago, Chaucer captured the mild annoyance of family and friends of an author, who, coming home from work, 'sittest at another book' until the eyes are dimmed (*daswed*). I therefore leave it to Chaucer's *House of Fame* (quoted in Webb 2007, p 135, and at en.wikisource.org/wiki/

The_House_of_Fame) to describe better than I could what Marie has had to put up with:

> For whan thy labour doon al is,
> And hast mad thy rekeninges,
> In stede of reste and newe thynges,
> Thou goost hoom to thy hous anoon;
> And also domb as any stoon,
> Thou sittest at another book,
> Tyl fully daswed is thy loke,
> And lyvest thus as an heremyte,
> Although thyn abstinence ys lyte.

Julian Stern
Faculty of Education & Theology
York St John University
September 2008

Preface

If you can't say anything nice, don't say anything at all.
 (Molly, aged 6, Afton Church of England primary school, UK)

Four education professionals sit around a table at a conference. We are asked to put words on cards into a diamond shape, with the most valued word for themselves, as educationists, at the top, and the others arranged below. One of the cards has 'tradition' on it, and this makes the three people argue. One says that tradition should be at or near the top, as tradition is so often ignored in schools, with pupils having too little connection to traditions, to authentic art, literature and sacred texts. Another says that tradition has been so damaging, with pupils and their families embattled and entrenched, that the word should be at the very bottom of the diamond. Two others want the word in the middle, useful but not dominant, already addressed in their schools and not in a damaging way. All are convincing for their schools, their contexts, themselves. What is the correct answer? They have all understood the significance of tradition, and all want to work with it in different ways. Schools are not abstract ideas, they exist in real places. All four education professionals may have been right, for their contexts.

The spirit of the school is also particular and emerges from the place and the time in which the school exists. As the architect Zumthor says,

When I come across a building that has developed a special presence in connection with the place it stands in, I sometimes feel that it is imbued with an inner tension that refers to something over and above the place itself.

 It seems to be part of the essence of its place, and at the same time it speaks of the world as a whole.

 When an architectural design draws solely from tradition and only repeats the dictates of its site, I sense a lack of a genuine concern with the world and the emanations of contemporary life. If a work of architecture speaks only of contemporary trends and sophisticated visions without triggering vibrations in its place, this work is not anchored in its site, and I miss the specific gravity of the ground it stands on. (Zumthor 2006, pp. 41–2)

This book is an attempt to understand and promote the spirit of the school, the spirit of particular schools, and it is a response and a celebration. It is a response to long-standing questions about what makes a 'good' school, a good particular school in a particular place. A response, for example, to parents and carers asking what school to choose for their children, and teachers and other professionals asking how to improve their schools. The response is not, I believe, generated by league tables of examination results, how well-dressed the pupils are, and whether the school buildings are ivy-clad or ultra-modern. However, it is easier to dismiss some kinds of response than it is to say something helpful.

It is always useful, when finding out about a school, to look around the school, listen carefully to what is being said, and talk with people in the school, during a normal school day. That is a better way of coming to understand the school than looking at statistics, uniforms, or design features, but it is a rather unreliable process, as it depends on the person doing the looking and listening. What should you look for and listen to? This book tries to answer that question. The answer is personal. The poet Rumi says, 'If anyone wants to know what "spirit" is, . . . / lean your head toward him or her. / Keep your face there close. / *Like this*' (Rumi 1995, p. 136).

As for the celebration, finding out about the spirit of the school involved talking with pupils, teachers and headteachers. What they said is a cause for celebration. Despite all the pressures, all the targets, all the controls, what came over was familiar to anyone who has worked with children. School staff are working hard to help children learn and grow, based on deeply felt principles that have not come pre-packaged from government websites. Children care about the people they are with, adults and children, and are fascinated by learning from those people. It might be thought that there is nothing new in that. It certainly is a message that might have been heard fifty, a hundred, or a thousand years ago. What is new to me is that while reading the transcripts, all I had previously read about the corruption of young people, and the destruction of professionalism, seemed like hopeless pessimism. The spirit of the school is alive and well. Best of all, it is familiar. That is to be celebrated.

So, what is the spirit of the school? What of the school promotes the spirit of the school? What do pupils and teachers and others do to contribute to the spirit of the school? This book considers the spirit of the school, ways of discovering the spirit of the school, and ways of comparing how much spirit there is to be found in different schools. Understanding spirituality is not the same as understanding religion, yet neither is possible without the other, so there will be consideration of a number of religious issues, too.

Although related, the spirit of the school is not the same as the school's 'ethos'. The difference between 'spirit' and 'ethos' in this context is that ethos refers to the character and dispositions of members of an institution, a description that is essentially internal to the institution and indicates the potential of the organisation. Spirit, in contrast, refers to transcendence. Spirit goes beyond individual people or individual institutions, and is an active or 'lively' characteristic incorporating events and emotions. Ethos is essentially internal, passive and continuing; spirit is essentially transcendent, active and changing. The spirit of the school is not easy to capture, but must be understood if schools themselves are to be understood.

Research into spirituality involves, I believe, investigating three dimensions of humanity: community, learning, and dialogue. The spirit of the school is generated by and in turn supports and promotes all of these. It is underpinned, that is, by the meaning of life. Community is described by relationships, including opportunities for friendship. Learning is a creative process, with school learning centred on becoming human. Through dialogue people make community and learn: dialogue is how people come to be themselves by relating to others. Schools are generally hierarchical, and in such schools, the spirit of the school will also be in part determined by the nature of the hierarchy, investigated here in terms of the leadership practised in the school, in particular, more magnanimous or 'great-souled' leadership.

This book is an academic book and a professional book. One of the peer groups to which I am proud to belong is that of university-based academics studying education and the meaning of life. Many years ago, when I was a student studying philosophy, people would occasionally ask me what my philosophy of life was. At the time, I thought that a very poor question, as I saw philosophy as an approach, a set of processes, an attempt to be clear. Now, with some embarrassment, I have to admit that it is exactly the right question to ask of philosophers. So this book is a book that tries to place what I believe in a context of academic researchers, philosophers and psychologists and educationalists, those studying schooling and those studying religion and spirituality. It is a conversation with long-dead members of the academy, including Aristotle, the original academician, and with those who are still very much alive. However, I am also a school teacher, and the peer group of school-based professionals is as important for this book as that of academics. Teachers, headteachers, and pupils are voiced in this book, albeit pseudonymously, and the teaching profession is intended as the audience most needed for the work represented here. Supporting and promoting the spirit of the school is the work of teachers, and I hope that what follows, here, will help with that task.

Chapter 1

Introduction: exploring humanity, spirituality and religions in school

The egotistic individual in civil society may in his non-sensuous imagination and lifeless abstraction inflate himself to the size of an atom, i.e., to an un-related, self-sufficient, wantless, absolutely full, blessed being.
(Marx and Engels, in Selsam and Martel 1963, p. 311)

The project

This chapter is an introduction to the book and to the *Spirit of the School* project. It touches on what spirituality is, what it could mean to promote spirituality, how spirituality might be investigated, and, as a result of that investigation, how the idea of spirituality might be further clarified. These topics raise important existential questions, research questions, and questions about pedagogy and education policy. That is why there is both an academic and a professional audience intended for the book. It follows on from *Schools and Religions: Imagining the Real* (Stern 2007a), a book that explored the nature of schooling and promoted the idea of action philosophy. That book ended with the claim that action philosophy is good to know: the point, however, is to change. Here, the change is built in to the book, with children and adults explaining, for example, how their school can become more of a community, and providing the stimulus for further developing the spirit of the school.

The research explores theories of learning from the social constructivist tradition, theories of community from the philosophy of John Macmurray, and theories of dialogue from the philosophy of Martin Buber. Those theories suggest that schools are forms of community like families, friendship groups, and religious communities, in which people are treated as ends in themselves and not as means to further ends. Schools are unlike other social groups that are, typically, driven by external aims. An approach to spirituality is also developed from those theories. Spirituality is seen as essentially relational. The spirit exists in the between. More of that, later. There are many more possibilities for spiritual development in schools as dialogic learning communities than in other social

1

groups, given these approaches to schooling and to spirituality, and there is likely to be a greater impact on schools, too, of the spirituality of members of school communities.

Having outlined the purpose of the project, the theories of schooling and the approach to spirituality, the rest of the book explores and further justifies those theories. By the book's conclusion, it is hoped that the theories are further clarified and strengthened. It is also hoped that education will be improved and that schools will be in a position to become more spirited.

Spirituality to and into dualism

The term 'spirituality' is well described by Swinton as a 'slippery concept', at least 'within Western culture' (Swinton 2001, p. 12). Nesbitt reminds readers 'of Priestley's image for attempting to define the spiritual of sending a child to "collect wind in a jar so that it can be examined"' (Nesbitt 2004, p. 126). Attempted definition 'is not only futile but totally counter-productive' because 'it is a characteristic of spirit and the spiritual that it is dynamic' (Priestley, quoted by Wong in Ota and Chater 2007, p. 73). Nevertheless, some kind of definition is worth considering. It is important to be clear, if that is possible, though it is equally important to avoid oversimplifying what are deeply held and fully lived philosophies and ways of life. As Wittgenstein says, slipping along may seem an ideal way to travel, but sometimes, when we want to walk, we need to get 'back to the rough ground' (Wittgenstein 1958, p. 46e, applied to education by Dunne 1997, title and xi). Here, there will be an account of various approaches to spirituality, and a position on the subject that is used in the rest of the book. It is not an attempt at a comprehensive historical or contemporary account, as either of those would need entire books of encyclopædic proportions. Instead, it is an attempt to put in historical and contemporary contexts the approach to spirituality used in and tested by the *Spirit of the School* project. The research reported in the following chapters will clarify the project's approach to spirituality: the foundational issue, of what spirituality is, will be explored throughout the book and in the book's conclusion there is, finally, a definition of the spirit of the school.

There are four themes in the current chapter: pre-dualism, dualism, materialism (associated also with positivism) and post-dualism (variously described as holistic and/or relational theories). Each is named, here, using philosophical language, but all are also embedded in various religious traditions. A useful and characteristic philosophical starting point is the work of Aristotle, who wrote *On the Soul* (Aristotle 1984, pp. 641–92) to provide his own account of contemporary theories of the soul or spirit. The account would be familiar to many writing in the twenty-first century, with debates reported on whether the soul is a separate substance in its own right, and if so, what kind of substance. Unlike later dualist philosophies, the philosophers reported by Aristotle generally identified four substances, four types of 'stuff', in the world: water, air, fire and earth. The soul was described by Hippo as being of water, by Diogenes as being of air, and by Democritus as being of fire. Spirit as breath is perhaps the most popular of those theories in later philosophy, and is embedded in the words themselves, as '[t]he term spirit comes from the Latin *spiritus* (Hebrew *ruach*, Greek *pneuma*), meaning breath, wind, and even life principle' (Robinson et al. 2003, p. 21). There are also popular senses of the spirit as fire, as in the 'spark of life', and the spirit as water, as in Emoto 2004 and Marks 2004 for whom 'one cannot understand water unless it is viewed as a mediator – not only between life and death, but also between the physical and the spiritual worlds'. Aristotle goes on to say that only one of the four substances is not attributed to the soul: 'earth has found no supporter unless we count as such those who have declared soul to be, or to be compounded of, *all* the elements' (Aristotle 1984, p. 646, original emphasis). The soul is therefore called 'incorporeal' (Aristotle 1984, p. 646), or not of the earth but possibly of water or air or fire. The term 'incorporeal' has been much used in later philosophies to mean something quite different: that the spirit is not of any material, as in 'our intention . . . [is] to explore the most elemental human instinct to engage with that which is non-material' (West-Burnham and Huws Jones 2007, p. 17), or not of the planet Earth, as in '[t]he secular assumption that there is no reality beyond the physical world is ultimately sterile' (Hall and Taylor 2005, p. 7).

It was the term 'incorporeal' that influenced modern philosophy, especially that of Descartes. Descartes' approach also followed a tradition of Gnostic Christian thought, with Gnosticism being assuredly dualist and influential despite its rejection from the Christian mainstream. As the theologian Thatcher says, dualist traditions right up to the guidance on spirituality provided by UK governments in the twentieth century, 'consciously commend the dualism between body and spirit which Christianity has had to struggle against for most of its history' (in Astley and Francis 1996, p. 123). Descartes (notably in the texts collected in Descartes 1912) presents a model of argument for dualism, separating body from mind, with mind being the same substance as spirit: 'because we have no conception of the body as thinking in any way at all, we have reason to believe that every kind of thought present in us belongs to the soul' (quoted from Descartes' *Passions of the Soul*, in Lokhorst 2006). It is worth summarising his argument here, while avoiding some of the details of the debates on Cartesian philosophy that have been the staple of philosophy classes for several hundred years. He starts from the famous proof of the existence of thinking, based on the idea that many things could be doubted, but if doubting is going on, then thinking is going on. *Cogito ergo sum*, I think therefore I am, which adds 'I' into the argument. Descartes then goes on to a proof that God exists, because you can conceive of something perfect, and the idea could not be more perfect than the reality. From the existence of a perfect and therefore good God, he went on to prove that other things, including bodily substance, exist, as only a malign or imperfect god would have tricked people into thinking that such things exist.

Descartes' philosophy has an instability at its heart, and this instability is what has led to its being correctly seen as the stimulus for much of modern philosophy. It appears to be a radically dualist philosophy, with two quite distinct substances, mind and body. As Barbour says, it is 'difficult to imagine how two such dissimilar substances could possibly interact' (Barbour 2000, p. 131). Yet Descartes could imagine how this happened in people: through the pineal gland, this being the point at which mind could affect body. Though the soul is described as being joined to the body as a whole, 'nevertheless there is a certain part of the body where it exercises its functions more particularly than in all the others, [. . . which] is not the heart at all, or the whole of the brain [. . . but] is a certain very small gland situated in the middle of the brain's substance' (quoted in Lokhorst 2006). He continues to describe the interaction, as '[t]he slightest movements on the part of this gland may alter very greatly the course of these spirits, and conversely any change, however slight, taking place in the course of the spirits may do much to change the movements of the gland' (quoted in Lockhorst 2006). Hence, 'my mind and body compose a certain unity' (Descartes 1912, p. 135). It is not Descartes' most convincing account, as noted by his contemporary Spinoza, who responded with one of philosophy's great put-downs: 'Such is the doctrine of this illustrious philosopher (in so far as I gather it from his own words); it is one which, had it been less ingenious, I could hardly believe to have proceeded from so great a man' (Spinoza 1955, p. 246).

The implausibility of Descartes' 'scientific proof' of the interaction of mind and body at the pineal gland (like the implausibility of so many of his scientific conclusions) should not blind one to his consistent belief in an interacting-dualism, not recognised by Barbour or by many who describe him simply as a dualist. In this way, Descartes may be seen as leading to the dialectical philosophies of Kant and then Hegel. Others treat the strength of Descartes' proof of the existence of thinking or mind, and its primacy over body, and the weakness of his proof of the existence of body, as a version of idealism (as in Costello 2002, p. 9). Still others concentrate on his arguments for body being sufficiently independent of mind. The substance mind is restricted to God and to people, and people rarely use their minds in such as way as to affect their bodies. This is used to found a materialist, positivist, world view, and as grounds for philosophical empiricism. In religious terms, Descartes' work might be seen as leading to a materialist atheism. As Armstrong describes it, 'Descartes saw the human being as the sole living denizen of an inert universe; Hobbes imagined God retreating from the world, and Nietzsche declared that God was dead' (Armstrong 2000, p. 365).

It is therefore possible to see how the apparently dualist Descartes also encouraged materialism (because he helped show how most human and all other activity could be mechanically explained), idealism (because there's a better proof of the existence of thinking than of anything else), and dialectical philosophy (because there seems to be a battle between mind and body). This may be framed positively: Descartes provided a dense but richly ambiguous philosophy, whose minute inconsistencies exploded into the variety of modern philosophy, rather as the material universe is said to have exploded, at the Big Bang, into the rich and diverse universe we currently inhabit. It may also be framed negatively, as in Conford's account from his introduction to a collection of writings of Macmurray. 'Descartes' starting-point led inevitably to atheism', he says, but since Macmurray 'considered atheism false, it followed that the Cartesian mode of thought must be mistaken' (Conford in Macmurray 1996, p. 21). Accepting 'the splitting of experience into mind and matter, the spiritual and the secular, ideal freedom and material subservience to law' would mean that religion, 'if not rejected outright as illusory, becomes a question of pure subjectivity, while the organization of everyday life is surrendered to scientists, managers and technocrats' (Conford in Macmurray 1996, p. 21).

After dualism

Materialist accounts of the universe do not necessarily reject the spiritual. A wholly materialist approach to spirituality may be built on the scientific rational view that everything can be explained in material, substantive terms – or at least has the potential to be explained in this way even if science has not yet yielded tangible evidence to support its theories. Materialists thus view 'spirit' as composed of matter just as the physical body is, and the term 'spirit' may be regarded as a cultural and linguistic synonym for emotion and other higher functioning aspects of the mind (as described in Mason 2000). Writing a book with the subtitle *The Biology of the Human Spirit*, Hay seems close to this materialist tradition, with spirituality 'a built-in, biologically structured dimension of the lives of all members of the human species' (Hay 2006, p. 49). Hay also notes the views of the materialist Marx, saying that 'in the 1844 manuscripts he [Marx] revised Feuerbach's picture of species-being as a kind of inbuilt human solidarity (or relational consciousness) by adding a dynamic, socially constructed aspect' (Hay 2006, p. 229). Essentially human, essentially dynamic, essentially social, Marx's view is explicitly a rejection of the absolute individualism of Stirner, whose philosophy is an extreme version of Cartesian solipsism. Marx's views, early in his life, are worthy precursors of the relational and post-dualist philosophies of the twentieth century. In a passage co-written with Engels in 1844, Marx notes that '[t]he members of civil society are not atoms', as '[t]he specific property of the atom is that it has no properties and is therefore not connected with being outside it by any relations determined by its own natural necessity' (in Selsam and Martel 1963, pp. 310–11).

> The atom has no needs, it is self-sufficient; the world outside it is absolute vacuum, i.e., it is contentless, senseless, meaningless, just because the atom has all its fullness in itself. The egotistic individual in civil society may in his non-sensuous imagination and lifeless abstraction inflate himself to the size of an atom, i.e., to an unrelated, self-sufficient, wantless, absolutely full, blessed being. Unblessed sensuous reality does not bother about his imagination; each of his senses compels him to believe in the existence of the world and the individuals outside him and even his profane stomach reminds him every day that the world outside him is not empty, but is what really fills. Every activity and property of his being, every one of his vital urges becomes a need, a necessity, which his self-seeking transforms into seeking for other things and human beings outside him. (Marx and Engels *The Holy Family*, in Selsam and Martel 1963, p. 311)

Among the many striking features of this passage, one worth highlighting is the materialist Marx rejecting the atomistic, positivist, impersonal materialism by which his later philosophy is so often characterised. Hay himself uses the writing of Marx to demonstrate how the spiritual cannot survive when 'privatised' in an individualistic world. 'Using the language of Emmanuel Levinas, the privatising of spiritual awareness makes it easier to lose touch with the 'face' of the other and hence of the sense of unconditional obligation' (Hay 2006, p. 231).

As Sacks describes it, '[o]ne of the governing presuppositions of modern thought was the concept of the isolated or atomic self, the "I" with which thought and action supposedly began', as in Descartes, Hobbes, and Adam Smith (Sacks 2003, p. 150). 'One of the great intellectual discoveries of the twentieth century', he continues, 'is that this "I" is a fiction, or at the very least an abstraction' (Sacks 2003, p. 150). From the social psychology of George Herbert Mead, for whom personal identity develops in conversation with 'significant others', to Wittgenstein's rejection of 'private language', the personal is seen to be other than the individual. Indeed, the biblical account of Adam and Eve is used by Sacks to demonstrate the antiquity of this view. Adam, seeing Eve for the first time, says

> 'This is now bone of my bone, flesh of my flesh; she shall be called woman [*ishah*] because she was taken from man [*ish*].' What is lost in translation is that biblical Hebrew has two words for man, *adam* and *ish. Adam* (meaning, taken from the earth, *adamah*) signifies man, the biological species. *Ish* means roughly the same as the English word, 'person'. The subtle point of the biblical text is that this verse is the first in which the word *ish* appears. Adam must pronounce the name of his wife before he can pronounce his own. He must say 'Thou' before he can say 'I'. (Sacks 2003, pp. 150–1)

That move from self to other is described by Wright in his account of the development of spiritual education. That development starts with authors such as Gadamer, Erricker, and Jackson who write of 'the horizon of the child', and moves outwards to those who write of 'the horizons of alternative spiritual stories' (Wright 1999, pp. 43–4). The dialectic of the argument moves to a third stage, 'the emergence of spiritual literacy' (Wright 1999, p. 45), by which the different stories can be discussed. It is the purpose of spiritual education, in this model, to develop 'a spiritual literacy grounded in academically sound, aesthetically informed, morally responsible and spiritually sensitive discourse' (Wright 1999, p. 47). It is an attempt to overcome solipsism and dualism, and therefore also introduces the whole tradition of philosophers attempting this same movement.

Spirituality overcoming dualism

From the pre-dualist Aristotle, to dualism and its successor, materialism, the fourth and final stage of this account of the spirit may be described as post-dualist, and is more often known as relational or holistic. Marx, Hay and Sacks have already been characterised in this way, and a further important example is that of Macmurray. He stressed the need to go beyond Cartesian dualism, as that is both flawed and leads inevitably to a materialist atheism (see especially Macmurray 1991a, pp. 18–23 and 74–81, and see also McIntosh 2001, Stern 2001b). Macmurray's concern with a spirituality made of personal relationships and with how people form communities is a philosophical approach with a lot in common with more recent 'care ethics' theorists. This has been pointed out by Almond (in Fergusson and Dower 2002, p. 160), who writes of Macmurray's contemporary relevance despite, regrettably, his less fashionable position in professional philosophy when he was alive. Noddings is one of the leading contemporary care ethicists and a philosopher of schooling – and nursing – as caring, community and relationships (e.g. Noddings 2003a, Chapter 8 on 'character and spirituality', Noddings 1984, Edwards 2001, p. 109 and pp. 114–19). She is therefore an important signifier of the influence of explicitly post-dualist accounts such as that of Macmurray.

Macmurray's approach to spirituality is also related to that of Buber, whose philosophy of spirituality is likewise centred on relationships and, for him, the dialogue by which relationships are made (see Buber 1958 *passim*, Friedman 1999, and Friedman in Buber 2002a). Buber considered the problem of treating people as 'it', matched by an equally problematic approach to a private life of feelings, a division also described by Sennett (1978) as created in the nineteenth-century cities of Europe and America. Both positions need to be overcome. In modern society, he said, in a passage reminiscent of that of Marx and Engels quoted above, all too often:

> Institutions are 'outside,' where all sorts of aims are pursued, where a man works, negotiates, bears influence, undertakes, concurs, organises, conducts business, officiates, preaches. They are the tolerably well-ordered and to some extent harmonious structure, in which, with the manifold help of men's brains and hands, the process of affairs is fulfilled.
>
> Feelings are 'within,' where life is lived and man recovers from institutions. Here the spectrum of the emotions dances before the interested glance. Here a man's liking and hate and pleasure are indulged and his pain if it is not too severe. Here he is at home and stretches himself out in his rocking-chair. (Buber 1958, pp. 62–3)

This is inadequate as 'the separated *It* of institutions is an animated clod without soul [a translation of the word 'golem'] and the separated *I* of feelings an uneasily-fluttering soul-bird' (Buber 1958, p. 63). What is missing is the sense of a person: 'institutions know only the specimen, feelings only the "object"; neither knows the person, or mutual life' (Buber 1958, p. 63). The move is from *individual* to *person*. Buber concludes his recorded conversation with the therapist Rogers, 'if I may say expressly Yes and No to certain phenomena, I'm *against* individuals and *for* persons' (Buber 1998, p. 174). Buber and Macmurray both describe relations as at the heart of spirituality. We only know people through particular kinds of relationships and we only *are* people in and through our relationships. Knowing the person is an *action*, not a 'state of mind' but a kind of 'imaginative leap' to the reality of the other person. The action of knowing is therefore an act of 'inclusion': 'It is inclusion – imagining the real – that banishes the illusion that we are confined to our skins or our own private experiences, as so many people think' (Friedman 1999, p. 410).

Buber, like Sennett, blames 'modernity', and Taylor provides a compelling historical-cultural account of the nature of emergence of the 'individual' in the modern world. 'The first source of worry', he begins, 'is individualism' (Taylor 1991, p. 2). Worrying, perhaps, but not without its positive features, as 'people are no longer sacrificed to the demands of supposedly sacred orders that transcend them' and '[m]odern freedom came about through the discrediting of such orders' (Taylor 1991, pp. 2–3). However, such individualism and 'freedom' ends up with a 'society structured around instrumental reason' that 'can be seen as imposing a great loss of freedom, on both individuals and the group – because it is not just our social decisions that are shaped by these forces' (Taylor 1991, p. 9). It may seem as though, as Bloom argues, '[e]verybody has his or her own "values," and about these it is impossible to argue' (Taylor 1991, p. 12), and yet even this can be positively framed in terms of 'being true to oneself' or 'authentic', which has value. Authenticity, according to Taylor, should be 'retrieved' from those who see it as entirely individualistic, 'justify[ing] ignoring whatever transcends the self' (Taylor 1991, p. 22).

The idea of authenticity may be a modern 'turn' in culture, developed by writers such as Rousseau at the end of the eighteenth century, but 'it can be seen just as a continuation and intensification of the development inaugurated by Saint Augustine, who saw the road to God as passing through our own reflexive awareness of ourselves' (Taylor 1991, pp. 26–7). It is a reflexive movement encouraged by psychotherapeutic interventions, themselves characteristic of modernity. As Guignon says of the 'authenticity' movement and therapy:

For the many professional therapists who have learned from the insights of the British psychoanalyst D W Winnicot, the program of transformation involves therapeutic interaction aimed at freeing

clients from the constricting demands of the "false self" to enable them
to access and express the "true self" within. (Guignon 2004, p. 6)

Modernity may, as Macmurray and Buber say, have created an empty
individualism, but the way out of this must recognise the 'inward turn'
described by Taylor, whilst avoiding 'the dark side of individualism . . .
which both flattens and narrows our lives, makes them poorer in meaning,
and less concerned with others or society' (Taylor 1991, p. 4), an entirely
self-serving 'true self' as an end-point. Contemporary research on spirituality needs to 'admit' and work through this 'inwardness' at the same time as
it can overcome the damaging forms of individualism. Relational theories
must incorporate what might be called the relationship with oneself.

Contemporary empirical research on children's spirituality undertaken
by Hay and Nye (Hay with Nye 2006, Hay 2002) describes spirituality in
terms of relational consciousness, and this incorporates and goes beyond
the relationship to the self, the '[w]ho am I?' question, by working outwards
to '[w]here do I belong? [w]hat is my purpose? [t]o whom or what am I
connected or responsible?' (Hay with Nye 2006, p. 77). This is a position
supported by UK government guidance for work on spiritual development
in schools, which refers to '[a]n awareness of oneself' as well as – and
building out to – '[r]elationships – [r]ecognising and valuing the worth of
each individual; developing a sense of community; the ability to build up
relationships with others', with 'steps to spiritual development [that] might
include: recognising the existence of others as independent from oneself'
(SCAA 1995, pp. 3–4). Relationality has become the central concept in
many contemporary debates on spirituality: its 'central importance . . . as the
locus of spiritual education means that the visibility of relationality can be
used as a measurement of the effectiveness of systems' (Ota and Chater
2007, p. 190). As Dearey says, 'relationship is a focal metaphor for the
nature of spirituality' (Dearey 2008, p. 2), characterised as 'a discourse
extending through time and across communities' (Dearey 2008, p. 3).

Complementing relational approaches to spirituality, there are several
approaches referred to as holistic, especially from those working in the
health sector, where 'holistic healthcare' has its own history and status.
Robinson refers to an approach to spirituality having

a strong sense of holism – involving the integration of affective, cog-
nitive and physical elements and making it impossible to isolate the
spiritual from the physical. The spirit is a dynamic reality that
expresses itself in the body. This can apply also to groups. (Robinson
et al. 2003, p. 21)

Robinson's view 'contrasts sharply with the more dualistic view of the spirit as quite separate from the body' (Robinson et al. 2003, p. 21) and is 'relational' as '[e]ssentially, . . . spirituality is relation and action centred and about making connections with these different aspects of life' (Robinson et al. 2003, p. 23). Reference is made to empirical evidence for such a view of spirituality and the authors conclude with a working definition of spirituality:

- Developing awareness and appreciation of the other (including the self, the other person, the group, the environment and, where applicable, deity).
- Developing the capacity to respond to the other. This involves putting spirituality into practice, embodying spirituality and thus the continued relationship with the other.
- Developing ultimate life meaning based upon all aspects of awareness and appreciation of and response to the other (Robinson et al. 2003, p. 23).

Defining spirituality again

On the basis of such work, this chapter suggests that spirituality itself overcomes dualism. The chapter tentatively hypothesises spirituality as that which unifies the two elements of a much more 'contingent dualism', a dialectical dualism based around historically embedded I-Thou relationships (as in Buber 1958). Spirituality in any form must by definition incorporate transcendence, a going 'beyond', or it is not spirituality: hence the necessary relationship between spirituality and some kind of dualism or pluralism. The spiritual should, it is suggested, also incorporate immanence, as implied by Taylor's work on authenticity, and made explicit by Yovel in his account of philosophers from Spinoza to Hegel, Marx and Freud (Yovel 1989a, 1989b). For Yovel, immanence is contrasted with transcendence of an absolute dualist kind. Discussing Hegel, for example, he says that 'philosopher of the spirit' 'not only denies the idea of transcendence, but sees the realm of immanence as divine' (Yovel 1989b, p. 27). What immanence contributes to spirituality is the possibility of it being historical, an emerging aspect of life: it is only non-transcendent in the sense that it is not of an entirely other world. It is much more than the limited 'secular immanence' described by Sennett as characteristic of nineteenth-century literature. That was based on an 'ordering of natural phenomena' that led to a 'doctrine of secular immanence', with '[p]ersonality [as] one form of this belief in immanent meaning in the world' (Sennett 1978, p. 150).

The spirituality put forward in this chapter is personal, communal, human, inclusive and creative. If spirituality is impersonal then it has no meaning to people, and yet if its personal aspect is solipsistic, rather than communal, then it would, equally, be meaningless. Thatcher congratulates government guidance on spirituality for schools for its 'emphasis on "relationships with other people and, for believers, with God"', but notes that 'the view of the pupil which dominates the document is the individual, autonomous self for whom even "recognising the existence of others" is a problem' (in Astley and Francis 1996, p. 123). Spirituality is therefore put forward as 'human', a dimension of all humanity, a part of this world, as also described above by Marx. And yet it should not be thought of as exclusively human: if it were so, there would be a problem of human alienation from the rest of the world, a 'radical anthropocentrism' (Taylor 1991, p. 58) that itself would be a dualism to be overcome. The worldly nature of spirituality is well captured by Wong, who promotes 'a more mundane form of transcendence' from our 'ordinary experience', exemplified by 'an everyday conversation that opens up a space of intersubjectivity' (Wong in Ota and Chater 2007, p. 74). Taylor makes a similar argument for the moral and spiritual significance of the 'ordinary life', 'concerned with production and reproduction, that is, labour, the making of the things needed for life, and our life as sexual beings, including marriage and the family' (Taylor 1989, p. 211). 'There is a power in the ordinary things of everyday life, as Edward Hopper's paintings seem to say', suggests Zumthor: 'We only have to look at them long enough to see it' (Zumthor 2006, p. 17). That is, the spiritual is ordinary, and is both inclusive and creative.

Policy on the spiritual

Schools may be expected to promote spirituality. This expectation is statutory in the UK, 'expressed first amongst the aims of school education, in the 1944 Education Act and again in the Education Reform Act 1988' (Hall in TES 1998). Elsewhere, there is a range of policies, positive and negative, promoting or restricting consideration of the spiritual. Policies have been developed on spirituality in schools, as for example in the UK (established through statute), Norway (established initially through the core curriculum, Royal Ministry of Church, Education and Research 1994), and, negatively, through restrictions on considering anything associated with religion in US and French state-funded schools (though see Sink et al. 2007 on US private schools). Policy, or formalised good practice, can be based at individual, school, local, national or international levels. There is an increasing move to international policies affecting spirituality, including educational policies relating, for example, to special needs (as in the Salamanca Statement, UNESCO 1994), or religious issues relating to discrimination (as in the 1981 *UN Declaration on the Elimination of All Forms of Intolerance and Discrimination Based on Religion or Belief,* www2.ohchr.org/english/law/religion.htm) or religious rights (as in the 1992 *UN Declaration on the Rights of Persons Belonging to National or Ethnic, Religious and Linguistic Minorities,* www2.ohchr.org/english/law/minorities.htm). In a recent report for UNESCO, Delors wrote of learning as 'the treasure within'. For him, 'learning to live together' is characterised by 'developing an understanding of others and their history, traditions and spiritual values and, on this basis, creating a new spirit which, guided by recognition of our growing interdependence and a common analysis of the risks and challenges of the future, would induce people to implement common projects or to manage the inevitable conflicts in an intelligent and peaceful way' (quoted in ODIHR 2007, p. 40).

The presence of understanding may create a new spirit; its absence might be the best way to deny or destroy the spirituality of young people. Other suggestions of school characteristics that could prevent or destroy spirituality would include fear, loneliness, a stress on technique alone, or the promotion of – or failure to go beyond – ugliness. Spirituality may then be seen to be promoted by the contrasting characteristics: fear might be replaced with feeling safe or having 'faith' (in Macmurray's sense of faith as absence of fear, in Macmurray 1979), loneliness replaced with the possibility of friendship (Aristotle 1976, p. 278), technique replaced with meaning-making (Dunne 1997), ugliness overcome by beauty (Schiller 1967, fifteenth letter, Eco 2004). As Samier says,

> The social problems associated with a widespread, single-minded reliance on technological rationality in society are numerous. Society becomes devoid of spirit, substantive values, emotion and authentic self-expression. As these represent the source of morality, ethics, culture, art and aesthetics, a society without them can be very ugly indeed. (Samier et al. 2006, p. 83)

In the policy context in England of personalised learning and of *Every Child Matters* (DfES 2004a), there is a renewed enthusiasm for consideration of the more personal and holistic aspects of schooling, including a specific inclusion of spirituality in one local authority interpretation of the policy (Hedley 2007). Several studies of children's spiritual development (such as Wright 1999, Hay 2002, Hay with Nye 2006) have stressed the relational nature of spirituality, and have described the impact of religion on spirituality while accommodating non-religious forms of spirituality. Studies of and guides to spiritual development in schools (such as Ofsted 1994, Davies 1998, Hartland 1999, West-Burnham and Huws Jones 2007, and also Wright 1999) have described possibilities of spiritual development within schools. The *Spirit of the School* project is primarily an investigation, at school-level, into the impact school has on the spirituality of members of the school community, and the impact the spirituality of members of the school community has on the school. These are brought together to answer the question 'what promotes the spirit of the school?'

Policies on promoting spirituality imply ways of investigating and measuring spirituality, in order to confirm that it has indeed been promoted. Many people think that spirituality is by its nature immeasurable, and yet this flies in the face of the history of spirituality. It may be hard to measure, of course, but being hard to measure is quite different from being immeasurable. The philosopher's example of something being hard to measure in any definite way, that is yet clearly understood, is of baldness. It is hard to say what the dividing line is between being bald and not being bald, and yet some people are definitely one or the other. More significantly, religious organisations have always measured spirituality, whether it is in order to appoint saints or gurus, or to judge sinners: to weigh people in the balance, in order to allocate them to the appropriate afterlife. Dante's *Divine Comedy*, for example, describes a magnificent, fine-tuned, measuring device. Along with such absolute measuring devices, there may be more dynamic measures, for example trying to measure whether spirituality has increased or decreased over time. However, it should be noted that it must matter what spirituality means, in any system of measurement. As Thatcher says, government guidance suggests that '[i]t doesn't matter what beliefs anyone has, as long as they have them, and as they acquire them they can be seen to be developing spiritually . . . [: t]his is the price to be paid for the wholesale neglect of the question of truth, of which beliefs are true and which conduct is right' (in Astley and Francis 1996, p. 126). In such a relativistic view, where all that is needed is having any system of beliefs and expressing it clearly, Thatcher continues to say that Hitler would qualify as having good evidence of spiritual development. Measuring spirituality should be possible and, although there are dangers of assuming that measurement is the same as promotion (illustrated by the saying 'you don't fatten a pig by weighing it'), the focus on spirituality stimulated by attempts at measurement may in itself help promote spirituality.

Spirituality, religion and ethos

The complexity of policy related to spirituality requires some consideration of the distinctions between spirituality, religion and ethos. Understanding spirituality, as described here, involves understanding transcendence and understanding relational issues. Failing to understand spirituality involves, in turn, treating it as a separate substance or, in Martin Buber's words, as 'an uneasily-fluttering soul-bird' (Buber 1958, p. 63, quoted above). If descriptions of spirituality therefore often have something of the ethereal about them, religion is in contrast often over-burdened with facts. Understanding religion is too often a study of inappropriately divided sectional communities, sets of beliefs, traditions and institutions, a kind of study of 'zoo facts'. It should, rather, involve understanding how people live religiously. As William Cantwell Smith says, it is not 'religion' but 'religiousness' that should be understood: 'It is not a thing but a quality: of personal life (both individual and social)' (Smith 1978, p. 138). If religion and spirituality are to be understood properly, spirituality should not be seen as the safer alternative to religion. As Copley says, '[a] society like ours that finds religion hard to handle seems somehow to live much more easily with spirituality' (Copley 2005, p. 83, in the chapter vividly entitled 'Spiritual Fruits, not Religious Nuts: Replacing "Religion" with "Spirituality"'). One response would be to restrict spirituality to religion, as in the UK government guidance from the 1970s:

> The spiritual area is concerned with everything in human knowledge or experience that is connected with or derives from a sense of God or of Gods. Spiritual is a meaningless adjective for the atheist and of dubious use to the agnostic. (DES 1977)

However, this avoids the interest in spirituality expressed by secular and godless traditions, and also avoids Copley's stronger criticism, that spirituality is too often a corruption of religion. This is well expressed by Rosen in a critique of the religious music of the nineteenth century. Rosen says that 'Mendelssohn's evocation of religion . . . represents no doctrine, and no particular issues are touched, but it is designed to make us feel that the concert hall has been transformed into a church' (Rosen 1995, p. 594). The music 'expresses not religion but piety', and '[t]his is kitsch insofar as it substitutes for religion itself the emotional shell of religion . . . [by] evad[ing] all aspects of controversy, of dramatic conflict' (Rosen 1995, p. 594). As Copley would no doubt say of spirituality as it is presented in many documents on schooling, '[r]eligion is drained of all its content and has become powerfully sensuous, a purely aesthetic form of the sublime' (Rosen 1995, p. 594). Copley describes spirituality as, in its worst forms, 'universal and inoffensive, the aromatherapy of the curriculum' (quoted in Mason 2000), whilst Rosen says of Mendelssohn's music that '[i]t created a feeling of pious devotion in the audience without making any awkward demands' (Rosen 1995, p. 595). Watson extends the argument by noting that spirituality should be considered seriously by both religious and non-religious people. Spirituality should not be fought over between religious and secularist groups: 'to speak in terms of [spirituality] being either religious or secularist is inappropriate because this suggests some kind of possessiveness or competition, which I see as the very antithesis of the inclusiveness of spirituality' (Watson 2004, p. 58).

By treating spirituality and religion as entirely independent of each other, as described by Watson (2007), it can be that spirituality becomes the name used for quite different qualities – although that is not Watson's aim. A report of a study by Egan, investigating 'successful schools' and commented on by Hopkins, said that their 'spiritual capital' was 'a crucial factor in their exam and inspection successes' (Stewart 2008). This spiritual capital 'was the same thing as . . . moral purpose'. Schools with moral purpose were 'those where heads could link their vision to practical action'. The example given of spirituality was where two pupils died in a car crash during a school holiday, and the headteacher opened the building up to visits from pupils and teachers. Egan was reported as saying that spirituality was made up of 'a strong ethos, a refusal to accept low performance, strong relationships, a strong pupil voice and student self confidence' (Stewart 2008). Much of this activity is valuable, but it hardly needs the term 'spirituality' to capture purposive moral action. Similarly, West-Burnham and Huws Jones say that spiritual development 'has almost always been interpreted in a religious way which, for many, can be restrictive and insular', so '[t]his is not a book about religion or faith, its approach is essentially humanistic' (West-Burnham and Huws Jones 2007, p. 4). Ignoring the possibility that humanism may also be found 'restrictive and insular' by many, the authors go on to note that '[t]here are multiple pathways into spiritual and moral understanding; all have validity according to historical and cultural norms' (West-Burnham and Huws Jones 2007, p. 4). The *Spirit of the School* project may be humanistic in the sense that it puts forward a view of spirituality based on essential human characteristics. However, it does not do so in order to avoid offending the non-religious or the anti-religious (or the religious), and it makes no attempt to promote a religious and spiritual relativism in which all 'pathways' have validity. As Dearey describes the situation, '[t]here are real differences between secular and religious spiritualities, but any absorption of one into another, even if it is only conceptualised for the purpose of arriving at an understanding of 'spirituality' which may be convenient for operational purposes, will seemingly discredit one or the other, and contradict the necessary relation of unity and diversity that has, from a religious perspective, its basis in God's immanence in relation to the world' (Dearey 2008, p. 46).

Parallel issues arise with respect to ethos and spirituality, as those with respect to religion and spirituality. When describing 'the spirit of the school', the most common response to the author from those with a professional interest in the topic was, 'isn't this just the school *ethos?*' Ethos refers to characteristics and dispositions of an organisation (OED 2005): it is essentially internal and continuing, and may express the potential of the organisation. Spirituality, in contrast, refers to going *beyond* the organisation, and is therefore a more lively and active dimension of organisations. Spirituality, like religion but unlike ethos, is best understood as dynamic rather than as a set of traditions and beliefs. This is already identified by Aristotle, for whom 'movement' is one of the three characteristics that all philosophers attribute to the soul (Aristotle 1984, p. 646). It is increasingly true of religion, too, as patterns of religious engagement become more fluid. Schreiner, discussing European approaches to religious education, notes how institutional religion has lost influence in the changing social systems of the world. Social changes include 'secularisation, individualism, pluralism, and globalisation', coinciding with 'the emergence of modernity' (Schreiner et al. 2007, p. 13). Although it may be possible to link modernisation with secularisation, the link is not secure. Indeed, 'there are good arguments to support [. . . Berger's view of the] De-secularisation of the World' (Schreiner et al. 2007, p. 13). It is, according to Berger and others, institutional religion, and not all kinds of religion and spirituality, that has lost power and influence. Religion and spirituality have become more complex and de-institutionalised, in some cases, even individualised – as in Davie's accounts of religion as 'life-style' (Davie 1994, Davie in Berger 1999). Religion seems to have become more like the fluid and dynamic spirituality, then, and both are further from the nature of ethos.

Perhaps the broadest account of school ethos is given by Dunne, who describes how 'very many teachers . . . still manage to create a humane space for their pupils' learning . . . [because] they have not lost the sense that practice has the sort of open texture that I have described and because they bring to it (in addition to competence in their subject matter) the variations it calls for of good temper, friendliness, love of

truth, and ready-wittedness, as well as of the larger virtues of courage and
justice' (Dunne 1997, p. 379). He continues that '[t]eachers can continue
to bring these qualities to their teaching only if there is a shared ethos
among their colleagues which prizes and sustains them'. Ethos, for
Dunne,

> is at the heart of what I have been calling a practice, and I am
> claiming that, against all the odds, there are schools and staffrooms
> in which it is still recognizable. . . . If individual teachers depend on
> the ethos of a school, it is no less true that the latter is itself highly
> vulnerable to the overall ethos of a society, expressed in and con-
> ditioned by the ways it organizes institutions, allocates resources,
> disposes of power and wealth. (Dunne 1997, p. 379)

This view puts ethos in a wider social context, yet still gives ethos an
essentially inward-looking nature, albeit subject to external influences. The
spirit, however, reaches beyond the essential conservatism of the present,
the here and now, the internal. Spirituality leaps out beyond, to the past,
the future, the 'other'. It includes leaps of the imagination, such as Buber's
imaginative leap to other people – the leap out of solipsistic individualism.
It is a leap requiring imagining not the fantastical but the real: 'getting in
touch through the imagination with what the other is actually feeling,
thinking, willing, and perceiving "and not as a detached content but in his
very reality, that is, as a living process in this man"' (Friedman 1999, p. 409,
quoting Buber 1998, p. 60). 'Imagining the real' or 'experiencing the other
side' of the relationship is for Buber an act of inclusion, yet 'goes hand in
hand with remaining on one's own side of the relationship' (Friedman in
Buber 2002a, pp. xiii–xiv). The spirit of the school is suggested as connecting, actively, within and beyond the school, whereas the ethos of the school
is essentially inward-looking and descriptive.

Researching humanity: community, learning, and dialogue

The *Spirit of the School* project builds on earlier research (in Stern 2007a),
which attempted to describe what is essential to humanity, or more precisely what it means to be a person, and did this in terms of three characteristics: community, learning and dialogue. It should be noted that what
is essential to humanity is not necessarily unique to humanity: a celebration of humanity need not be in the form of an exclusivist humanism,
cut off from the rest of the world. Buber discusses in *I and Thou* how there
can be a form of dialogue even with a tree (Buber 1958, p. 21). Further,

dialogue might be regarded as possible with people who are no longer alive, as in the dialogic approach to literature of Bakhtin (e.g. Bakhtin 1981), for whom physical death is not absolute death. As Taylor says, '[o]ur "conversation" with the absent and dead is, of course, mediated by the works of oral and written culture, by sayings, sacred writings, works of thought, poetry, and works of art in general', but '[t]hese are originally conceived as figuring in a conversation' (Taylor 1989, p. 526). He concludes that '[o]ne thing a work of art is in its essence, I would say, is a bit of "frozen" potential communication' (Taylor 1989, p. 526). Dead writers are remembered; only the unremembered suffer from 'absolute death', that is, 'the state of being unheard, unrecognized, unremembered' (Friedman 2002, pp. 355–6).

For living people, as well as the dead, existence is not a straightforward issue. We may 'crumble away to dust', as one philosopher said of himself when he considered himself alone and separate from his wife. For John Macmurray, '[w]e are all more or less unreal', and '[o]ur business is to make ourselves a little more real than we are' (Macmurray 1992, p. 143). This is a form of 'self-realisation':

Our own reality is not self-contained. It consists in our capacity to realize the independent existence and value of what is not ourselves. To be ourselves we must live beyond ourselves. If we misapprehend the character of the world in which we live, we are infected with illusion. The unreality that results is in us, not in the world outside us. It is *our* unreality. The more real our apprehension is of what is not ourselves, the more real we are in our own selfhood. This is the essential nature of personality. To realize ourselves, therefore, is to realize the world that is not ourselves. The self which is indifferent to the nature and significance of what is other than it, is indifferent to its own reality and cannot realize itself. (Macmurray 2004, pp. 160–1)

We achieve self-realisation through learning, then, and we do this in community, through dialogue ('real' dialogue, Buber 1958, p. 22). This 'becoming more real' is itself a creative learning process, then, and allows for friendship too. People are social beings, and this can be expressed in communities through the possibility of friendship. It was in that context (of the philosophy described in Stern 2007a) that schools were described as necessarily communities, and therefore necessarily places with the potential for friendship (described in greater detail in Chapter 2, below). We learn, are creative, and become more human in schools, and we make community and friendship through dialogue.

There is a danger that a view of schools as friendly, communal, creative places might suggest a romanticised and over-optimistic view of organisations as easily 'democratic'. It is therefore worth stressing that schools are typically hierarchical communities, and undemocratic (as in Stern 2002). In such hierarchical organisations, there are leaders and followers. However, just because there is a hierarchy, does not mean that there cannot be egalitarianism: 'an equalitarian and co-operative attitude can be, not only worked for, but practised to a considerable extent in *any* society' (Stern 1971, p. 525, emphasis added). Rather than the absence of hierarchy, a form of egalitarianism may be based on other qualities held in common among people who are in some way genuinely different. As Taylor says of gender equality: 'If men and women are equal, it is not because they are different, but because overriding the difference are some properties, common or complementary, which are of value' (Taylor 1991, p. 51). Leaders in a hierarchical system may be 'equal' in various ways with those whom they lead, yet may still retain distinctive qualities. They may, in particular, have the characteristic of magnanimity or being 'great-souled'. That term is used by Aristotle, to describe the 'crown of the virtues', the virtue available to leaders who already exhibit all the other virtues of good leadership. It involves working for the people being led, a simple yet rarely addressed aspect of leadership, often confused by consideration of 'democracy' and 'distributed leadership' that fails to describe leadership in hierarchies (see Stern 2002).

In order to make the *Spirit of the School* project more than a recasting for spirituality and schooling of the earlier work on religions and schools, what was added was research conducted in schools, research with people learning and teaching together. The research was intended to encourage sincerity, also described as 'more than not lying' (Stern 2007a, pp. 165–8). Research in the form of meaning-making, commonly found in ethnography, can be of a kind described by Moustakas: research that 'keeps us forever awake, alive, and connected with what is and with what matters in life' (Moustakas 1994, p. 65). Research as defined by the UK's Research Assessment Exercise of 2008 (the assessment of UK academic research, Hefce 2005) is, incidentally, rather similar to creativity as described in educational debates: both require originality, an understanding of context, and self- and peer-evaluation.

For the *Spirit of the School* project, a set of research tools was developed that can be used by schools and researchers alike. These tools are adapted from a number of approaches: that of Hay and Nye studying spirituality in language and looking for evidence of 'relational consciousness' (Hay with Nye 2006), elements of grounded theory (including an openness to responses, and coding-based analysis of some data, as in Strauss and Corbin 1990), elements of ethnography (as described by Baszanger and Dodier in Silverman 1997), and elements of school development techniques (of Dalin and Rust 1983: a study of the mutuality of an institution's creativity and its adaptation processes). As Hick says, '[w]e live amidst unfinished business; but we must trust that continuing dialogue will prove to be dialogue into truth, and that in a fuller grasp of truth our present conflicting doctrines will ultimately be transcended' (Hick 1974, p. 155). Schools can be places for dialogue towards truth. Those researchers privileged enough to be able to complete school-based research, working with pupils and adults in schools as co-researchers, will themselves be able to take some part in this dialogue. Researchers should be 'vivisecting' schools: that is, studying them while they are alive, joining them with their communities, joining them across national boundaries, and engaging them with universities.

The structure of the book

The philosophical development of the earlier work (Stern 2007a), the further clarification of that philosophical framework, and the methodological approach of the *Spirit of the School* project underpin the structure of the chapters of this book. Each chapter can be read on its own, as accounts, respectively, of spirituality, community, dialogue, learning, leadership, and research. Chapter 2 investigates schools as communities and the possibility of friendship, centred on the communal philosophy of Macmurray. Is the school community one that stretches beyond the school, in both space and time, and is it one in which friendship becomes distinctively possible? Are some schools simply less communal, less open to friendship, and why? From this foundation, Chapter 3 investigates learning in school, centred on Vygotskian learning theories. School subjects are often ignored in educational research, or seen simply as means to promote generic skills rather than as having any meaning in themselves. It is the meaning, and the meaning-making, of subjects that is addressed here, along with how inclusive and how creative that learning might be. Pupils and teachers and other members of school learning communities, past and future, are connected through dialogue, and it is the nature of dialogue that is investigated in Chapter 4, which is centred on Buber's approach to monologue and dialogue. Chapter 5 addresses hierarchical issues in schools, and whether school leaders might be described as 'great-souled', a term that comes from the work of Aristotle. In Chapter 6 the focus moves to the value of the research process itself in understanding and promoting the spirit of the school, while acknowledging the idea that '[f]undamental to spirituality is the absence of force' (Rabbi Hugo Gryn, quoted in Chichester Diocesan Board of Education 2006, p. 4). Whereas Chapter 1 works towards a definition of spirituality, Chapter 6 includes, on the basis of the theoretical and empirical research (i.e. the conversations with books and with people), a final summative description of the spirit of the school.

Each of Chapters 2 to 6 illustrates the arguments with evidence drawn from book-based and school-based research, with the school-based research in Chapters 2, 3 and 4 focused in a section referred to as 'the spirit of the schools', and in Chapters 5 and 6 spread through the chapter. The research was completed in thirteen schools with pupils aged six to seventeen (with the majority between seven and fourteen), teachers, and headteachers. Those schools all volunteered to take part in the first stage of the research, with others already lined up to take part in the next stage. Of the thirteen schools represented here, nine were in the UK (six primary schools, three secondary schools, five with Church of England foundations, one with a Roman Catholic foundation, and three with no religious foundation), and four were schools in Hong Kong in China (two primary schools, two secondary schools, two with Protestant church foundations, one with a Roman Catholic foundation, and one with no religious foundation). Altogether there were 144 participants: 16 pupils, 13 teachers and 4 principals were involved in Hong Kong, and 65 pupils, 37 teachers and 2 non-teaching staff, and 7 headteachers (one of whom was head of one school and 'executive head' of another) were involved in the UK.

Following the six chapters, the Appendix includes the whole of the *Spirit of the School* toolkit, the activities and questions used in schools involved in the project, and notes on the origins and implications of those activities and the methodological principles underpinning them. Beyond the scope of this book, but to be published in other articles and books, is a set of systematic comparisons of different types of school, primary and secondary schools, schools with and without religious foundations, schools in areas of greater social deprivation or greater wealth, or schools in different countries. Although the book summarises a considerable amount of research, it is therefore also a starting point for a bigger project, aiming to promote the spirit of the school in many contexts and countries.

Chapter 2

School communities and the possibility of friendship

Happy or unhappy moments, it's all in our memories.

(15-year-old boy, School 1, Hong Kong)

Introduction

As the previous chapter explains, the *Spirit of the School* project explores what spirituality is, what it could mean to promote spirituality, and how spirituality might be explored, founded on theories of learning (from the social constructivist tradition), community (from the philosophy of Macmurray), and dialogue (from the philosophy of Buber). Macmurray's philosophy suggests that schools are forms of community like families, friendship groups, and religious communities, in which people are treated as ends in themselves and not as means to further ends. Communities are unlike other social groups that are, typically, driven by external aims. Whereas a society 'is an organization of functions', a community 'is a unity of persons as persons' (Macmurray 1996, p. 166). The 'personal' is defined in terms of the possibility of friendship. Indeed, Macmurray remarkably suggests that '[a]ll meaningful knowledge is for the sake of action, and all meaningful action for the sake of friendship' (Macmurray 1991a, p. 15). In schools that are Macmurrian communities, friendship will be possible and the possibilities for spiritual development will therefore be that much greater than in other social groups.

The *Spirit of the School* project has been investigating school communities and the possibility of friendship. The model of friendship emerging from this research, and to be analysed and explored in this chapter, is compared to the philosophies of friendship of Aristotle (e.g. 1976), Buber (e.g. 1958, 2002a), Macmurray (e.g. 1991b), Lynch (2005), and theoretical frameworks developed by Lawrence-Lightfoot (2000, 2003), Hey (2002), Epstein (2002) and Noddings (1994, 2003b). It is also derived from the participants in the research, such as the boy (quoted below) who describes the people who have remained his friends, despite them now being in other classes, because 'we had some common experience which had made a deep impression in my mind'. The interviewer asks 'you had some happy moments together, right?' and the boy answers with considerable pathos: 'Yes. Happy or unhappy moments, it's all in our memories.'

Community

Studying community can become a complex matter, as so many writers have such strong, and such contrasting, understandings of communities. Human communities are generally thought to be relatively small (in contrast to societies), and to have something in common (the etymological source of the word 'community'). The greatest disagreement is over what might be common to members of a community. It is possible to describe two broad if overlapping traditions: one tradition saying that what is held in common is a set of views, norms, or beliefs, the other saying that what is held in common is a set of activities or relationships. This is a disagreement, like so many disagreements, well represented in the work of Plato and Aristotle: Plato wants agreement, Aristotle wants activity. Plato approvingly describes Socrates stressing the need for common beliefs in a community, and the need for agreement, whereas Aristotle fears too much unity in a community. The 'dictum of Socrates' that 'it is best that the state should be as much of a unity as possible' is simply 'not true' (Aristotle 1962, p. 56): creating unity would be 'as if one were to reduce harmony to unison or rhythm to a single beat' (Aristotle 1962, p. 65). A state must have citizens of variety in it, to fulfil different roles, and this is what makes a community. There is a need for working towards, more than believing in, a common purpose (the state as a community), and good as that work is, even that work is not what defines human goodness as a whole:

> A citizen is one of a community, as a sailor is one of a crew; and although each member of the crew has his own function and a name to fit it – rower, helmsman, look-out, and the rest – and has therefore his goodness at that particular job, there is also a type of goodness which all the crew must have, a function in which they all play a part – the safe conduct of the voyage; for each member of the crew aims at securing that. Similarly the aim of all the citizens, however dissimilar they may be, is the safety of the community, that is, the constitution of which they are citizens. Therefore the goodness of the citizen must be goodness in relation to constitution . . . On the other hand we do say that the good *man* is good in virtue of one single perfect goodness. Clearly then it is possible to be a good and serious citizen

without having that goodness which makes a good man good. (Aristotle 1962, p. 107)

Aristotle explicitly rejects 'the extremist unification of the state' (Aristotle 1962, p. 64), and this is based on a belief in a degree of self-determination of each person, or at least of each male freeman. As Howie says, this has a particular relevance to education: for Aristotle, 'education is not something imposed on students from outside by a teacher; rather it is an internal process of personal exploration and self-questioning' which 'is something which the learner must do for himself' (Howie 1968, p. 31).

The contrast between community theorists who emphasise a common belief, and those who emphasise a common activity, can be traced again in early nineteenth-century philosophy. Hegel focuses on the '*consciousness* of the community – which thus makes the transition from mere humanity to the God-man, to the intuition, consciousness, and certainty of the union and unity of divine and human nature – that the community begins; this consciousness constitutes the truth upon which the community is founded' (Hegel 1988, p. 469). A community for Hegel 'presupposes shared ideals and purposes' (Hawkesworth in Alperson 2002, p. 323). In contrast is the position of Feuerbach, for whom community is created through direct relationships, rather than abstract beliefs. 'The single man for himself possesses the essence of man neither in himself as a moral being nor in himself as a thinking being', he says, but instead '[t]he essence of man is contained only in the community and unity of man with man; it is a unity, however, which rests only on the reality of the distinction between I and thou' (Feuerbach, quoted by Jung in Fergusson and Dower 2002, p. 176). Jung suggests that Feuerbach thereby creates a tradition of 'heterocentric thinking and doing' (Jung in Fergusson and Dower 2002, p. 176). What it certainly does is emphasise the sense that common beliefs are not what make community or individuality: what is needed is activity, in relationships between people. It appears that Marx in some ways returns to Hegel's views, in his rejection of Feuerbach. Marx criticises Feuerbach's 'abstraction', and goes even further in describing activity, work, as the human and communal essence. However, Marx seems to externalise the social relationships, such that 'human essence is no abstraction inherent in each single individual', as '[i]n its reality it is the ensemble of the social relations' (Marx and Engels 1970, p. 122). Marx then returns to the need for a common set of beliefs about these social relations, a class consciousness, as a necessary precursor for changing the world.

In the twentieth century, there is again a contrast between those who write of community and other social bonds as dependent on beliefs, and those who concentrate more on activities. Social contract theorists, notably Rawls (1972), look for the possibility of agreement, abstracted from activity and from knowledge of one's own position in society, as the form of legitimation of any social system. The need for abstraction and for a belief in the legitimacy generated by intellectual agreement rather than activity, has been criticised by a number of writers on community, especially feminist writers and care ethicists, well represented in Alperson's collection of articles on diversity and community (Alperson 2002). Nussbaum for example writes of the family as a 'privileged community' (Nussbaum in Alperson 2002, p. 212), and this family basis is focused on activity, caring. It is a reflection also of the approach of Macmurray, who saw family, friendship group, religious community, and school as the four models of community in general. He uses the biblical account of the Good Samaritan to support the Christian nature of community as activity not belief, as in that account Jesus is asked to say 'who is my neighbour?' As Macmurray says, 'the Samaritan shared his material possessions with the Jew in his need, while the priest and the Levite made their natural community as members of the same nation and the same faith an ideal matter which did not express itself in action' (Macmurray 1996, p. 111). That is, community cannot be assumed, as a result of common beliefs or any nominal membership: it can only be the result of particular activities.

A pupil at Afton primary school (Church of England, UK) describes the active nature of friendship, and how that overcomes or subverts the school's or the government's achievement orientation. Molly, aged six, is responding to the question asking for the times when the school made her feel good about herself, and describes a boy in the year below her.

> Well, [name], he's in year one [aged five or six] and he's kind of a bit wild, and a bit naughty sometimes, but he's my best friend, and erm he he made me feel happy one day because I was on the bars on outside and I was stuck, 'cos I had my leg twisted kind of the other way, and he helped me off and he didn't hurt me or anything and I had a sticker on me because I was being good in school at numeracy, and I gave it to him because he really did help me . . . and it felt really really joyful and happy to me.

This is the *Spirit of the School* equivalent of the Good Samaritan narrative. The community that is the school cannot be defined in terms of achievements in numeracy. Even when numeracy skills are, quite rightly, celebrated, the sticker celebrating that achievement can have far more meaning to two children, as a joyful celebration of helpful activity in community.

Seeing schools as communities encourages the activity-based approach to community. Notwithstanding the common beliefs and norms that may be promoted within schools, it is as communities of practice that schools can best be understood, in the tradition, as described here, running through Aristotle and Feuerbach to Macmurray. Schools as communities of practice will also be understood by those working in the tradition of learning theory promoted by Lave and Wenger (1991). They see learning communities in this way, having developed a model of 'situated learning' involving increasingly legitimate and decreasingly peripheral participation. They refrain from describing schools as learning communities. This is a challenge to those working in schools, and is justified by them because they are more interested in learning than instruction, and because schooling presupposes the possibility of 'decontextualised' learning, that is, learning outside the 'situation' in which the practice is based (Lave and Wenger 1991, pp. 39–41, and see Fielding 1999). However, the argument is made in the *Spirit of the School* research, as it was previously (in Stern 2007a, pp. 29–34), that the practice situated in schools is that of being human: '[t]he golden aim of education [is] to teach the children how to live' (Macmurray 1968, p. 114, quoted at greater length below, in Chapter 6). It is not simply a 'practical' education: the living might involve contemplation. The contemplative life promoted by both Plato and Aristotle, and many religious traditions since their time, is therefore not excluded from this practice-based schooling. Yet it is appropriate to call the education *situated*, situated in community, in life, and not apart from life or merely a *preparation for* life.

The current research on the communal nature of schooling is therefore based on the work of Macmurray, a philosopher whose work gained additional publicity towards the end of the twentieth century when his views were promoted by the then leader of the British Labour Party, Tony Blair, who wrote the foreword to a collection of Macmurray's writings (Macmurray 1996, and see also McIntosh's chapter in Kim and Kollontai 2007). Blair is reported as saying: 'if you really want to understand what I'm all about, you have to take a look at a guy called John Macmurray. It's all there' (Kirkpatrick 2005, p. 157).

Macmurray's community philosophy centres on the nature of personhood in community, in contrast to our existence in *social* groups. Communities are positive and personal; societies are negative and impersonal. Both community and society are vital, but they are differentiated by the intentions of their members. In communities, people treat each other as ends in themselves; in societies, people treat each other – and the society – as means to further ends. As has been said in another context (Stern 2007a, p. 21), in society, there is nothing inappropriate about treating people as a means to an end, such as treating a taxi driver as a means to facilitate travel from one place to another. In community, in contrast, such a way of treating people is wrong, as in the frequent complaint of parents about their children treating them like taxi drivers.

In these ways, Macmurray follows Buber on community, who distinguishes 'community' from 'collectivity': '[c]ollectivity is based on an organized atrophy of personal existence, community on its increase and confirmation in life lived towards one other' (Buber 2002a, p. 37). Macmurray similarly says that people should 'use the term "society" to refer to those forms of human association in which the bond of unity is negative or impersonal; and to reserve for the contrasted forms of association which have a positive personal relation as their bond, the term "community"' (Macmurray 1991b, p. 147). Hence, whereas a society 'is an organization of functions', a community 'is a unity of persons as persons' (Macmurray 1996, p. 166). Macmurray exemplifies communities with families, schools, and religious orders. Schools, it should be noted, are *necessarily* communities (as described in detail in Stern 2001b). They are necessarily places where people treat each other as ends in themselves.

> [W]hen we try to teach, we must deal with living human beings. We, the teachers, are persons. Those whom we would teach are persons. We must meet them face to face, in a personal intercourse. This is the primary fact about education. It is one of the forms of personal relationship. It is a continuing personal exchange between two generations. To assert this is by no means to define an ideal, but to state a fact. It declares not what education ought to be, but what it is – and is inescapably. We may ignore this fact; we may imagine that our task is of a different order; but this will make no difference to what is actually taking place. We may act as though we were teaching arithmetic or history. In fact we are teaching *people*. The arithmetic or the history is merely a medium through which a personal intercourse is established and maintained. (Macmurray 1968, p. 5)

Friendship

If community has a long academic tradition, friendship is rather less enthusiastically studied. Yet for two of the philosophers central to an understanding of community, Aristotle and Macmurray, friendship is the

quality most needed for communities to exist. Communities are, for Macmurray, places of friendship, and it is only in community that friendship,
and through that – remarkably – freedom, are fully possible. For him,
'expressing our own reality in word and action . . . is freedom, and the
secret of it lies in our capacity for friendship' (Macmurray 1992, p. 150).
A 'secret' doubly so, as friendship is so little studied since Aristotle retired.
Perhaps the lack of clarity in the nature of friendship made it hard to
study. Perhaps the term was spoilt by the Romantic view of being a friend
of humankind, as in the 'fraternity' of the French revolutionary call for
liberté, égalité, fraternité. Or perhaps it was spoilt by the sexualisation of
friendship since the late nineteenth century, as theorised by Freud, from
which time all friendships were a little suspicious (see Vernon 2005,
Chapter 2 and *passim*). Certainly the reaction to friendship in schools is
most often one of embarrassment and concern at the risk of inappropriate exploitative or sexualised behaviour. It is right, of course, to be concerned about exploitation and the sexualisation of school relationships,
yet that does not need to take with it all forms of friendship. If it did,
schooling would be much the poorer.

Having said that friendship is something of a secret, in recent years it
has somewhat come out of the closet. Books on the philosophy of friendship (such as Lynch 2005, Vernon 2005) are in the mainstream of popular
academic philosophy, and they follow a cultural interest in friendship
generated not least by the popularity of the television series *Friends*: an
account of friendship-centred, rather than family-centred, life that is
typical of what Roseneil (2004) describes as our post-heteronormative
society. She quotes Nick Hornby, who says in his novel *About a Boy*: 'I just
don't think couples are the future' (N Hornby 2000, p. 276). There is
even some work on friendship in schools, although this is generally
restricted to friendship between pupils, and is often carefully separated
from anything that might be thought suspicious, as in Lewis's account of
friendship, seen 'in the way it is seen by the Quakers (the Religious
Society of Friends), as a way of being together that involves unconditional
positive regard and a wish and concern for each other's well-being . . . you
can be friendly to people you have yet to meet' (Hayes 2007, p. 122,
original ellipsis). As friendship, then, becomes more important, its
analysis also becomes more important. Here, friendship will be considered in three ways, in terms of freedom and fear, irreplaceability, and
difference.

Friendship, freedom and fear

According to Macmurray, 'Freedom in Community is the first condition as well as the final goal of true education. Friendship then is the condition of freedom in community' (Macmurray 1968, pp. 33–4). It is important to link friendship with freedom as friendship is and must be by its nature voluntary or a matter of free choice: you can choose your friends, but not your family. This is why friendship can be so important to young people, as it is one of their first conscious expressions of free choice. As Epstein says, 'young people may form themselves in "conditions not of their own choosing", but they are highly agentic in their making and breaking of relationships, and the ways they use these to distinguish between self and Other' (Epstein 2002, p. 149). That is, young people 'do' friendship in 'becoming' themselves. Hey, in an article in the same collection as that of Epstein, describes this relationship well, as friendship is 'one of the few social and interpersonal relations in which young children can exercise any form of social control' (Hey 2002, p. 227):

> Friendship has a key position here, since it draws so heavily upon the discourse of individual freedom. Historically, friendship premises itself on ideas about 'choice' and uniqueness and it thus makes a particular claim on young people, since it appears as an ideal or first practice of the 'reflexive' self. Friendship viewed in this light offers a rich theoretical yield not only because it emerges as a common-sense manifestation of the 'freedom' to choose forms of sociality but because it is lived by these young people as an ontology and epistemology of the self through the 'other'. (Hey 2002, p. 239)

The making of the self, through friendship, is therefore an important theme of friendship and freedom. It is freedom as described also by Maritain, 'that freedom which is spontaneity, expansion, or autonomy, and which we have to gain through constant effort and struggle' (Maritain 1971, pp. 10–11). We are, according to Macmurray 'all more or less unreal' and '[o]ur business is to make ourselves a little more real than we are' (Macmurray 1992, p. 143). We can only do this, though, through others. Hence, '[t]o be a friend is to be yourself for another person' (Macmurray 1979, p. 5). So why is friendship not more common or more easy? It is, he says, 'natural' that when two people meet, they should 'care for one another as friends', yet it is all too rare '[b]ecause we are afraid' (Macmurray 2004, p. 172): 'We are full of deep-seated, half-conscious fears that will not allow us to trust one another, or to give ourselves away.

We have learnt the arts of self-defence; to keep ourselves to ourselves, to give others no handle against us' (Macmurray 2004, p. 172).

If fear works against friendship, so too do tyranny and injustice. The psychoanalysts Mitscherlich and Mitscherlich write about the possibility of post-war Germany working through its earlier, pathological, experience of authoritarian politics. Their purpose, they say, 'is to improve the prospects for the "friendly German"' (Mitscherlich and Mitscherlich 1975, pp. xxvii–xxviii). It is the association of authoritarianism with 'unfriendly behavior – in the widest sense of the term' (Mitscherlich and Mitscherlich 1975, p. xxviii) that links this work with the contemporary writing of Macmurray, and with the long-distant writing of Aristotle. For Aristotle, 'in a tyranny there is little or no friendship . . . just as there is no justice', indeed, in a tyranny the relationship of leader to led 'is like that . . . of master to slave' (Aristotle 1976, p. 278). The work of Aristotle is still the benchmark for studies of friendship, and has some unlikely supporters (given the period in which he worked, let alone his misogyny) in post-structuralist feminist and post-heteronormative writers such as Roseneil.

The connection between friendship and fear, in Aristotle's terms, is related to only one kind of friendship, which is the kind that is most important to schooling. 'There are . . . three kinds of friendship' (Aristotle 1984, p. 1826), he says, 'those who love each other for their utility . . . those who love for the sake of pleasure . . . [and] the friendship of men [*sic*] who are good . . . [i.e.] those who wish well to their friends for their sake' (Aristotle 1984, p. 1827). Young people often focus on pleasure-related friendship, the elderly often focus on utility (Aristotle 1984, p. 1827), but all – all 'good' people – can have friends for their own sake. Friendships based on pleasure or utility are not related to freedom. Pleasure-seeking may seem like an act of freedom, but friendships based on pleasure are ultimately selfish and at the same time self-destructive. They typically include, for young people, those friendships that lead a person to do precisely what they themselves realise they should not be doing, whether that is cruel behaviour such as bullying or self-destructive behaviour such as the excessive use of legal or illegal drugs. Aristotle's third kind of friendship, what might be called 'full' friendship as it involves neither exploitation (for pleasure or utility) nor self-destructiveness (through seeking pleasure or utility), is between people who are, as friends, irreplaceable. It is this form of friendship that is most important in schooling.

Friendship and irreplaceability

Irreplaceability is critical to Macmurray's conception of friendship. In separating social from communal groups, he separates social and personal relations. The latter are by their nature unique.

> As husbands or wives, as parents, as brothers, or as friends, we are related as persons in our own right: and we are not replaceable. If I lose a friend I lose part of my own life. This is not a mere poetic metaphor. For we are what we are through our intercourse with others; and we can be ourselves only in relation to our fellows. (Macmurray 2004, p. 169)

Friends and family members are in one sense 'replaced': family members die, new ones are born, marriages break up and new relationships emerge, friends fall out and people make new friends especially when they move house or employment. Yet the uniqueness of friends and family members means that there is not a straightforward 'swap'. It would be cruel to say of someone whose friend has died, 'don't worry, you'll get another friend', just as it is cruel to say to a woman who has given birth to a baby who has died, 'you'll be able to have more babies'. 'Getting another friend' or 'having another baby' is not the point: the loss is still there, is still felt. In the same way, second husbands/wives will object to being thought of as 'replacements'. Recent recruitment advertising for teachers in the UK used the strapline 'no one forgets a good teacher', and this captures something of the irreplaceability of some teachers.

There is a risk here of making friendship a requirement, which would deny its freedom. That risk has even been described in terms of the 'governmentality of the soul' (Rose, quoted in Hey 2002, p. 227). Hey believes that initiatives related to 'emotional literacy' are similar attempts to 'pedagogise this reflexive knowledge in a mobilisation that at least recognises there is a *struggle* for the soul' (Hey 2002, p. 228). However, there must still be the *possibility* of friendship within communities, otherwise they would not be communities. Schools should therefore enable friendship and should avoid enforcing friendship. Organising schools in such a way that pupils work productively with a number of other pupils as well as on their own, organising non-lesson times in corridors and playgrounds and lunch halls in such a way that pupils can befriend and be befriended, helps enable friendship. Those pupils who go through a period in school, or even their whole lives at school, without friends will still be aware of the difference between being friendless in a school that allows for friendship, and being friendless in a school that either attempts to enforce friendship or that undermines friendship through fearfulness or tyranny.

Now communities, in all models, are likely to incorporate differences and divisions and conflicts, just as the smallest family will contain divisions even as it is united. Aristotle sees differences in terms of hierarchies, of leaders and the led, of old and young, of class and of gender, just as more recent writers see such divisions – albeit more critically. It is, for Aristotle, friendship that seems to hold such diverse communities together (Aristotle 1984, p. 1825). Aristotle is referring to 'states', but implying communities of fewer than 100,000 people: 'You cannot make a city of ten men, and if there are a hundred thousand it is a city no longer' (Aristotle 1984, p. 1850). Periclean Athens, by far the largest of the Greek city states, had a population including slaves of between 130,000 and 170,000 (Held 1987, p. 23). As Macmurray notes, 'Aristotle himself insists that the State must not be so large that all its members cannot know one another' (Macmurray 1968, p. 39). Macmurray is even clearer on this relationship, as '[t]he structure of a community is the nexus or network of the active relations of friendship between all possible pairs of its members' (Macmurray 1996, p. 166). This is 'a positive unity of persons' that 'is the self-realization of the personal', in which people, as friends, are 'related as *equals*' (Macmurray 1996, p. 167).

Friendship and difference and inequality

Friends are therefore related as equals, for Macmurray, even if they are not equal in other ways:

> This does not mean that they have, as a matter of fact, equal abilities, equal rights, equal functions or any other kind of *de facto* equality. The equality is intentional: it is an aspect of the mutuality of the relation. If it were not an equal relation, the motivation would be negative; a relation in which one was using the other as a means to his own end. (Macmurray 1991b, p. 158)

It is an important point that, as friends, there can be equality, even if, as colleagues, as teachers and learners, as members of different classes, there may be very significant inequalities. Aristotle explains it in a somewhat different way, yet still allows friendship involving inequality, 'e.g. that of father to son and in general of elder to younger, that of man to wife and in general that of ruler to subject' (Aristotle 1984, p. 1831): in each, 'the

love also should be proportional, i.e. the better should be more loved
than he loves' (Aristotle 1984, p. 1831). Friendship can itself equalise:

> Now since friendship depends more on loving, and it is those who
> love their friends that are praised, loving seems to be the character-
> istic excellence of friends . . . It is in this way more than any other
> that even unequals can be friends; they can be equalized. (Aristotle
> 1984, p. 1832)

Differences are there at the same time as they are overcome. In a more
contemporary phrasing, 'the getting of a self requires the getting of a
friend and this invariably involves the transmission of forms of "difference" that write social class, gender, sexuality, "race" and ethnicity' (Hey
2002, p. 238). In the research reported by Hey and by Epstein, children's
friendships were 'a key resource for their constructions of identity *and* the
negotiation of difference' (Epstein 2002, p. 149, emphasis added). These
differences are amongst pupils, but there is still the question of friendship
between teachers and pupils. The possibility of such friendship is a
requirement for Macmurray, as schools are communities. For Noddings,
the teacher–pupil relationship is based on the forms of dialogue that are
possible, or, as she says, the kinds of conversation that are possible. Real
conversation is a form of moral education.

> Many children and adolescents lack opportunities to engage in real
> conversation with adults. They have brief exchanges, of course, and
> perhaps more than enough warnings and direct instruction: wear
> your heavy jacket, wipe your feet, finish your breakfast, clean your
> room, feed the dog, and so on. Some badly neglected children do
> not even receive this, but I am referring to real conversation in
> which all parties speak, listen and respond to one another. For many
> young people, this is a rare experience. (Noddings 1994)

Teachers can talk with young people in a way that is fully engaged and
not condescending, even if it is between 'unequals'.

> Many parents and teachers make the mistake of treating children's
> talk as 'cute', and this habit is often carried even into the teenage
> years. Parents listen and smile when their teenager expresses an
> opinion on a political or social problem. The opinion is not taken
> seriously and the adults do not press the child for evidence, point
> out feasible alternatives, express their own views seriously or confess

their own confusion. In other words, these parents do not really converse with their children and the children do not learn to listen attentively or to construct persuasive arguments. (Noddings 1994)

How important this is for the nature of schooling, is the subject of the rest of Noddings' article (and see also Noddings 2003b). A real conversation is one in which 'the adult participants must be reasonably good people – people who try to be good, who consider the effects of their acts on others and respond to suffering with concern and compassion', and in which 'the adults must care for the children and enjoy their company' (Noddings 1994). It should be noted, here, that Noddings requires greater 'goodness' of the adults than of the children: this is exactly as Aristotle requires, as, for him, this inequality itself helps equalise the relationship. Finally, for Noddings, although the curriculum is important, it is not the end, the purpose, of the conversation. Just as Macmurray, quoted above, notes how '[w]e may act as though we were teaching arithmetic or history . . . [while] [i]n fact we are teaching *people*' (Macmurray 1968, p. 5), Noddings notes that in a real conversation, of the type she expects of teachers and pupils,

> we are aware that our partners in conversation are more important than the topic. Participants are not trying to win a debate; they are not in a contest with an opponent. They are conversing because they like each other and want to be together. The moment is precious in itself. The content of the conversation, the topic, may or may not become important. Sometimes it does, and the conversation becomes overtly educative and memorable on that account. At other times, the only memory that lingers is one of warmth and laughter or sympathy and support. (Noddings 1994)

That is precisely the kind of dialogue promoted by Buber, who rejects competitive 'discussion' as 'breaking apart' (Buber 2002a, p. 3, explored more fully below, in Chapter 4). Buber does, however, have a different view of the inequality involved in schooling. As teachers and pupils are unequal, they cannot be friends: 'the special educative relation could not persist if the pupil for his part practised "inclusion," that is, if he lived the teacher's part in the common situation', and if this were attempted, either 'the *I-Thou* relationship now comes to an end or [it] assumes the quite different character of a friendship' (Buber 1958, p. 165). That approach, however, is one rejected not only by Macmurray, but also by Korczak, another philosopher of education in the same tradition. Korczak promoted the idea that the 'educator and child must meet at the same level' (Boschki 2005, p. 115). Indeed 'the teacher must look up to the children' and 'must try to soar, must stand on tiptoe to reach up to the children's feelings' (Korczak, in Boschki 2005, p. 121). This is a more radically equalising relationship than that in Macmurray, and it stands as an example of the possibility of togetherness in educational settings that in other ways certainly supports the humanising philosophies of Buber and Macmurray, and their opposition to 'breaking apart'. Avoiding the temptation to break apart is also the theme of Lawrence-Lightfoot in her account of teacher–parent relationships. For her, this is needed to overcome the sense of teachers and parents as 'natural enemies', and to create a 'we' in a way that does not ignore difference (Lawrence-Lightfoot 2003, p. 42, p. 184). Maritain writes on the same topic describing 'the necessity of mutual help but also the inevitability of a reciprocal tension between the one and the other' (Maritain 1971, p. 24).

The spirit of the schools

Close to me

Research has been carried out within the *Spirit of the School* project on the communal and friendly nature of schooling, including interviews and other research activities with a range of pupils, teachers and headteachers. Research tools include the 'Salmon Line' work, developed out of personal construct psychology, and from interviews the deceptively simple question 'how can we make the school more of a community?' There was also one of the 'concentric circles' exercises, asking for responses on 'me and the people closest to me in school'. These activities and questions are described and analysed in detail in the Appendix, at the end of the book, but the 'close to me' activity is worth considering here in more detail. This activity involved pupils filling in a set of concentric circles with 'me' in the centre, and putting the names or descriptions of people within the circles. It may seem perverse to be researching friendship without asking explicitly about friends, just as it may seem perverse to be researching spirituality, creativity, and dialogue without asking explicitly about any of those terms. The intention is to investigate these concepts without getting caught in some of the stereotypes associated with them, and friendship, as has been described earlier in this chapter, has a riskiness about it, generated by the romanticisation and the sexualisation of the term. One of the most striking findings of the whole research project was generated by this oblique approach to friendship, and this finding is also relevant to the

Buber-Macmurray-Korczak disagreements over the nature of the relationships between teachers and pupils.

When talking about 'friends', in school contexts, adults talk about other adults, children talk about other children. Descriptions of friendship networks then look distinctly intra-generational. The only references to inter-generational personal relationships (other than narrowly pedagogic relationships) are likely to be family relationships: parents with children in the school, cousins of different ages, and so on. Yet when asked, in this research, about people who are 'close' to them, respondents comfortably mixed the generations. Pupils had both pupils and teachers and other staff mixed together in each of the circles, and teachers likewise had staff and pupils mixed in each of the circles. There was a tendency of pupils of all ages to include the class teacher (in secondary schools the 'form tutor' or 'personal tutor', or in some cases a subject teacher) and 'best friends' and classmates, along with relatives, in the innermost circle, and other school staff (especially teaching assistants and, for primary pupils, dinner staff) and pupils from other classes or year groups, placed more peripherally. Pupil and teacher responses were broadly symmetrical: teachers characteristically had their own class or form/tutor group and often a teaching assistant in the innermost circle, along with one or two teachers from a subgroup of the staff (for example, a department or a phase group). Other staff and pupils, and pupils' families, ranged outwards from this central group.

It appeared, therefore, that inter-generational 'closeness' was identified by participants from all the schools and all the categories of respondents. There seemed to be a little less inter-generational mixing in the responses of secondary school respondents, but this was by no means a strong pattern. Four of the thirteen schools had less inter-generational mixing. North Humber (secondary, UK) had few teachers put pupils in any of the circles, and where the pupils did mention staff, these were most often in the intermediate and peripheral circles. Similarly, in St Martin's (primary, Church of England, UK), there was very little mention of pupils by staff, although there were some staff mentioned by pupils. In Richardson (primary, UK) the staff included pupils in their circles, but the pupils mentioned few adults. Only two mentioned any adults, with one pupil mentioning three names of adults amongst 44 names in total, and another mentioning three names of adults (two of which were of the researchers, met for the first time that day and presumably included out of politeness), among 35 names in total. The lack of adult names in the pupil responses may have been associated with conversations between the pupils during the activity. One pupil, Jack, seems to have run out of names to put in the

circles, and other pupils (left unnamed in the transcript that follows) start
suggesting putting people whom they *dislike*, outside the circles:

Interviewer:	Well you do the ones you can think of
Jack:	I've just put a third
Interviewer:	Is that all you want to put Jack? That's fine. Well it's up to you to decide who you put on it
Pupil:	Who don't I like?
Pupil:	Ayub
Pupil:	That's a cool name
Pupil:	Miss, that one I've put it for this one
Pupil:	Jay, and Mark my worst enemy is going there
Pupil:	or Jay, Liam . . .
Pupil:	Nicole is my worst enemy and all
Pupil:	She's my worst enemy ever
Pupil:	Emily
Pupil:	No, don't . . .
Interviewer:	Lizzie is working hard
Pupil:	She had him in the middle though
Interviewer:	No, it's up, you leave Lizzie if she's doing her, her ideas
Pupil:	Desmond's my worst enemy . . .
Interviewer:	Right, how are we getting on? Have you got some more to put in . . .
Pupil:	Miss, that's all I can think of.

It was only in this school that closeness led to a discussion of enmity as
well as friendship, and it appears from the transcript to have been derived
from an attempt to help Jack over his expressed inability to think of more
than three names of 'close' people, and to have been exacerbated by the
later mention of 'my worst enemy'. Jack ended up putting six names in
the circles, all of pupils, and all in the first two circles. He did not write of
enemies, and in the end only two of the eight participating pupils wrote
down the names of what can be assumed to be enemies: names outside
the circle and at the edge of the piece of paper. Nevertheless, talk of
friends and enemies perhaps led the pupils (in contrast to the views of
their own teachers) to underplay their closeness to teachers and other
staff, and overplay the picture of friendship that is all too common, as
being typically and most appropriately being between people of a similar
status and power.

St Bede's (secondary, Roman Catholic, UK) had more inter-generational
responses from both pupils and staff than was common for secondary

schools, and there was also a significantly greater number of family relationships mentioned. Perhaps the family connections result from the
school drawing on a wide geographical area, with people committed to the
religious ethos being typically from family groups. In School 1 (secondary,
Protestant, Hong Kong), pupil CC (female, aged 14) responds to the
question about closeness with 'my classmates and the class teacher',
refining this to 'the chairman of our class committee' (roughly equivalent
to a prefect or chair of the school council in the UK system) and 'the class
teacher', as the former coordinates 'leisure activities' and the latter 'is very
kind to us'. The teacher's closeness is not only within lessons, but also
through 'extra-curricular activities' (as mentioned by CC and other pupils),
and CC 'always' has lunch with the teacher before going to 'play with my
schoolmates'. Pupil A (aged 15, male) in the same school says that the
teacher is 'more like a father' than a brother or teacher, and 'is more like a
friend'. This puzzling combination of roles is explained by CC in these
terms: 'during the lessons, he is a teacher to me, but after the lessons, he is
a friend to me . . . [because he will] talk about matters not related to the
lessons, like things [that] happen at home'. One of the teachers at this
school explains the communal nature of the school, in the first instance, in
terms of relationships between staff and the principal: 'there is no wall
between us', and 'if someone is unhappy, we will go and give our support'.
This has an impact on the pupils: 'I think the students know that their
teachers have a good relationship and they will learn from it.' She continues, 'this is the first thing', and it is a view echoed by the principal of the
school who says 'our relationship with the students starts from the relationship between us'. The second thing, the teacher therefore says, is the
teacher's relationships with pupils: 'they are related to their class in a way
just like a mother, a father or a big brother'. Pupils and teachers in School
1 all therefore describe strong intra-generational bonds which are related
to and supported by strong inter-generational relationships.

An extreme example of inter-generational closeness came from Ruislip
school (primary, Church of England, UK). Jonathan (year 3, aged 8) had
in the circle closest to the centre eight names, six of which were of adults
(indicated by the titles 'Miss' or 'Mises' [*sic*]), and only one of which was
of a pupil. Other pupil names were in the intermediate and outer circles,
but this preponderance of adult names suggested that Jonathan might
have been separated from potential friends through the close attention of
adults. Informal discussion with his class teacher confirmed that Jonathan
did indeed have a lot of attention from staff, in order to help meet his
special educational needs. The encouragement of educational inclusion
has meant pupils being more likely to be taught together in mainstream

schools, yet the very attempt to include can itself isolate the pupil from other pupils and potential friends of the same age. This seems to have happened to Jonathan.

The 'close to me' circles activity therefore raised a number of interesting ideas on how people in school related to each other, and provided some evidence for a more Macmurrian view, in contrast to Buber's view, of the possibility of inter-generational friendship in the school community. It may be better to say that some evidence is provided for a more Macmurrian and Aristotelian view of friendship itself, as something that is not necessarily hampered by significant, established and appropriate inequalities in a relationship, such as the inequality between the roles of teacher and pupil. The second important finding, that some pupils may be cut off from other pupils by their closeness to adults, especially if they receive intensive support from adults, has an importance for the analysis of inclusive education, as well as for the analysis of the communal nature of particular schools.

Working together: friends in deed

In Afton (a Church of England primary school, UK), Ruth (aged 10) describes the nature of the school community in a personal way. She was interviewed soon after a flood had affected the school, and says that:

> There was a big flood and it came all into the school about two foot deep into the school and we've all worked together to try and clean it up and even people that don't go to school have come in and helped us and all the parents and we've got loads of support, and I think it's really good because if we didn't have a big community and a family that we have all together, then it just won't be like this. We probably wouldn't even be back to school and we are all working together and we're finding things in places where to store stuff when the stuff, when the builders are coming in to fix it all in the summer, and next year I hope that it will be even closer because they found out how we can work together.

She continues that 'we're all working together at the moment' and 'we can prove to everyone that they can work together more now': indeed, as a result of this, in the future, 'it will be more like a bigger family'. As well as the flood, less dramatic problems can also illustrate the communal nature of Afton, with three teachers describing how the school makes them feel good about themselves:

Teacher 1:	I've not been here very long, and you've made me feel really welcome, the rapport between all of us, everybody gets on really well, mostly, we do, don't we, it's a really lovely atmosphere in here, and
Teacher 2:	but if somebody's having a bad day, grumpy, we all understand and sort of get over it, you know, like me last Tuesday
Teacher 3:	I'm still getting over that
Teacher 2:	Yeah I bet you are.

Anthony (aged 11, also in Afton) makes more of the description of the school in terms of friendship, when asked whether the improvements in the communal nature of the school would have happened as quickly if there had not been a flood.

> Well, I think it would have because we've got a big holiday on the way and so and leavers in like a few days . . . so people planning not to have arguments and everybody is trying to be friendly, work together so they wouldn't have, . . . because they want some like friends to play with over the summer and so there've been groups as well. . . . So, I think the flood did make more people in groups and teams but I think it would have gradually gone up anyway.

In such ways, therefore, the school is moving towards being more communal, in a way that enhances the possibility of friendship, with these two characteristics being seen as mutually beneficial. The examples given here, of working together in community, refer to friendship in action, in the activities of the school. This is repeated throughout the research responses, alongside the friendship expressed in personal support through difficult times. Friendship is an activity deeply embedded in schools. As Charlotte, aged 10 (Richardson primary school, UK) said, the most memorable time that the school makes her feel good about herself is 'when you've got friends'. William, aged 9, defined community as 'when the teacher looks after you'. The work towards friendship is not always this sort of direct personal support. Several respondents described the school's environment as itself part of what makes the school a community. Two nine-year-olds in Richardson linked the need for a better environment back to the school council, in an incomplete yet interesting interchange:

Jack:	It means the school needs, the school needs to be more better and the school needs to be more fitter

Interviewer:	It needs to be fitter? Well, what do you mean by that Jack?
Jack:	The walls needs to be cleaner
Interviewer:	Oh right you are thinking about the building, okay
Jack:	It needs to be clean and it's gone [unclear word]
Anne:	I swear like if the [school] council is somewhere important and any other like children
Interviewer:	So, the school council people are important
Anne:	Yeah.

Jack is wanting a cleaner school and Anne seems to link it to the importance of the school council. Both pupils were members of the school council, and so it appears that they were saying that the school council had asked that the school be cleaner, but had been ignored. A 'fitter' school is therefore not simply worthwhile in itself, it is a sign that the staff of the school were listening to the voices of the pupils expressed through the school council. BH, a teacher in School 1 in Hong Kong (secondary, Protestant), and the school's principal, in separate interviews describe the even more physical involvement of pupils in improving the School 1 environment.

I think this school puts an emphasis on students' experience. For example, letting them do volunteer work as a group. . . . During the lessons, we also taught them respect for others and care for the environment. All these things go on at this school. I think the school stresses that our students can learn these things through their daily experience. If they can learn these things, the school will be more like a community and not a group of isolated, unrelated individuals, like in some schools, when the bell rings, the school will be like an abandoned city within 30 minutes. Rather, our students don't want to leave the school even when the gate needs to be closed at 5:30. They want to stay and play ball games. I think this is what makes our school like a community. (Teacher BH, School 1)

The most important thing is to develop students' sense of belonging to school and see the school as their second home. The campus is owned by the students. That's why we let our students do a bit of the cleaning, maintenance and repair work of the fixtures. Any defects reported will be quickly fixed by our janitors. But if we let the students try and do some of the work, they will understand how hard the work is and appreciate it when our janitors are doing most of the work. In addition, we will try and upkeep our campus' condition. We are not a luxuriously furnished campus, but we will keep it clean and tidy. . . . [Interviewer: When you say 'letting the students do a bit of the work', what are they doing, say in cleaning?] They will wipe the tables and sweep the floor. We also have a cleaning week once a year. [Interviewer: So, they do all the cleaning?] Yes. For those who often break school rules, we will punish them by letting them do some service for the school. They won't be solely responsible for that task. We just ask them to do a small part of it. We mainly let them follow the janitors to see how hard they work for a certain period, e.g. washing the toilets and floor sweeping. We let them do just a bit of the work so that they can appreciate the hardship yet it is not too much to cause their resentment. Our janitors are adults and the school treats them well. They know what these children have done. When these children were asked to follow them for an hour to watch them work, they will give them lectures and advice like 'You shouldn't do that, the teacher loves you'. We complement each other's work. (Principal, School 1)

No doubt some would interpret pupils completing cleaning tasks as unreasonable or exploitative, although none of the pupils mentioned this in their responses. What is interesting is how the teacher and principal insist on the relational aspects of cleaning, in terms of work and respect for all members of the community, including the janitors, and their respect or love for the pupils even as they are being punished. Another clue to the meaning of cleanliness is given by a primary school teacher in Hong Kong. Working at the environment provided the 'strongest sense of belonging':

The most unforgettable experience come into my mind was our General Studies. I think that will be the same in other subjects, too. Every year we would take an inventory of all the teaching kits that we have and tidy up our General Studies Room. We will take out anything not useful. This task would take us a few days. We will work enthusiastically as we want to finish it as soon as possible. I feel great on those few days . . . It is really a big task. It's like a family who work together to clean up their home. We will tell each other, 'hey! let's come back early tomorrow to work!' It really feels like tidying up my own home. (Teacher A, School 2, a Roman Catholic primary school in Hong Kong)

Keeping the school clean and tidy is here likened to keeping a family home tidy, and that is noteworthy evidence of its communal significance. The school as a community is full of pleasant and unpleasant times and activities, and even the less pleasant times may help make the community, and help make friendships. 15-year-old pupil A in School 1 makes this very clear, in describing his continuing friendship with people who were his classmates 'a few years back' but are no longer together. The boy has talked about the people closest to him, including his brother who is also at the school and his current classmates:

> I think apart from classmates from the same class. It's my old class-mates and schoolmates in higher forms whom I want to make contact with. For my old friends, I want to chat with them about the times we had together. For those in higher forms, some of whom I have known them for some time, I want to chat with them because I don't usually have much chance to speak to them. . . . [Interviewer: How come you are so close to them?] When we were together a few years back at a lower grade, we had some common experience which had made a deep impression in my mind. I don't want to lose these friends so soon. [Interviewer: You had some happy moments together, right?] Yes. Happy or unhappy moments, it's all in our memories.

Memories, including unhappy memories, making friendship: this forms a powerful description of relationships bridging time and people, and not being weakened by the association with unhappy times. Even if Parsi Zoroastrians believe that 'misery is a sin to be confessed' (Hinnells 2007, p. 58), unhappiness as well as happiness contribute to spiritually significant friendships. This is a contrast to some views of spirituality as entirely consisting of beauty and pleasure. Such a view, an entirely positive view, of being 'spirited' can be evidenced by a request for photographs to decorate a cancer ward in England, suggesting that '[t]he photographs should portray the positive spirit and identity of the area served and could be of Spring, Summer, landscapes, or nature, and people enjoying them-selves', and that '[t]hings to avoid are sunsets, cloudy days, insects, and Autumnal and Wintry scenes' (Hey! 2008).

Conclusion

Schools are – must be – communities, and communities of a particular kind, similar to the community nature of the family home, where people treat each other as ends in themselves, not as means to external ends. Teacher BH in School 1 (secondary, Protestant, Hong Kong) says simply that pupils and teachers 'meet each other 40 hours a week' for 'five or six years'. 'It's a very long time', he continues, and 'within such a long portion of time in their life, of course we hope that they can make the school their home', and 'can have a feeling of "living" at the school'. If schools are communities of that kind, they must incorporate the possibility of friendship. Friendship itself is possible amongst pupils, amongst staff (as '[t]he tendency to sacrifice the adults to the children is as disastrous as it is widespread', Macmurray 1968, p. 37), and between teachers and pupils. This idea of schooling, and its link to friendship, means that successfully communal schools, or appropriately friendly schools, can be placed in the middle of a continuum between two opposing, and equally inappropriate, ideas of schooling. Having the best practice set in the middle of a continuum between two inappropriate forms echoes the method of Aristotle, for whom 'moral excellence is a mean . . . between two vices' (Aristotle 1984, p. 1751). As the model of schooling is itself derived in part from Aristotle's flexible and unromanticised view of friendship, this balanced view of school communities is entirely fitting.

The less successfully communal schools, the less 'spirited' schools, are of two kinds. At one extreme is the school dominated by external aims, a social organisation with an external purpose, in which friendship may occur, but in which the personal relationships are secondary to the social, external, functions of the school, and in which friendship is likely to be limited or peripheral and restricted to subgroups of members of the school. At the other extreme is the school in which friendship is made compulsory, in which people are pushed together by an insistent, oppressive, friendliness. This latter position might be illustrated from the early days of Steiner schooling. It appears, from this description and despite his claim that 'this love cannot be mandated' (Steiner 1996, p. 68), as though the expectation is that all the children must love their teachers:

It is December 21, 1919, and Rudolf Steiner is addressing a Christmas assembly of teachers, parents, and students of the newly formed Waldorf School. 'Do you love your teachers?' he asks the children. 'Yes,' comes the resounding reply. A few minutes later in his talk he repeats, '. . . I would like to ask you again, "Don't you all sincerely love your teachers?"' 'Yes, we do,' shout the children. These earnest questions and fervent answers are repeated many times in the next few years on his frequent visits to the school. (Steiner 1996, p. ix)

Either of the extremes may be characterised by a requirement to assent to a set of beliefs or norms, where those beliefs or norms are prioritised above the practices of the members of the school community, or where they exclude members of the school community – at least, as long as they allow continued membership to those thus excluded. The possibility of friendship is a delicate but vital requirement of schooling, the first principle, and for young people often the first example, of freedom.

Schools are friendly places, but they are not merely friendship clubs: they are learning communities. The following chapter considers the processes of learning in schools, then, and is followed by a chapter on dialogue, which is presented as the mechanism by which community, friendship and learning are all achieved.

Chapter 3

Learning together in the creative school

The spirit begins here as an instinct, as an instinct to the word, that is, as the impulse to be present with others in a world of streaming communication, of an image given and received.

(Buber 2002a, p. 230)

Introduction: inclusion and creativity

Inclusion and creativity are the concepts at the heart of this chapter, which describes the spirit of the school as involving learning together, generating stuff. As educational concepts, inclusion and creativity are popular and dangerous, attractive and corruptible. Both are used in debates on policy, and both are used in everyday conversations by education professionals. It is the significance of the concepts, in helping determine how people learn in school, that is explored here. Broadly, inclusion is about what and who is included in school learning, and creativity is about what and who is generated through school learning. The connections to spirituality should be, although seldom are, straightforward. All too often, inclusion is seen as a matter of getting everyone in the same place, and it ignores what happens in that place. All too often, creativity is seen as a matter of adding an artistic element to a crowded curriculum, and it ignores what happens the rest of the time. The more spirit a school has, the more inclusive, truly inclusive, it will be; the more spirit a school has, the more creative it will be. Communal, friendly, dialogic, magnanimous, inclusive, creative: these are the adjectives that best capture the spirit of the school.

The meaning of inclusion

Inclusion has been one of the most influential concepts in social and educational policies of the late twentieth and early twenty-first centuries, from the Salamanca Statement of 1994 (UNESCO 1994) through to issues of 'e-inclusion' (Abbott 2002, 2007). Two themes emerged, of *social*

47

inclusion, which was related to debates on poverty and alienation (as in Ranson 2000), and *educational* inclusion, which was related to meeting the whole range of learning needs (Frederickson and Cline 2002). The concept became something of a myth, an inspirational idea with an influence beyond its literal meaning (Crichton 2007). There were tensions in the concept, however, which were to an extent disguised by its mythic status. Educational inclusion could be seen as a deficit model, based on ensuring that all could be schooled together in mainstream schools, or as a reinvigorated version of the comprehensive ideal of the 1960s (Benn and Chitty 1996, Pring and Walford 1997, Stern 2007a, p. 26). These both worked against an achievement-driven policy that might allow for more distinct provision if it led to improved levels of achievement. The tension is expressed in a policy document from 2004: 'Raising standards in schools and inclusion must go hand in hand', it says, not based on a philosophical commitment to inclusion but because 'schools have a critical role in raising the educational achievement of children in care and other groups that have consistently underachieved' (DfES 2004b, p. 38). A second set of tensions was generated by the positive promotion of diversity. Following the events of 9/11, policy-makers and educationists increasingly recognised the presence of groups explicitly excluding themselves, religiously or politically. Inclusion was damaged by being seen by some such groups as a kind of imperial enforced assimilation. Hence, books were published with titles that retained the idea of inclusion only through linking it with diversity (as in Frederickson and Cline 2002, Grove and Smalley 2003). The combination of achievement and diversity, and the demotion of inclusion, was heralded in UK policy by the 2001 document *Schools: Building on Success: Raising Standards, Promoting Diversity, Achieving Results* (DfEE 2001).

At a deeper level, the tension in inclusion policies was, and remains, the question of the nature of the organisation or community in which people are to be included. If being included is to have any value, its value must depend on the value of that in which people are included. A school that is exploitative and driven by external targets, a school of fear or of meaningless learning, is not improved by becoming more inclusive. Inclusion in such a school is likely to be damaging. Clearly, inclusion in a 'good' school would be a good thing, and inclusion in a 'bad' school would be a bad thing, but schools are not so neatly divided into the good and bad. It is therefore difficult to determine the tipping point, the point at which inclusion in a school is likely to be a good thing. This tension is reflected in the ambivalence of a headteacher interviewed for the *Spirit of the School* project (and quoted in full in Chapter 6, below). He expressed an opposition to selective education and a preparedness to send his daughter to a selective school, on the grounds that the actual schools available were not suited to the girl, even if the principled opposition to selection was still maintained. What the girl was to be included in, he might have said, was not worthy of the inclusiveness implied by comprehensive schooling.

A more spirited school, in the model developed in this book, is one that will be more educationally and socially inclusive, but inclusion itself is not the aim: it has been moved to the sidelines. Inclusion on the sidelines is also a way of describing the importance of more spirited schools understanding and including those people and activities that themselves are 'on the sidelines'. When asked the question 'when do you feel most included in school?' a number of children in earlier research responded by saying when they were left to work on their own (Hatfield 2004). There will be times when the most inclusive thing that can be done is to leave someone alone. In the current research, this is recognised by many of the respondents who, when describing what sort of conversation they would like to have with someone who was troubled, said they would allow them to be on their own. As eleven-year-old Amy said, she would 'just let them be for a couple of minutes' (quoted below, in Chapter 4). To 'let someone be' is a kindness, in contrast to pushing someone out of a group or marginalising them (Messiou 2006), and this distinction is further explored with respect to headteachers in Chapter 5.

What inclusion has contributed to educational debates is the communal nature of learning. Spirituality as a dynamic relational concept is similarly tied to communal learning. Learning 'is a way of being in the social world, not a way of coming to know about it' (Hanks, in Lave and Wenger 1991, p. 24), and 'is not something that happens to a person on occasion; it is what makes him [*sic*] a person in the first place' (Kelly, quoted in Dryden 1984, p. 144). It is a short journey, then, from inclusive learning to spirited learning: both have existential implications, and both are essentially communal. Inclusive learning is worth fighting for, if inclusion is in a learning community and if it is of a kind that allows for privacy and aloneness. Just as the quality of the inclusion is as important as the 'fact' of inclusion, the quality of the learning is as important as the 'fact' of learning. Inclusion's relational nature is also the clue to its dependence on dialogue. A mere geographical inclusion, putting people in the same building, or social inclusion, avoiding selection in schooling based on ability or ability to pay, has little meaning. Indeed, it is people coming together with different beliefs, values, and practices, that seems to be the starting point, the stimulus for, inclusion, rather than its conclusion.

Dialogic inclusion is needed, bringing people together to do something new.

The meaning of creativity

The second key concept in this chapter is creativity, a concept that helps distinguish routine transferring of information from meaning-making and, more broadly, from 'generative' work in schools. This is set in policy contexts of creativity in education, notably the current UK government policy dominated by the documents developed by Robinson (DfEE 1999) and Roberts (Roberts 2006), and religious and philosophical issues related to creation, creativity, and human nature. The relation between creativity in its everyday sense, and creation in its religious usage, is well described by Buber's account of how '[c]reation happens to us, burns itself into us, recasts us in burning – we tremble and are faint, we submit' (Buber 1958, p. 108). He continues that '[w]e take part in creation, meet the Creator, reach out to Him, helpers and companions' (Buber 1958, p. 108). Creativity is, understandably, less poetically described in government documents. The UK's curriculum authority says that creativity 'involves the use of imagination and intellect to generate ideas, insights and solutions to problems and challenges', and that, '[c]oupled with critical thinking, which involves evaluative reasoning, creative activity can produce outcomes that can be original, expressive and have value' (QCA 2008). That is, there is reference to the agency of the person being creative (imagination, thinking, reasoning), the originality of the processes or products (generate, original, expressive), and the value of that generated (solutions, evaluative, value) (see also Stern 2007a, pp. 124–6).

One of the tensions in the concept is similar to that in inclusion, related to whether or how the concept complements achievement-oriented target-driven policies. The tension is recognised in policy documents themselves, which note that 'it is vital that creativity and attainment are not depicted as in competition – they are different sides of the same coin', and '[t]here is increasing evidence that headteachers are seeing creativity in the curriculum as the way of achieving the next step change in pupil attainment' (Roberts 2006, p. 15). Perhaps, but it is hard to see how high-stakes testing and league tables of school results are conducive to imagination, expressiveness and originality, let alone the ability to '[q]uestion and challenge conventions and assumptions' (Roberts 2006, p. 67). A second tension in the concept emerges from that first one. Creativity is something that by its nature cannot be generated, as it is itself generative. An active policy that aims to promote creativity is therefore liable to be self-defeating. A creativity policy, to avoid contradicting itself, may best focus on the negative, on preventing barriers (including policy-generated barriers) to creativity: a more apophatic approach. As a document from the Royal Opera House describes it,

> Creativity does not need generating. It is an innate quality in children and young people. However it does need nurturing and protecting from being constrained or even extinguished by fear of failure. (Royal Opera House response, quoted in Roberts 2006, p. 68)

Fear can be generated within schools, and pupils and teachers can, as a result of fear, extinguish creativity. For Buber, 'a real lesson . . . [is] one which develops in mutual surprises' (Buber 2002a, p. 241, explored further, below, in Chapter 4), and yet the surprise in creative work can itself be worrying. The current chapter investigates, then, how people learn together, in and beyond school subjects, and how that learning is creative, in the sense that people make themselves, in learning, as well as making new meanings, new things. It is, most of all, an attempt to negate the fear that restricts creativity, that limits inclusion.

Inclusive learning

Inclusion cannot be taken for granted. To be included must mean to be included in something, and the quality of that 'thing' must warrant the inclusion. Furthermore, even if the community or organisation is of a kind warranting inclusion, being included may nevertheless mean being offered privacy, rather than being forced into working with others all the time. How people are included in schools, then, is a personal matter, an educational matter, and a spiritual matter. Inclusive learning is explored here, and the possibilities of such learning are related to the nature of the school as a learning community, to the nature of subjects studied, and to the nature of the people involved in the learning. The starting point, here, is how inclusion should not require setting aside or being intolerant of the very qualities that make up the people who are to be included. It is not real inclusion in a school, if everyone leaves their humanity at home.

Weak inclusion

A person may apparently be included, but only by rejecting elements that are important to them. For example, a requirement to 'set aside' religious or political beliefs or practices in order to be 'included' in the school is not truly inclusive or is, at best, a very weak form of inclusion. Whether the school has a religious foundation or is described as secular, it cannot be inclusive to the extent that the beliefs and practices of the pupils are simply ignored or actively bracketed out. It should be noted that this is a problem, or a potential problem, equally for 'religious' and 'non-religious' schools: an enforced secularism can offend as much as an enforced religiosity. Of course, there may be appropriate times when people should 'suspend their belief or disbelief', as when engaging in literature or virtual realities. Houston describes work with virtual reality as an example of 'the expression of a human need to create realities within realities in which we can suspend belief in one set of commitments in order to engage in an alternative set' (Houston 1998, p. 95). However, he is also clear about the moral dangers of unlimited immersion in such real-ities, and the moral significance of even brief periods in there. Within Christianity, the moral dangers are expressed by Matthew 5:28: 'I tell you that anyone who looks at a woman lustfully has already committed adultery with her in his heart' (quoted in Houston 1998, p. 82).

At the extreme of virtuality, there can be a loss of a sense of reality, or a replacement of an understanding of gradations of reality with the position of the sociologist Schutz, for whom '[e]ach world *whilst it is attended to* is real after its own fashion; only the reality lapses with the attention', as '[r]eality means simply relations to our emotional and active life; whatever excites and stimulates our interest is real' (Schutz 1973, p. 340). The willed suspension of belief or disbelief is therefore significant and dangerous, but cannot be discounted, as it is characteristic of many forms of religious, literary, and technical practices: indeed, of all forms of playing. Playing games in order to avoid other more 'real' responsibilities may be danger-ous, but avoiding all playfulness is just as dangerous. And an 'acted neutral-ity' may at times 'free the subject from factional concerns or pressures' and allow 'the reconsideration of established positions, the adoption of fresh points of view, the investigation of neglected or suppressed topics' (Donovan, in McCutcheon 1999, p. 246). The school curriculum can be investigated for its ability to provide safe opportunities for the suspension of belief or disbelief, and to return to or move on from those suspended beliefs or disbeliefs. Weak inclusion, or the weak reality of 'virtual' reality, has its place, but this is a limited place in a strongly inclusive school.

Strong inclusion

The way in which the school community is inclusive would need to be one that embraces diversity. There is an episode of *The Simpsons* ('The Fat and the Furriest', 15:5, 2003), when Homer Simpson helps a bear. They give each other a hug, and Homer ends up with a ripped shirt and bleeding back. 'I don't know why they go on about bear hugs', he comments. The lesson to be learned is that inclusive diversity may be uncomfortable. It is all too easy to promote diversity only when it is the sort of diversity that includes little disagreement. A place that really embraces diversity will welcome people who disagree with them, will welcome their own worst enemies. Some schools that want, admirably, to tackle racism or to encourage academic success, want to tackle them with a 'zero tolerance' policy on racism or failure. However, Stoll and Myers criticise such positions. 'Most of us learn through and from our mistakes', whilst zero tolerance 'suggests this is not an option and that we must turn away from, reject, punish and blame those who fail' (Stoll and Myers 1998, p. 5, and see also Olsen and Cooper 2000, p. 97). Instead, they say that the '[m]ature way to tackle these issues has to be through joint acceptance of the problem and working together to find remedies . . . [through] co-operation, not confrontation' (Stoll and Myers 1998, p. 5). There is a need to talk with people, engage people, whether or not they are racist, whether or not they are failing academically. Being intentionally 'intolerant' is a bad example to set. This may be able to be achieved in a number of different types of school. As a report on Church of England schooling commented:

> Our view is that Church schools are a legitimate expression of diversity within the educational system. We question the assumption that religion is by its nature inescapably divisive, and the philosophical corollary of this assumption that only a 'secular' understanding of the world can be truly inclusive. (Dearing 2001, pp. 16–17)

Notwithstanding the religious or non-religious status of the school, and the dangers and opportunities provided by that status, an inclusive learning community will need to include, in some way, people and practices from a range of religious and other traditions. Thinking of a religion as a neat set of beliefs and practices and organisations, all tied together in the name of a god, a sacred person or a holy book, makes a lot of sense. It is how religions are most often described in popular textbooks and on television. Those same books and television programmes are full of facts and figures: there are so many million followers of this religion, and so many more million followers of that religion; this country is 42% this religion, 55% that religion, and 3% non-religious. However, this is misleading. The religious education researcher Teece suggests that one of the problems is that religions are often understood naturalistically, non-religiously, sociologically, phenomenologically, anthropologically, or historically: religions are not always understood 'religiously' (in Stern 2007a, p. 95, and see Baumfield et al. 1994). People are religious or non-religious in different ways. For some, being religious is evident in everything they do; for others, there is almost no evidence of religion in what they do and believe. But most people are in between, even those who do not think of themselves as religious at all. Taylor refers to 'secular humanism' as having 'its roots in Judaeo–Christian faith; it arises from a mutation out of a form of that faith' (Taylor 1989, p. 319). The writer Jack Priestley tells the story of the English atheist philosopher Bertrand Russell talking to the Indian atheist politician Pandit Nehru, saying that they had their atheism in common. Nehru apparently replied that they should remember: Russell was a Christian atheist, while he, Nehru, was a Hindu atheist.

There are religious groups, or approaches to religion, that may upset or annoy many of those who say they believe in multi-religious, interfaith, inclusion. Put together a group of professional specialists in religious tolerance, and mention fundamentalism, Plymouth Brethren, Paganism, Mormons, or Voudou, let alone Satanism or witchcraft: some will be surprised and fascinated, others appalled. There should not be such surprise. Deep in most religious traditions is an absolute and fundamental rejection of other religious traditions. In most of the big 'respectable' mainstream religions, non-believers are said to go to hell, even if this is said rather quietly, with hell often portrayed in contemporary traditions as being without God rather than as a fiery expanse. There has since the seventeenth century been a 'decline of Hell' (Taylor 1989, p. 318, following Walker 1964), and 'many theologians . . . are reticent about the doctrine of hell' (Bowker 1997, p. 420, but see also Cain 2002). If going to hell is still a mainstream if far from universal religious judgement on those of different traditions or practices, then it is difficult to see how much further beyond the pale a tradition can go. Religious inclusion, to have any meaning, must include 'hell-bound' traditions among which are many of those that have all too often been excluded from multi-religious and interfaith projects.

Inclusion of the curriculum and of people

Religion and religious inclusion in school learning communities is complex, then, and controversial. Understanding religiousness is just one example of how a school can be an inclusive learning community. The same risky embrace of diverse ways of life can be described, for example, of political views and national identities. What is important is an inclusion that brings in such diversity, and the curriculum is that which brings in to the school the diversity beyond the school. Religious education, history, and social studies subjects are the subjects that might be expected to bring in religious and political diversity; science might bring in diverse views of evolution or life or medical ethics; English, languages, art and music may bring in all kinds of cultural diversity and radically diverse ways of describing and interpreting the world. Each subject in its own way can have this function, along with many other functions. Analysis of the curriculum can therefore help people understand the degree of inclusiveness of subjects, yet on its own the curriculum is not enough to make for inclusive learning. The personal dimension of inclusion draws in the people of the school community. How people are included, and whether they are included as themselves, or as abstractions of themselves, or as means to ends beyond themselves, is the central question.

Inclusion, then, involves bringing people into the school, without the determined 'bracketing out' of aspects of those people. Along with the pupils and teachers, other people are to be included: other school staff, families of pupils, members of local communities, and people from well beyond the school building. Who is included, and what the school can do to enable greater inclusion, is worth further analysis. With respect to families, engagement with schools may be filled with uncertainty and potential conflict: visiting parents may, according to Hornby, be unsupportive, uncooperative, hostile, complaining, threatening, abusing, suffering from their own personal marital or family problems, vulnerable, and expecting too much or too little (G Hornby 2000, Chapter 9). Yet the *exclusion* of family members is unthinkable, and forms of inclusion must go beyond a bland expectation to talk only about 'the well-being of the parent's own child' while supporting 'the largely taken-for-granted value system of the school' and helping 'with fund-raising, or transmitting information' (Munn 1993, p. 1). Part of the complexity of family involvement in school is that created by the child's wish to be independent, to be 'an individual by contrasting himself [*sic*], and indeed by wilfully opposing himself to the family *to which he belongs*' (Macmurray 1996, p. 129). It is a complexity that cannot be avoided, and in recent years accounts of positive engagement with families, that are not at the expense of children, are becoming more common (e.g. Bastiani 1997, Bastiani and Wolfendale 1996, DfES 2003a, b, G Hornby 2000, Lawrence-Lightfoot 2003, Munn 1993, Stern 2003a, Topping 1986, Vincent 2000, Wolfendale 2002).

Through the use of books and computers, people can be brought into the school from the past, and from the other side of the world. Looking at the pictures on the walls of the school, or the pictures in the books used by pupils, the types of people being included, and those being excluded, become evident. It may be that women are excluded, through being made 'invisible' (Spender 1982), or that the populations of whole continents are excluded. Within school subjects, every pupil and teacher can include people, themselves and their own experiences, families and members of local communities, and more distant people. One of the ways that schools help with this form of inclusion is through the use of homework, a process by which school can not only be taken out into the world beyond school, but also a process by which the world can be brought into the school (Stern 2006a, introduction and Chapter 3 'bringing the world into the classroom'). The social and educational implications of this 'pushing out' and 'bringing in' are explored by learning theorist Engeström, who investigates the approach of Davydov, '*to push school knowledge out into the world* by making it dynamic and theoretically powerful in facing practical problems' (in Daniels 1996, p. 161, original emphasis), and of Lave and Wenger who promote 'pushing communities of practice from the outside world into the school' (in Daniels 1996, p. 164). It is this second 'drawing in' of people to the school that is of particular significance for inclusion. Engeström supports the idea of learning that can 'transcend the institutional boundaries of the school and turn the school into a collective instrument' (in Daniels 1996, pp. 168–9). The spiritual implications of these ways of bringing people into schools, as well as expanding beyond schools, are explored throughout the current book, following on from work on computers (e.g. Stern 2003b), and on sacred text (e.g. Stern 2006b, Chapter 2, 2007a, Chapter 6). Those publications develop a model of creative learning in which the 'output' of schooling, the 'pushing out into the world', is itself a spiritual matter.

Making sense: the spirit of creativity

Learning cannot be seen as a passive activity. It is necessarily 'constructive' or 'creative'. Creativity is typically associated with arts education, but it has a much more comprehensive role in schooling, and is central to many of the characteristics typically associated with spirituality such as relationships, flow, imagination, delight and despair. If spirituality overcomes dualisms, the spirit is itself creative and is about creating humanity itself. 'Pushing out into the world', to use Engeström's description of schooling, is also a good description of the birth of a child. Childbirth is itself the archetype of creativity or generation. As Klass notes, this creativity cannot be captured by scientific description alone, as '[n]o matter how scientifically we might now understand human reproduction, the baby feels like a new creation' (Klass 1999, p. 5). For Buber, the spirit 'steps forth' when a child begins to speak, and the growth, learning, and spirit of the child develop through learning. Although 'the spirit was in the child before it tells its story, . . . [t]he child "has spirit" for the first time when it speaks' (Buber 2002a, p. 229). Having been a potential before speech develops, dialogue or communication is how spirituality emerges. 'The spirit begins here as an instinct, as an instinct to the word, that is, as the impulse to be present with others in a world of streaming communication, of an image given and received' (Buber 2002a, p. 230). This concern with children's first words is shared with Macmurray who wrote extensively, and unusually for a philosopher of his time, on the conversations between mothers and children (Macmurray 1991b, Chapter 2). Since that time, further research on even younger children, has suggested that there is meaningful 'reasonable' communication at an even earlier stage, before the first words are spoken (notably Trevarthen in Fergusson and Dower 2002, p. 97). However, the power of meaningful speech, recognised by Buber and Macmurray, and its signalling of being 'spirited', is an important foundation for work on creative learning.

Agency, originality and value

The description of creativity given earlier in this chapter is one in which people make themselves in learning, as well as making new meanings and new things. The three concepts capturing much of creativity are agency, originality and value. Agency implies creativity as making, that is, a generative or spontaneous in contrast to a passive or externally directed process. It involves the creator being responsible for what is created. The second of the three concepts, originality, implies a novel in contrast to a copied, imitated or routine process, related to context: that is, the relationship of the process to other processes known to the person. Value is embedded within the concept of agency: a person's responsibility is itself implied by the person being in a position to make evaluative judgements. That is, the person knew and understood something of what they were doing as they were doing it. It is also embedded in originality, as the scope of originality, the agent's horizon, can also determine the degree of value. A six-year-old child is likely to have little experience or understanding of the artistic products of large social groups and different historical periods: the horizon is close. What is 'beautiful' for that six-year-old child, then, is likely to be determined by a very small-scale originality, and the product may be said to be less 'beautiful' when set in a broader group with a wider horizon. 'Beauty has never been absolute and immutable but has taken on different aspects depending on the historical period and the country: and this does not hold only for physical Beauty (of men, of women, of the landscape) but also for the Beauty of God, or the saints, or ideas' (Eco 2004, p. 14). Hence, value is generated by the evaluation of the creator and of a variety of peer groups. Among the peer groups of significance in school are other pupils. As Craft says, '[i]t is . . . important to . . . make use of peer review and self-evaluation by pupils, as this may produce a variety of value judgements, contributing to an evaluation profile' (Craft et al. 2001, p. 21).

Creativity, like spirituality, is in and of a place, then, and stretches beyond that place: it has a horizon. The peers who are evaluating are the 'we' of creativity, those who are this side of the horizon. As Owen says, '[i]t makes more sense to talk of 'our' creativity than 'my' or 'your' creativity', 'so when it comes to our own thoughts about how we make our own children more creative, and how to prevent their creativity being killed off, then starting with ourselves – and how we are creative *with* our children – is an excellent place to start' (Owen 2007). Evaluation is a moderating process, with both 'yes' and 'no' in it. Owen goes on to say:

> There are two easy routes to killing creativity in your children (if that's what you want to do!).
>
> Route One: say 'no' to everything they suggest, think about, play with and are curious about. Be sure to block initiative, stifle unacceptable behaviour and generate fear about the consequences of their actions. Worry them about their appearance, their status in other people's eyes and what their attitudes and behaviour might say about you than it might say about them.
>
> Route Two: say 'yes' to everything they suggest, think about, play with and are curious about. Be sure they understand there are no such things as boundaries of any sort, that all kinds of behaviour in any circumstances are completely acceptable. Encourage them to think that all their ideas are perfect and require no further modification from any other source at all. Offer free, unconditional, unending praise for any kind of behaviour and have an unending supply of house points for every time they do something you think is creative. (Owen 2007)

Free unconditional unending praise is suggested as a possible problem in Northcliffe school (secondary, UK), whose headteacher refers to 'a very bizarre combination of optimism . . . based on low expectations' or 'phoney optimism'. How real creativity, rather than universal praise or universal criticism, can be promoted in schools, and the opportunities thereby created for spiritual development, is also embedded in and emerges from individual subjects, individual processes and activities of the school. It is worth educational researchers considering some of these school subjects, not least because so much of education research ignores the substance of school subjects and investigates instead features of schools such as 'effectiveness' or 'standards' or 'skills' that are regarded – incorrectly – as independent of those subjects. As the sociologist Bernstein said, since the 1960s, much of the research on education was 'culture free' and ignored the distinct 'bodies of knowledge' to which school subjects were related (Bernstein in Daniels 1993, pp. xvii, xx). Since the re-emergence of educational research based on the approach of Vygotsky, children and learning have become more 'contextualised' and the research more 'socio-centric' (Bernstein in Daniels 1993, p. xxii). Teaching is now more likely to be seen as having 'a profoundly creative character' (Davydov, quoted by Daniels 2001, p. 29), through, and not independent of, school subjects.

Creativity, discipline and authenticity

The idea of originality in artistic creativity and its parallel in personal creativity, the making of the self, is seen by Taylor as having been developed roughly 200 years ago, when art became '[n]o longer defined mainly by imitation, by *mimēsis* of reality, art is understood now more in terms of creation', that is, '*poiēsis*, making' (Taylor 1991, p. 62). At a personal level, '[i]f we become ourselves by expressing what we're about, and if what we become is by hypothesis original, not based on the pre-existing, then what we express is not an imitation of the pre-existing either, but a new creation' (Taylor 1991, p. 62). Taylor insists that this approach to creativity and to personal authenticity is a positive feature of modernity, of the current 'sources of the self: the making of the modern identity' (Taylor 1989, title). At the same time, he worries about 'the slide to subjectivism' (Taylor 1991, p. 55) and a 'social *atomism* . . . [that] tend[s] to see fulfilment as just of the self, neglecting or delegitimating the demands that come from beyond our own desires or aspirations, be they from history, tradition, society, nature, or God; they foster, in other words, a radical anthropocentrism' (Taylor 1991, p. 58, original emphasis). In school contexts, the personal and artistic tension between traditional imitation, *mimēsis*, and original making, *poiēsis*, can be illustrated by the use of the term 'discipline'. An academic school subject can be called a 'discipline', a set of rules and practices which must be followed by those learning the subject, just as the school may be expected to impose 'discipline' on its pupils, through rules on behaviour. The term 'discipline' comes from the same root as 'disciple'. A disciple is one who learns, its first meaning, and one who follows, its second meaning (SOED 2007). An academic discipline may be regarded as a framework for learning, or as a restriction on freedom or originality; personal discipline may be seen as a framework for communal or social living, or as a denial of individual personality or authenticity.

Holding these two ideas of discipline together, Macmurray described UK politics, in a BBC radio programme broadcast in the early 1930s, as a contrast between a version of discipline and a version of freedom. He says the 'modern spirit' is characterised by the contrast between Nietzsche and Marx. Nietzsche 'is the protagonist of Fascism, because Fascism wishes to call a halt in the struggle for freedom and go back to the old idea of authority and discipline, to the old Roman tradition of Europe from which the modern spirit has been in revolt', whilst Marx 'is the protagonist of Socialism, for Socialism reasserts the faith in freedom and equality, and demands that we shall not call a halt and retrace our steps, but carry the struggle through to the bitter end' (Macmurray 1933, p. 188). He concludes that '[i]t is between these two that the modern spirit has got to make its choice' (Macmurray 1933, p. 188, the final words on the 'makers of the modern spirit'). However, this contrast, presumably intended to promote socialism and Marx as against fascism and Nietzsche, exaggerated Macmurray's views of the contrast between discipline and freedom (and between Nietzsche and Marx), which in other circumstances he put together, albeit in tension. He says of schooling that 'in the choice of subjects and the organisation of curriculum, I should make it a first principle of choice that the development of disciplined imagination and spontaneity of emotional expression are all-important' (Macmurray 1968, p. 44). Macmurray goes on to say that people should not, in fact, contrast 'freedom' and 'discipline', as '[d]iscipline is the condition of all freedom in human life, and all training is discipline' (Macmurray 1968, p. 33). Behavioural discipline in a school 'may be willingly and gratefully welcomed by its pupils or it may be imposed and enforced', with the latter to be avoided as it 'means that the motive for accepting it is fear, and to enforce discipline is to use fear as an educational motive: I will not say that this is never justifiable, but I will say that it can only be justified as a last resort; and that it implies a confession of failure' (Macmurray 1968, p. 33).

For subject disciplines, Macmurray 'would seek to use the normal and necessary subjects and disciplines of any curriculum as a medium for the development of spontaneity of feeling and imagination; within an atmosphere of positive community and co-operation' (Macmurray 1968, p. 44). One of the examples he gives is of history:

> History . . . can be taught as an exercise in intellectual technique which extends the range of knowledge and understanding. But it can also be used as an instrument of imaginative self-transcendence and of emotional expression. It can be dramatised and re-enacted; not merely in the mind. In this way it becomes a medium of cultural development. (Macmurray 1968, p. 44)

Teachers, like pupils, must be disciplined, and 'must have gone through the process of learning to be human with at least a fair measure of success', and 'must be qualified on the artistic side – I mean he must not be bookish or merely intellectual . . . but . . . be alive and creative; his imagination must be active and disciplined' (Macmurray 1968, p. 154). In the teaching of literature, a teacher 'who doesn't like poetry, for example, cannot teach poetry to children', as '[e]ven if he masters all the latest methods of poetry teaching, and carries them out faithfully and well, he will only waste the children's time, and – what matters less perhaps – his own' (Macmurray 1968, p. 154). From other sources could be added music, which can enable spiritual development through being able to 'promote discipline, inner strength and resilience through practice to achieve an ideal sound or technique' (Chichester Diocesan Board of Education 2006, p. 25), maths, which involves 'appreciating the beauty and perfection of mathematics' (Chichester Diocesan Board of Education 2006, p. 20), or design and technology, which involves 'appreciating variety, beauty, ingenuity, achievement, magnificence, and simplicity in design' (Chichester Diocesan Board of Education 2006, p. 22).

It is on the 'education of the emotions', a phrase that might suit various school subjects such as personal, social, emotional or character education, that Macmurray best describes his views on the nature of behavioural discipline. 'The traditional methods', he says, 'which are now for the most part happily superseded, or at least out of favour, have been that of a stern discipline of punishment and repression' (Macmurray 1995, p. 37). Although 'in its worst forms this old-fashioned discipline was barbarous', and 'has been largely replaced by a more humane conception', at least these 'older disciplinary methods, if they rested upon fear, yet avoided the more subtle dangers of exploiting the child's natural affection and reverence for authority' (Macmurray 1995, p. 37). What was worse, he said, was to have methods that 'rest on an appeal to the child's "better nature"', as those 'exploit . . . the child's natural affection and reverence for authority' (Macmurray 1995, p. 37). The consequence of this view of discipline and the emotions is a clear view of emotional education:

> Emotional education should be . . . a considered effort to teach children to feel for themselves; in the same sense that their intellectual training should be an effort to teach them to think for themselves. So long as we start with the assumption that we know how people ought to feel, and that it is our business to teach our pupils to feel in that way, the less successful we are the better. We have to realize how feeble and ineffective our own emotional life is, and to realize that for that very reason our notions of what is good feeling and what is not are also feeble and probably false. Then we shall perhaps begin to discover what we can do to develop in children the rich capacity for a spontaneous emotional life which has been so stunted in ourselves. One of the first results of such a fundamental change of attitude would be, I doubt not, that we should recognize that it is as ridiculous to put the emotional training of children in the hands of teachers whose emotional life is of a low grade or poorly developed, as it is to commit their intellectual education to teachers who are intellectually unintelligent and stupid. (Macmurray 1995, p. 39)

Macmurray has a strong view of subject disciplines and of behavioural discipline, and this underpins his views of schooling, all of which in turn have helped generate the *Spirit of the School* research. Inclusive and creative subjects bring in people and cultures, and enable pupils to make, re-make, with originality, things or ideas of value. The spirit of the school can therefore be described in part through subjects. These would be, as Macmurray says, the 'normal and necessary' subjects, rather than a new set specifically designed to promote spirituality. Subjects vary so much between systems, according to the age of the pupils, the country, and the fashions of the day, that treating any single subject, let alone a whole curriculum, as uniquely required of schooling would be misleading. A curriculum may also be driven by skills, by themes or topics, or by vocational disciplines, so the very existence of subjects is not guaranteed, although it is worth stressing the need for 'discipline'. For learning to be inclusive it must be able to connect to, to bring in, people and cultures and ways of living from the past and from beyond the confines of the school. One of the ways that schools can create unnecessary barriers to the involvement of parents and carers in the education of their children is to create a curriculum with such arcane and unrecognisable elements, subjects or themes, that only professional educators, and pupils, can understand.

The spirit of the schools

How people are included in schools and how they learn, create, are personal matters, educational matters, and spiritual matters. As it is described here, spirituality is that which overcomes dualism; it bridges, it brings together. Spirituality also goes beyond (it involves transcendence), yet, like a bridge, it remains on this side of the duality (it involves immanence). People may apparently be included, but only by rejecting elements that are important to them. People may apparently be encouraged to be creative, even visionary, but only by repeating other people's creations, other people's visions. If the curriculum is so boxed and the teaching so predictable that it is all known in advance, then where is the room for originality and for responsibility? Many of the questions and activities carried out in the *Spirit of the School* project (described in the Appendix) helped generate ideas on inclusion and creativity. The Salmon Line activity, describing the extent to which the school is a community and how it might become more of a community, generated a number of ideas on inclusion. More explicitly, the second of the 'circles of importance' activities, asking 'to what do I belong, in school?', and the follow-up question 'when do you feel most included in school?', addressed the nature of membership and inclusion. Inclusion as an act of 'bringing in' was investigated through asking 'about a time in school when you talked about something important to you', and 'what, from your life outside school, is something that is studied in school?' For creativity, the activities exploring the nature of learning included the 'what is typically said?' work in various classroom activities and at playtime. Both inclusion and creativity were illustrated by responses to the questions asking about recent or memorable times that the current school, and for adults also the schools they attended as children, made the respondents feel good about themselves.

There is a complex relationship between the empirical research and the literature-based work of the *Spirit of the School* project (described in Chapter 1 in terms of 'conversations with books and with people'), belied by the presentation of key empirical findings in this separate section towards the end of the chapter. Theoretical positions have been immensely influenced at all stages by the process of the research, the informal discussions with pupils and school staff, as well as with co-researchers and with researchers and other participants in a number of conferences and presentations. The cyclical nature of action research and, as is presented here, action philosophy (mentioned in Chapter 1, and derived from Stern 2007c and 2007a, pp. 1–2), makes it difficult to separate different influences. However, the work on inclusion and creativity has been informed by how participants in the research describe their own learning. For example, despite the sense in which all subjects can be creative, a striking feature of the research was the predominance, in people's memories of how the school made them feel good about themselves, of 'traditionally' creative subjects. Respondents repeatedly talked about musical performances, school plays, sporting achievements, and the products of art and craft lessons. Similarly, despite the sense in which literature, art and computers can provide access to people and ideas from around the world, respondents highlighted the 'traditional' interactions with visitors to the school, and visits from the school to adventure parks and galleries and churches. If it appears to be technologically naïve or Luddite, then that is regrettable. Nevertheless, the research prioritised the physical presence of objects and people and places, and underplayed their virtual presence through the technologies of books, computers, or mass media. As Blumberg says, in her argument for 'technology-free space in religious education':

> The teacher and the other students in the class may be spiritual models for a learner. The students learn to struggle with belief, faith, doubt, joy, and sorrow through the relationships they develop. For some, it is the relationship with the teacher that is most meaningful. For others, the relationships to their fellow students create deep and lasting bonds. . . . The participants [in Blumberg's research] believed that face to face, either an authority figure or another friend was the most positive and powerful of the learning experiences they identified. . . . In both groups [i.e. teachers and students], there was a feeling that technology may have gotten in the way of their communication. (Blumberg 2008, p. 9)

The remainder of this section therefore looks at some of the ways in which the *Spirit of the School* participants viewed inclusion and creativity in their schools.

Inclusion in and out of groups

A combination of group work and individual work is explicitly recognised by the pupil Anthony (aged 11, in Afton primary Church of England school, UK): 'I think this school has quite a high community because we can help each other if we want and we can work individually if that's how we feel.' He continues:

> we started clubs afternoon like last year and it's got more of the school into groups, so we can do stuff together but, and so by next year we might have another thing like what puts you into groups, like creative arts groups, because that's where you work into groups of like five or six, and you go and do stuff like, we do like playmaking and things like that and we've got, it's like it's year six and five together to do things which we can do together and then say in English, Maths sometimes you just want to do on our own.

This sense that there is a wide range of group activity and yet opportunities for individual work underpinned by the possibility of help (as 'it's nice knowing that people who will help you can help you') is a subtle grasp of the value of inclusion in Afton. Help is not to be of a kind that creates a dependency, as Henry (aged 9) notes of the pupils working well together even before the flood:

> before the flood anyway we had all these clubs going on and the field were perfectly dry, there was loads of sport and everyone got on, we worked in groups, and we managed to get along, and if the teacher had to go out of the classroom, then we would just get on with our work and it would be quiet.

The inclusive nature of another school, Ruislip (a Church of England primary school in the UK), is illustrated by an account that, interestingly, includes a rejection by one of the respondents of the Christianity that underpins the school, while still feeling comfortable engaging and 'believing' (also discussed below, in Chapter 6). It is also illustrated by the way in which the subjects are organised, analysed in terms of Daniels' classification and framing. According to Daniels (2001, Chapter 5), classification (how 'bounded' a subject is) and framing (how dominated by the teacher a subject is) can be stronger or weaker – and weaker classification/framing makes for a more inclusive schooling. Starting with the nature of school subjects and the boundaries between them (what Daniels, following Bernstein, refers to as the 'classification' of subjects), this is illustrated by the conversation in Ruislip school following an account of a visit to York Minster:

Interviewer:	So, what sort of lesson, tell me what sort of lesson that was?
Lucia:	It was
Jonathan:	It was kind of history
Lucia:	It was history and RE
Jonathan:	RE.

Having difficulty explaining which subject was being studied suggests a weaker classification of subjects, and is further illustrated by Lucia's description of circle time as having taken place possibly in English: 'once in circle time we talked about, I think it was in English I think, and we talked about good changes in our life and bad changes'. According to Daniels, weaker classification of these kinds is likely to help in making the classrooms more inclusive of pupils with emotional and behavioural diffi-culties, as 'collaborative patterns of staff working . . . [is one of the] key indicators of what we define as good practice' (Daniels 2001, p. 139). In the respondents' subsequent description of a typical history lesson, there is also an excellent description of weaker 'framing', where the teacher is clearly opening up the subject to pupils by working from what they already know. Jonathan starts the description with what could well be a 'strongly framed' statement by the teacher of 'right, we're going to learn, you're going to be learning about ancient Egypt', but as Terence joins in (opening his contribution with 'I know what to do'), the description becomes more weakly framed:

Terence:	When it's the first lesson that we've done it, out of the whole time, then she just asks us 'What do we know?'
Jonathan:	about Egypt
Lucia:	Yeah
Interviewer:	Okay
Terence:	and like what we did, I think it was the
Jonathan:	The last topic
Terence:	Tudors or Victorians, we, we did one and then right at the end we got a different colour . . . and wrote all the new things that we had learned
Jonathan:	Yeah, . . . like if you didn't know that much, you will put it in red . . . if you
Terence:	and then right at the end
Jonathan:	It was

Terence:	it was done in a different colour
Jonathan:	If you like, if you know a lot of it, you'll put green and if you kind of know stuff, . . . you put in yellow.

For English or literacy lessons, the respondents have greater difficulty saying what a teacher might typically say, despite descriptions of English or literacy work on persuasive writing. With encouragement from the interviewer, who clarifies the imaginative requirement of the exercise, and helpfully leaves the sentence unfinished ('well, if, if she was to have done, what sort of thing, it doesn't have to be something that she actually said, what sort of thing do you think she might'), Jonathan finally suggests:

Jonathan:	She, you have to do, we're doing like a poster
Lucia:	poster
Jonathan:	of
Terence:	persuading people to drink water
Jonathan:	people to drink water more
Interviewer:	Okay. So what would she say to you?
Jonathan:	She could be saying that, you could draw poster of somebody drinking water or something.

This seems fairly weakly framed (as it does not involve the teacher giving explicit and narrowly defined tasks), and yet the respondents still have difficulty describing what a pupil might be saying, eventually, with prompting from the interviewer, involving pupils giving examples of words with particular beginnings, which are good examples of much more strongly framed teaching:

Interviewer:	Okay and what would the child be saying in the picture about that? What sort of ideas might they have do you think?
Terence:	I don't know really
Interviewer:	What sort of things do you say? What sort of things do you talk about in literacy and English?
Jonathan:	About water
Interviewer:	Letters or sounds or your writing, what sort of thing would you say?
Jonathan:	In physics we learned about sound
Interviewer:	Do you? What sort of sounds you're doing at the moment?
Jonathan:	[*unclear*] weren't with us
Interviewer:	Okay, it doesn't matter. How about you then Jonathan? It doesn't matter

Jonathan:	We do SH, CH, we do everything, we do like letters what end in like SH or something
Interviewer:	okay
Jonathan:	because this morning I came out with loads of answers for CH. It had to be at the beginning.

Religious education in a religiously sponsored school might be expected to involve some stronger 'framing', as it might be thought that such a school would promote the sponsoring religion (i.e. in this case Christianity). There is some evidence of this, in the emphasis given to 'God and Jesus' (repeated for further emphasis), and to prayers that fit Christian models of prayer:

Interviewer:	So, if it was an RE lesson what might your teacher say to you then, for RE?
Terence:	As far as we're doing in RE, we're doing
Jonathan:	We are doing religion of God and Jesus. We're doing stuff about God and Jesus
Interviewer:	So, what might the teacher mention about God and Jesus do you think? Would she ask you a question or ask you to do something? . . .
Lucia:	In our RE lesson last week, Mrs . . . told us to think of a line to go in our prayer when we went to York Minster . . .
Terence:	and this was our prayer in the crypt
Interviewer:	Oh, lovely, lovely. So, did you think of something?
Lucia:	Yeah, . . . we each thought of a line
Interviewer:	So, what sort of line did you come up with? What might the pupil, the child in the picture say? What sort of thing if she was asked, she was asked to put a line together? What sort of lines did you come up with? Can you remember any?
Terence:	I can, it was stuff like 'Thank you God for food and water' . . . 'Thank you God for letting us come to this wonderful place' . . . things like that.

Of course, writing a prayer to be said in a Christian church might be expected to be typically Christian. There is evidence later in the interview when Terence 'objectifies' the Christian nature of what he has said, suggesting he has understood and would therefore be in a position to reject stronger 'framing' by the school, and perhaps even the 'framing' by the interviewer in saying 'that's good' to his religious statement. Terence's position is complemented by Jonathan's clear rejection of Christianity, accompanied by an acceptance that he nevertheless 'believes': 'I'm not Christian but I still believe' (discussed further in Chapter 6, below). Religious education at Ruislip also includes work on other religions (as indicated in the relevant syllabus – East Riding of Yorkshire Council 2005 – as well as the church's guidance). Terence and Lucia refer to learning about 'Jewish', 'Hindi' and Buddhism, to provide evidence of weaker framing in the subject than might be expected.

Other examples of weaker framing include reference to work on a stained glass window for the new school hall, which will be designed by the pupils. They describe this with some excitement (evidenced by all talking together), and link it also to the school trip to York Minster. Although the final design will be picked by the manufacturer, it will have been designed by a pupil:

Jonathan:	They start doing the roof [of the new school hall] now, they have to do, put the windows in and we're going to get a big stained glass window
Terence:	stained glass window [at the same time]
Jonathan:	and we're going to design it
Interviewer:	What the design? You're going to design it?
Lucia:	Yeah
Jonathan:	Yeah, like York Minster
Interviewer:	Like York Minster? You're going to have the rose window?
Jonathan:	No, no at York Minster like if you are above it, it like a cross shape
Terence:	Yeah . . .
Interviewer:	So, you're designing your own window
Lucia and Jonathan:	[together] Yeah
Interviewer:	That's great
Jonathan:	and we have to give it to this man or woman, I can't remember and she or he is going to pick which one to do.

The 'show and tell' work in circle time is also mentioned, and is another example of weaker framing, as 'sometime somebody [a pupil] gives, brings some stuff to show and we have to sit in a circle and we pass 'em all along . . . and we have to, like, and look at it'. Including people through the work itself is a helpful description of the possibility of inclusive learning.

Made up

The phrase 'made up' has a number of meanings. It can mean that something is not true: the person has invented the account, rather than
described reality. It can mean that something has been constructed or
manufactured: the material has been 'made up' into a suit. In colloquial
English, it can also mean pleased or satisfied, especially for someone else,
as in the statement 'I'm made up for you'. The fictionalising, manufactur-
ing, and satisfying meanings are all related, because all indicate forms
of creativity and how that creativity is also a personal, communal and
pleasurable matter. One event at Richardson seems to illustrate all three
senses. Recently, the school had suspended the normal curriculum in
order to have a 'super learning day', where pupils and teachers would
work together on the theme of health, with teachers working with pupils
they may not have previously worked with, and pupils grouped according
to their choices of topics and not according to their ages or classes.
Gloria, a teacher, describes the day as one of the most memorable times
the school made her feel good about herself:

> but one thing that sticks in my mind is our last super learning day
> and, and it was lovely, the staff were all very enthusiastic, the
> children, every child was totally involved. [Interviewer: Why did it
> make you feel good about yourself then?] I'm not sure if it's a
> personal thing but I'd say we'd done a good job, we, we worked as a
> staff and because we'd all played our parts and worked together the
> whole day was a success and we got a lot out of it, . . . and the
> children learnt a lot which was obviously . . . the idea behind it . . .
> and . . . it was lovely, there was a real buzz . . . and it was good.

Central to this description are enthusiasm (the 'real buzz'), teamwork
(among teachers and with pupils), and learning by teachers (who 'got a
lot out of it') and by pupils. The headteacher of Richardson also
mentions this super learning day, and adds to the inclusive and creative
dimensions of the description, in response to a question about a time
when she talked about something that was important to her:

> Last week we had one of our work super learning days which we do
> every term where the children work in mixed aged groups, so we
> have like a special day, so instead of the children working . . . all year
> six together, the children are in teams and they work with their
> teams. . . . We've had children from four to eleven working together

and our theme for this one was about healthy living, . . . so each
teacher was doing something related to healthy living. So one
teacher would be doing exercise, one teacher would be doing you
know fruit and vegetables, healthy eating, . . . that kind of thing, one
teacher was doing relaxation, they were doing yoga and talking
about lavender and things and it was my role to, to start the day with
an assembly and finish the day with an assembly. So, I started it by
bringing lots of things from home and talking what's important
healthwise in our house. . . . So, I've brought things like my trainers
. . . and said I don't wear them very often but you know when I do,
it's because you know when we are walking whether we are on
holiday or . . . whatever and I brought a card in that my little girl had
got because she'd come second in an ice-skating competition . . .
and I've always said you know that was important for her because
she'd done well and it was nice to know that other people thought
she'd done well because it, . . . you know, so I brought things like
that in that were important to me, to show the children that it's not
just about what happens in school, it's about . . . what happens
outside.

Bringing in to the school and pushing school learning out of the
school: both were recognised in these descriptions. An interesting characteristic of the day was its cross-curricular nature: the subjects appeared to
be weakly classified or even unclassified. This is also well described by
Charlotte, aged 10, a pupil at the same school, in describing a class visit to
a football stadium. She says that the school makes her feel good about
herself 'when Miss Sue takes us on trips', and continues:

like yesterday we went to the [name of football stadium] and it's, we
had to do like electric about, well yeah science and like art, we had
to make this car and we had to blow a balloon up and put it on it and
the balloon just made it like go off.

Charlotte and the other pupils carry on to describe in detail the
making of the car. The 'making up' of creativity is also well described by
the headteacher, in response to the question about how the school made
her feel good about herself:

Year two [aged 6 to 7] did their class assembly and they stood up in
front of the whole school and an audience of parents and carers and
showed what they've been doing in class this year, . . . and it was

delightful, the children stood up and it's hard isn't it, when you are only seven and they told what they've done and they read poems that they'd written individually and collectively and they were using words like 'alliteration' and 'onomatopoeia' and I just thought . . . for seven that was, . . . it was a lovely assembly not just because they were using those words but the way they were so excited about sharing what they'd done and I, I thought that was lovely and I thought the children, you know, did it well and the teacher had just let the children do it and write it really, . . . so she just took a back seat and just let them share what they had done. [Interviewer: So, it made you feel good because?] Because the children had the confidence . . . to stand up . . . and tell us, tell the children and the parents what they had been doing and obviously by what they're doing you could see that they were working very hard, they were proud of what they had achieved. . . . It was . . . their poems, they had put it together . . . I mean she'd obviously helped them with pictures and things and put the order together but it was all based on everything that they had written.

The weaker framing of the work, exemplified by the way the teacher 'took a back seat', combined with the involvement of the wider school community, including parents, and the proper pride of the pupils in their own work, combine to produce an authoritative account of the spirit of that particular school.

Conclusion

Richardson's headteacher, who had been in post 'just over a year', was clearly getting to the stage in her own role when she was sufficiently aware of the school's (and therefore her own) good qualities, to be able to celebrate them. Indeed, at one moment in the interview, she makes the decision to add to her 'circles of importance' activity on 'what beliefs and ideas are most important'. 'I'm going to put in here', she says, 'I'm going to have celebration in there, into my beliefs and ideas that are most important.' Being ready to celebrate, and to use celebration to share across and beyond the school, is a good way of including (bringing in to the school, including the diverse people and practices within the school) and a way of creating (making things that are put up for evaluation by a wider audience), that can generate proper pride in learning. A similar description came from Morag (aged 9, at Long Barrow primary school,

Church of England, UK), incorporating learning, relationships beyond the school, achievement, and pride:

> We have like an achievement assembly and we get certificates, like if we've done something, like to help people or like doing something good in our work or something like that. It's just sort of like, yeah, makes you a bit more, like, cheerful and things like that, and proud.

Anyone would be 'made up' for such pupils, actively involved, learning together in a creative school, valuing their work sufficiently to be able to present it to a wide audience, and having the strength to feel a proper pride.

Chapter 4

Monologue or dialogue?
Stepping away from the abyss

. . . mutual surprises.

(Buber 2002a, p. 241)

Introduction

For some strange reason, many English people are poor at languages other than English. Typically, an English-schooled person will have learned to speak French. When they go to France, they find that they can indeed say what they have learned, and yet the French person to whom they talk says something unpredictable and incomprehensible in return. The French, like the English, are unpredictable in their conversations: in neither nation do people speak quite as they do in textbooks. So it is not enough to learn to speak in French: it is necessary to learn to *listen* in French. The same is often true of new teachers. They know how to speak 'teacher', what to say in the classroom, and they may plan in great detail their script for the lesson. What is harder to do is to work out how to *listen* in 'teacher', how to respond to the unpredictable comments made by their pupils. Dialogue is mutual and, if it is real dialogue, it is surprising: hence the Buber quotation in the chapter heading.

This chapter explores Buber's approach to dialogue, and why that approach is of such importance to schools and to learning more broadly conceived. Buber's 'dialogic principle' is far more than an encouragement to talk. Dialogue in learning has an ontological significance and helps form both a groundwork for schooling, answering the question 'why do we school?', and a task for schools, answering the question 'how do we school?' He expresses this double value of the dialogic principle in his preface to *Between Man and Man*, the central text used in this chapter. There, he refers to 'education' rather than 'schooling' (Buber 2002a, p. x), as he is keen to alert the reader to other forms of learning, and clearly considers there are important distinctions between school-based education (as described in Smith 2000), let alone learning beyond formal institutions. Dialogue is central to learning, and both have an historical significance as well as an immediate educational significance. The world is moving close to an abyss, and dialogue may move us away from that abyss.

Moving away from the abyss is a persuasive if not complete justification of schooling, an answer to the question 'why do we school?' To answer *how*, rather than why, we school, Buber and others embed dialogue in a kind of apprenticeship model of learning and of schooling. Apprenticeship in learning has become fashionable in recent years, through the work of Lave and Wenger (1991, Wenger 1998) and Gardner (1991, pp. 121–5), but its underpinning by Buber helps strengthen their argument, by applying the model more clearly to schooling and to becoming human. Lave and Wenger 'do not talk . . . about schools in any substantial way, nor explore what our work has to say about schooling' (Lave and Wenger 1991, p. 39). Gardner recognises that 'apprenticeships may well be the means of instruction that builds most effectively on the ways in which most young people learn' (Gardner 1991, p. 124), and he goes on to commend education that involves 'the melding of certain features of apprenticeship with certain aspects of schools and other institutions, such as children's museums' (Gardner 1991, p. 125). Buber's approach draws out the wider social and political significance of dialogue, learning and becoming human as an apprenticeship in becoming more human, more real, within schools. This parallels the educational philosophy of Macmurray (1968, and explicated in Stern 2001b). Buber traces the history of the development of learning, from apprenticeships to formal schooling. 'There was a time, there were times, where there neither was nor needed to be any specific calling of educator or teacher', but instead there was 'a master, a philosopher or a coppersmith, whose journeymen and apprentices lived with him and learned, by being allowed to share in it' (Buber 2002a, p. 106). The learners 'also learned, without either their or his [*sic*] being concerned with it, they learned, without noticing that they did, the mystery of personal life: they received the spirit' (Buber 2002a, p. 106 [Buber and his translators use non-inclusive masculine pronouns throughout his writings, and they are retained here when quoted directly]).

Despite the difficulties of retaining an apprenticeship model, as teachers must be conscious of their roles as teachers, 'the master remains the model for the teacher', as 'if the educator of our day has to act consciously he must nevertheless do it "as though he did not"' (Buber 2002a, p. 107). In and beyond individual subjects of the curriculum, dialogue answers the why and how questions of schooling. This chapter does not look in detail at individual school subjects (though they are addressed in Chapter 3, above), yet the implications of each element of dialogue for every subject can be derived from this account. Buber's is a strictly dialogic description of apprenticeship, in which 'the spirit' is given and received, in which there is an inequality in the relationship (there is a 'master' and a 'pupil'), and in which dialogue itself makes the process mutual and unpredictable (progressing in 'mutual surprises'). Apprenticeship models of learning in school seem to have had a relatively small impact on schools policy, in contrast to the influence on further education. There is considerable interest in the links between schooling and vocational or work-related learning, but much of the schools policy related to this has distanced itself from apprenticeship. In the UK for example, 'apprenticeships' have struggled to gain high status, and 'practice' is seen as 'anti-academic'. Courses are therefore described as 'pre-vocational' (i.e. not yet vocational), as 'practical' or as suited to pupils who are 'less academic' (i.e. who are failing exams).

However, dialogue has had more of an impact on school policy, most particularly since the ratification of the United Nations Convention on the Rights of the Child (UNCRC) (UN 1989, in a simplified version UNICEF 2008, ratified in the UK in 1991, not yet ratified by the US). That document built on earlier conventions (especially the Declaration of the Rights of the Child, UN 1959), and promotes the idea that a 'child who is capable of forming his or her own views' should have 'the right to express those views freely in all matters affecting the child', and these views should be 'given due weight in accordance with the age and maturity of the child' (UN 1989, Article 12, p. 4). Further, it asserts 'the right of the child to freedom of thought, conscience and religion' (UN 1989, Article 14, p. 4). The convention has influenced international policy (Council of Europe 1996, on family life participation), national policy (such as the UK's *Children Act*, DoH 2004, and *Children's Plan*, DCSF 2007), age-group policy (for early years and childcare, Fajerman et al. 2001), and subject teaching (Lindon 1999 on world religions and early years practice, Hull 1998 and Ipgrave 2001, 2003, 2004 on religious education more generally). Dialogic implications of the convention are highlighted in the *Children's Plan*: '[t]o ensure that Government aims and policies reflect the priorities of children, young people, families and communities and build on best practice, we will establish an ongoing dialogue and consultation with children, young people, parents and professionals' (DCSF 2007, p. 165). Since the convention was agreed, just as the Cold War ended, further stimulus to dialogue with and between children has been provided by the reaction to different forms of international conflict, especially since 9/11.

Dialogue answers the why and how questions of school. This chapter moves from the consideration of dialogue in general (with its implications for individual subjects) through dialogue in conflict, dialogue in classrooms through dialogue beyond schools. It concludes with detailed evidence from schools.

Dialogue and duellism

The various essays published in Buber's *Between Man and Man* (Buber 2002a) develop the work of the earlier and better known *I and Thou* (Buber 1958, first published in 1923). They include *Dialogue* (first published in 1929), which explicitly attempts to 'clarify the "dialogical" principle presented in *I and Thou*, to illustrate it and to make precise its relation to essential spheres of life' (Buber 2002a, p. ix). There, Buber distinguishes three kinds of dialogue: technical dialogue (roughly, exchanging information), real or genuine dialogue (which for Buber has existential and religious significance), and 'monologue disguised as dialogue'. Technical dialogue 'is prompted solely by the need of objective understanding . . . [and] belongs to the inalienable sterling quality of "modern existence"' (Buber 2002a, p. 22). Genuine dialogue happens 'where each of the participants really has in mind the other or others in their present and particular being and turns to them with the intention of establishing a living mutual relation between himself [*sic*] and them . . . [and is] continually hidden in all kinds of odd corners and, occasionally in an unseemly way, breaks surface surprisingly and inopportunely' (Buber 2002a, p. 22). Monologue disguised as dialogue happens when 'two or more men, meeting in space, speak each with himself in strangely tortuous and circuitous ways and yet imagine they have escaped the torment of being thrown back on their own resources' (Buber 2002a, p. 22). The life of real dialogue involves a 'strengthening sense of reciprocity', while one of only monologue 'will not, even in the tenderest intimacy, grope out over the outlines of the self' (Buber 2002a, p. 24).

The ten-year-old Holly (Long Barrow Church of England primary school, UK) answers the question asking for times 'when you talked about something important to you' by describing what might be real dialogue, even though, and partly because, little was said:

when you feel ill or something and you would rather not tell somebody, there's . . . teachers that would just sort of . . . look after you, . . . you would come inside and they would just be like, oh do you want this or do you want that, and they wouldn't exactly ask you what's wrong with you because . . . they just sort of . . . see that you don't really want to discuss it, . . . so they just sort of . . . help us in a different way.

Dialogue is possible with few words; monologue, conversely, is possible despite many words being exchanged. Even philosophers risk living in monologue, as Buber wrote (in 1961) that '[m]any modern – and that means often de-Socratizing – philosophers have fallen, with the totality of their thought world, into a monologizing hubris' (Buber 1998, p. 103). This may help explain Buber's self-identification as a poet, rather than as a philosopher, as reported of a conversation with Macmurray: 'I see no difference between us', Buber said, '[i]t is simply that you are the meta-physician and I am the poet' (Costello 2002, p. 322).

'Real' conversations are similar to 'real' lessons or tutorials, and must involve dialogue, just as real embraces and, surprisingly, real duels. All involve that same existence in the between, as a person 'is a creature of the "between," of the happening between man and man that cannot be reduced to a sum of two individuals or to a merely psychological reality within the minds of each' (Friedman in Buber 2002a, p. xviii).

> In a real conversation (that is, not one whose individual parts have been preconcerted, but one which is completely spontaneous, in which each speaks directly to his partner and call forth his un-predictable reply), a real lesson (that is, neither a routine repetition nor a lesson whose findings the teacher knows before he starts, but one which develops in mutual surprises), a real embrace and not one of mere habit, a real duel and not a mere game – in all these what is essential does not take place in each of the participants or in a neutral world which includes the two and all other things; but it takes place between them in the most precise sense, as it were in a dimension which is accessible only to them both. (Buber 2002a, pp. 241–2)

Although it may seem strange to include duels in this list of real dialogic encounters, some evidence was generated, in the empirical research, for the importance of conflict – conflict itself, not its resolution – in bringing people together. A headteacher, in response to a question about how legislation and other regulations might have stopped him doing something he wanted to do, presented a fascinating picture of how personal identity is understood at times of difficulty. He describes how he managed to take a boy on a school trip, despite his parents being reluctant for him to go.

The boy actually cried on the morning that his mum brought him to school and she said he's crying and he won't come into school. So I said 'Well, we are going on a trip', so she said 'Well, can I, can you put him in one of the other classes, he doesn't want to go?' So, I bluffed, played a bluff on her really and said 'Look he either goes on the trip with me or you take him home and that's all that we're doing', and erm she said 'Well, I'd like him to go on the trip' and I said 'Right, come on the trip with me', and I actually picked him up and carried him into the school, and we had a big kicking session, where we didn't want to go, where we didn't want to do anything, after that had gone we, we calmed down again, we put the boy on the coach, went on the trip and he was fine and halfway between here and Leeds, he said 'this is the first time I've been out of the village', and all the legislation and all the rest of it just doesn't cover things, things like that really.

In analysing that account, what is most striking is that the pronouns used are 'I', 'he' and 'she', until the point at which the boy started kicking. Then, the pronoun used is 'we' (i.e. from 'we had a big kicking session'), with a reversion after 'we calmed down again' to the use of 'he' and 'I'. This use of pronouns suggests that, despite the conflict being problematic, it was indeed a time of 'inclusion', or in Buber's terms a period of real dialogue, of I and thou being described in terms of 'we'. The word 'we' may be used without sincerity, as in the question often put by medical professionals to patients, 'how are we feeling today?' Here, however, the word seems to indicate a period of struggle that, in the struggle, was of existential significance for both people, as '[o]nly men who are capable of truly saying *Thou* to one another can truly say *We* with one another' (Buber 2002a, p. 208). Whereas '[d]istance provides the human situation', 'relation provides man's becoming in that situation' (Buber 1998, p. 54). The two struggling people may have been granted a form of unity: 'in moments and forms of grace, unity can arise from the extreme tension of the contradiction as the overcoming of it, which is granted only now and in this way' (Buber 1998, p. 54). This is at the heart of dialogue rather than the Hegelian dialectic, a contrast well described by Wegerif. Wegerif highlights the need to consider dialectical models as based on the resolution of conflict, whereas dialogic models allow for meaning resting in the conflict itself. The author 'recovered' by Wegerif's clarification is Bakhtin, who 'associates the ambition to grasp everything with Hegel's dialectic and writes that this attempt to "erase the divisions between voices" would close down the infinite potential for meaning of dialogue' (Wegerif 2008, p. 358). This is, Wegerif continues, 'a "prophetic attitude", always open to the possibility of the "unexpected"' (Wegerif 2008, p. 359), rather like Buber's 'surprises'.

A similar struggle, and a similarly important act of inclusion, may take place between teachers and parents or carers of children. The sociologist Waller wrote in the 1930s about parents and teachers as 'natural enemies'. Both 'wish the child well, but it is such a different kind of well that conflict must inevitably arise over it' (quoted in Lawrence-Lightfoot 2003, p. 43). Teachers are likely to recognise the significance of parents, but they may also see parents as a barrier to the effectiveness of the teachers. However, in recent UK policy documents, the role of parents is highlighted. The *Children's Plan* notes that 'government does not bring up children – parents do – so government needs to do more to back parents and families' (DCSF 2007, p. 5), and 'services need to be shaped by and responsive to children, young people and families, not designed around professional boundaries' (DCSF 2007, p. 6). If teachers are of value, then their value is therefore not as the only people interested in children's flourishing. Their value must instead be in specialist or professional understanding, and indeed they are described by one sociologist as 'society's professional adults' (Lawrence-Lightfoot 2003, p. xxi). As a result of their different roles, encounters between teachers and parents and carers can be hostile, anxious, or defensive, but they can also be intimate, celebratory, and productive. Participants can feel consumed, tolerated, marginalised, or rejected, but they can also feel included, empowered, or recognised. Being engaged in an 'inevitable conflict' can mean being ready for a dialogue of difference, a real dialogue. In that sense, the rhetoric of 'every child matters' (i.e. the policies generated from DfES 2004a) should be reframed to include adults, as 'every person matters' (Stern and James 2006).

Recognising the inevitability of significant conflict, and hoping to work through that conflict, is a different approach from hoping for a universal consensus and ignoring difference. As the architect Fehn says of his work, '[t]he intellectual world meets the landscape, and in the ensuing duel beauty is born' (quoted in Yvenes and Madshus 2008, p. 39). An interest-ing recent example of actively ignoring conflict comes from the nursing profession. The Nursing and Midwifery Council says that practitioners should 'promote and protect the interests and dignity of patients and clients, irrespective of gender, age, race, ability, sexuality, economic status, lifestyle, culture and religious or political beliefs' (NMC 2004, p. 5). That is helpful in many ways, but there is a problematic use of the word 'irrespective'. The meanings of 'irrespective' in the OED include 'not respectful, disrespectful', and 'existing or considered without respect or regard to something else; without taking account *of*, independent *of*' (OED 2005). The NMC phrase therefore seems to mean that the practitioners are *not* to respect gender, age, race, ability, sexuality, economic status, lifestyle, culture and religious or political beliefs: they are, instead, to respect 'patients and clients' *without*, or at least *independent of*, respecting their gender, age, and so on.

Recognising the value of dialogue within conflict, rather than 'independent of' conflict, allows for a more valuable inclusion in schools, an inclusion that does not deny the humanity of the participants. Schools can then be engaged in helping people become more human, an existential task.

Existential vocationalism and abysmal dialogue

The importance of dialogue, in schools, is made clear here and throughout Buber's writings. Real schools (as in Stern 2001b, 2007a, Chapter 4, based on the related philosophies of Buber and Macmurray) will be those in which real dialogue takes place, and in which lessons develop 'in mutual surprises'. If teachers are monologic, they will be typical of many contemporary people, as '[t]he mark of contemporary man is that he does not really listen' (Friedman in Buber 2002a, p. xiv). If teachers are dialogic, they will be more inclusive. Dialogue involves 'imagining the real' (*Realphantasie*, Buber 1998, p. 71, translated by Simon as 'realistic imagination' in Schilpp and Friedman 1967, p. 562). This is an act of inclusion that 'goes hand in hand with remaining on one's own side of the relationship' (Friedman in Buber 2002a, p. xiv). All such acts are possible in schools, as

> If we want to do today's work and prepare tomorrow's with clear sight, then we must develop in ourselves and in the next generation a gift which lives in man's inwardness as a Cinderella, one day to be a princess. Some call it intuition, but that is not a wholly unambiguous concept. I prefer the name 'imagining the real', for in its essential being this gift is not a looking at the other, but a bold swinging – demanding the most intensive stirring of one's being – into the life of the other. (Buber 1998, p. 71)

Levinas later emphasises the centrality of this to Buber's philosophy, and he notes how this inclusion (*Umfassung*) 'should be distinguished from the psychological phenomenon of *Einfühlung* [usually translated as 'empathy'] where the subject puts itself completely in the other's place, thus forgetting itself' (Levinas 1989, p. 68). When being empathetic, 'the I forgets itself, and does not feel itself as a Thou of the Thou', whereas 'in the *Umfassung* the I sharply maintains its active reality' (Levinas 1989, p. 68).

Buber, distinctively, sees the inclusion in schools as somewhat one-sided, with teachers including pupils in a way that pupils would not include teachers. '[T]he true relation of the educator to the pupil is based on inclusion', but 'however intense the mutuality of giving and taking with which he is bound to his pupil, inclusion cannot be mutual in this case' (Buber 2002a, pp. 117–19).

> The educator stands at both ends of the common situation, the pupil only at one end. In the moment when the pupil is able to throw himself across and experience from over there, the educative relation would be burst asunder, or change into friendship. (Buber 2002a, p. 119)

He bases this one-sidedness on his view that '[a] great and full relation between man and man can only exist between unified and responsible persons' (Buber 2002a, p. 138), with school pupils not being thought by him as entirely 'unified and responsible'. Perhaps being a specialist in adult education, having organised adult education institutions in Germany until 1938 and in Jerusalem from 1949 (Schaeder in Glatzer and Mendes-Flohr 1991, p. 3, and Smith 2000), Buber was focusing on the distinctions between the education of children and of adults, such that 'the latter involved full mutuality, the former . . . a more asymmetrical relationship' (Smith 2000).

Possible ways of understanding and critiquing Buber's asymmetry are explored in the account of friendship (above, in Chapter 2), and it is, in any case, clear that the lack of full mutuality of relationships between pupils and teacher is, for Buber, part of a stage for children who are moving towards adulthood and the possibility of complete mutuality: helping Cinderella become a princess (Buber 1998, p. 71, quoted above), as he so poetically describes the situation. However asymmetrical the relationships may be, then, schools are still seen as places where people can be included, while remaining on their own side of the relationship: an inclusion that is not suffocating. Teachers are not – should not be – propagandists (Buber 2002a, p. 72), but should help children become what they can be, in mutuality. This is what might be called existential vocationalism, a calling to being or to becoming more real as oneself, as in the account given by Friedman:

'When I get to heaven,' said the Hasidic rabbi Susya shortly before
his death, 'they will not ask me, "Why were you not Moses?" but
"Why were you not Susya?"' Why did you not become what only you
could become? This is the existential guilt that comes when one
realizes one's vocation and fails to respond to it. (Friedman in Buber
2002a, p. xvii)

Here, it is argued that the possibility and the presence of real dialogue
is a defining characteristic of schools as learning communities, and that
monologic conversation in school is both tempting and harmful.
Dialogue is all the more important in an age of 'homelessness', an age
when we stare into the abyss, as Buber notes in 1938, pre-dating the
Shoah/Holocaust and the other horrors to come in and after World
War II.

In the history of the human spirit I distinguish between epochs of
habitation and epochs of homelessness. In the former, man lives in
the world as in a house, as in a home. In the latter, man lives in the
world as in an open field and at times does not even have four pegs
with which to set up a tent. (Buber 2002a, p. 150)

Since that time in the 1930s, the homelessness would surely be seen as
even greater, through the wars, the development of weapons of indiscrim-
inate mass destruction, and more recently problems related to the Earth
as home and environmental sustainability. How prescient was Buber? He
was not simply concerned with deaths, but rather with the state of living
humanity. A 'secure' present and future had been sketched by Hegel, a
century and a half previously, who 'compulsorily combined the course of
the stars and of history into a speculative security' (Buber 2002a, p. 172).
A more tortuous but eventually secure future was described by Marx, who
'confined himself to the human world, ascribed to it alone a security in
regard to the future, which is likewise dialectic, but has the effect of an
actual security' (Buber 2002a, p. 172). However, '[t]o-day this security has
perished in the ordered chaos of a terrible historical revulsion':

Gone is the calm, a new anthropological dread has arisen, the
question about man's being faces us as never before in all its
grandeur and terror – no longer in philosophical attire, but in the
nakedness of existence. No dialectical guarantee keeps man from
falling; it lies with himself to lift his foot and take the step which
leads him away from the abyss. The strength to take this step cannot

come from any security in regard to the future, but only from those depths of insecurity in which man, overshadowed by despair, answers with his decision the question about man's being. (Buber 2002a, pp. 172–3)

It is not that Buber was depressed by this vision of the presence of the abyss. He worked tirelessly through Germany in the 1920s and 1930s, and Jerusalem through the 1940s and on to the 1960s, seeing dialogue as the basis for strength in decision-making. And yet the abyss was there, with 'the peculiarity of the modern crisis' being 'man's lagging behind his works' and unable to 'subdue and render harmless the golem he has created' (Buber 2002a, 187). Three examples are given of the creation of such a golem, from industry, economics and politics. In industry, machines 'were no longer, like tools, an extension of man's arm, but man became their extension, and adjunct on their periphery, doing their bidding'. In economics 'it is as though the business of the production and utilization of goods spread out beyond man's reach and withdrew itself from his command'. Finally, in politics, '[i]n the first world war, and on both sides, man learned with ever greater horror how he was in the grip of incomprehensible powers, which seemed, indeed, to be connected with man's will but which threw off their bonds and again and again trampled on all human purposes' (Buber 2002a, pp. 187–8). Buber's 'golem' is explained by the translator as an 'animated clod without soul', a 'clay figure, possessed of no divine soul, made by a Rabbi in order to prevent attacks on Jews', whose 'end is either its destruction by the Rabbi, or his by it; for it could only destroy or be destroyed' (Buber 2002a, p. 248). Humanity can, through dialogue, destroy the golem at some point in the future, and this is a task that adults must therefore enable through their teaching of the young.

Lessons in dialogue

As well as having been influenced by policy, dialogue has been promoted in schooling in many forms, from Socratic dialogue (Lipman 2003), through religious dialogue (Ipgrave 2001, 2003, 2004), to the dialogic classrooms of Alexander (Alexander 2004, 2006). Buber is not unusual, then, but it is helpful to describe some other accounts of school dialogue. For the philosopher Oakeshott, schooling involves a 'conversation of mankind', albeit one described by White as evoking 'the wide-ranging, unfocused atmosphere of an upper class dinner party' (White 2007, p. 26, with a more sympathetic account in Pring 2004, pp. 20–1). Oakeshott's views parallel those of the literary critic Leavis, whose reputation is over-shadowed by claims that he was elitist, or rather that he was elitist and snobbish, making an 'attempt to maintain privileged definitions of culture and to articulate them . . . in ways that define and legitimate hierarchies of aesthetic, cultural and social power' (Bates in Samier et al. 2006, p. 213). Despite himself writing of the 'minority' on whom 'depends our power of profiting by the finest human experience of the past' (Leavis 1948, p. 144), Leavis had an attitude to the majority, and especially to the working class majority, dominated by shame: 'shame, concern and appre-hension at the way our civilization has let them down – left them to enjoy a "high standard of living" in a vacuum of disinheritance' (Leavis and Leavis 1969, p. 5). He saw 'high' culture as talking across time, and the possibility of that dialogue, even as an activity engaged in by a minority, as politically and morally essential. The possibility of such dialogue was threatened by a rejection of the old, of 'tradition', of the 'difficult', of that which is not seen as immediately 'relevant' or 'functional'. White sees dialogue in schools as more universal, and of more immediate functional-ity, with 'a more serious and vital purpose' (White 2007, p. 26). However, both of these philosophers see conversation as broadly social, with useful outcomes such as becoming 'better-informed contributors to the national and global conversation' (White 2007, p. 25).

Buber might take from Leavis a sense of the personal importance of the dialogue, while rejecting his elitism (as he does in Schilpp and Friedman 1967, pp. 723–4), and he might take from White the sense of a global conversation, but he has a discrete account of the nature of the conversation itself. It is 'real' conversation (or 'real' dialogue), that distin-guishes schooling. Schools are helping children (and adults) become the people they can be (as for Susya, in the previous section of this chapter, above), and being 'responsible' in the form of 'attentiveness'. 'Genuine responsibility exists only where there is real responding', and this involves responding '[t]o what happens to one, to what is to be seen and heard and felt' (Buber 2002a, p. 18). Such a person will be 'attentive', as 'the attentive man . . . faces creation as it happens', and '[i]t happens as speech, and not as speech rushing out over his head but as speech directed precisely at him' (Buber 2002a, pp. 18–19). Some examples from schools that might be thought of as dialogic are not genuinely dialogic. 'Discussion', for example, is described as appropriately named (as 'breaking apart'), and is a 'curious sport . . . which is indulged in by men who are to some extent gifted with the ability to think' (Buber 2002a, p. 3). This approach is closer to that of Taylor, for whom '[t]he general feature of human life that I want to evoke is its fundamentally *dialogical* character' (Taylor 1991, pp. 32–3). Taylor expresses that same idea of dialogue as what makes us 'full human agents': 'with important issues, such as the definition of our identity . . . [w]e define this always in dialogue with, sometimes in struggle against, the identities our significant others want to recognize in us' (Taylor 1991, p. 33).

Lessons should involve real dialogue, and be full of surprises. Some modern accounts of such forms of schooling are couched in terms of creativity, and Buber, too, writes of creativity as at the heart of education because it is essentially dialogic. Art is simply 'the province in which a faculty of production, which is common to all, reaches completion', and '[e]veryone is elementally endowed with the basic powers of the arts', so '[w]hat the child desires is its own share in this becoming of things: it wants to be the subject of this event of production' (Buber 2002a, p. 100). This cannot be routine production, but 'spontaneous' production, and hence 'real education is made possible – but is it also established? – by the realization that youthful spontaneity must not be suppressed but must be allowed to give what it can' (Buber 2002a, p. 104). As a minimum, this means teachers being accepting of what pupils say: the 15-year-old male pupil A (School 1, Protestant, Hong Kong) described this in response to being asked about whom he was closest to: 'I usually talk to those beside me about homework', he says. 'We will teach each other and learning more' and 'our relationship also grows', and this is also related to the teacher's position, as 'the teacher always talks to us, and he won't reject us when we ask him/her questions'. In contrast to dialogic schooling, mono-logic schooling is characterised by the self 'curving back on itself', or in Buber's terms 'reflexion' (Buber 2002a, p. 26, noting the translator's explanation on p. 246). Monologic reflexion is criticised by Buber. This might be thought to be a criticism of the 'reflective practice' described by Schön (1983, 1987). However, dialogue is specifically promoted by Schön (e.g. Schön 1987, p. 100ff, on the 'dialogue between coach and student'), and has as its theoretical base the work of Dewey, who had a more social, at times even communal, view of reflection (as in Dewey 1916). Dewey also has views similar to those of Buber on 'apprenticeship' in living as the basic form of education (Dewey 1916, p. 6). Pfeutze compares Buber and the American pragmatism of Dewey's assistant and close friend G H Mead (in Schilpp and Friedman 1967, pp. 511–42, and see also Ryan 1995, p. 79).

The 'temptation' to monologue is described by Buber in terms of his encounters as a child with a horse. He had become close to the horse, and visited it regularly, but then, once 'it struck me about the stroking, what fun it gave me, and suddenly I became conscious of my hand' (Buber

2002a, p. 27, also reported in Buber 2002b), and this consciousness, this experience of his self 'curving back on itself', spoilt the relationship with the horse.

> The game went on as before, but something had changed, it was no longer the same thing. And the next day, after giving him a rich feed, when I stroked my friend's head he did not raise his head. A few years later, when I thought back to the incident, I no longer supposed that the animal had noticed my defection. But at the time I considered myself judged. (Buber 2002a, p. 27)

Buber's approach to dialogue and its implications for schools can be described in two forms (as described in the following section). One is the dialogue specifically between pupils and teachers, the other is the dialogue that reaches beyond the school. Dialogue is personal, with real dialogue being distinguished from the no doubt useful 'social conversation' that characterises many other descriptions of schooling. It is a creative and a spiritual matter, with spirituality being an 'everyday' issue for Buber. 'Dialogue is not an affair of spiritual luxury and spiritual luxuriousness, it is a matter of creation, of the creature, and he is that, the man of whom I speak, he is a creature, trivial and irreplaceable' (Buber 2002a, p. 41).

Dialogue within and beyond schools

Dialogue between pupils and teachers is at the heart of schooling, therefore, and is not a luxury. Indeed, teachers who avoid dialogue are described at one point by Buber as potentially Satanic. Monologic teachers may try to promote their own views, and be 'propagandists' (as above, from Buber 2002a, p. 72), and more than this, a teacher 'who prompts me with an answer in such a way as to hinder my perceiving is the *hinderer*, let him be for the rest who he will' (Buber 2002a, p. 80, emphasis added). The 'hinderer' is the translator's rendering of the Hebrew שטן 'Satan', justified by reference to the Bible (Numbers 22:22 'adversary', and Numbers 22:32 'to withstand') (Buber 2002a, p. 248). With such a warning, it is important to return to what, positively, the teacher can do. It is not, essentially, either a matter of 'pour[ing] information into the student's head as through a funnel', or of 'regard[ing] all potentialities as already existing within the student and needing only to be pumped up' (Friedman in Buber 2002a, pp. xvii–xviii). Rather, it involves 'foster[ing] genuine mutual contact and mutual trust, . . . experienc[ing] the other side of the relationship, and . . . help[ing] his pupils realize, through the selection of the effective world, what it can mean to be a man' (Friedman in Buber 2002a, p. xviii). By helping pupils realise what it can mean to be a person, teachers can provide what is known in the US as the 'education of character', which 'takes place through the encounter with the image of man that the teacher brings before the pupil in the material he presents and in the way he stands behind this material' (Friedman in Buber 2002a, p. xviii).

'Character education' is close to UK forms such as 'personal and social education', or 'moral education' (as in Berkowitz and Bier 2007), or perhaps (in a Buber-esque form) 'spiritual development' (for which, see Stern and James 2006, and Chapter 1, above). Buber stresses the education of the 'whole person', yet 'it is advisable not to over-estimate what the educator can even at best do to develop character', for 'as soon as my pupils notice that I want to educate their characters I am resisted precisely by those who show most signs of genuine independent character: they will not let themselves be educated, or rather, they do not like the idea that somebody wants to educate them' (Buber 2002a, pp. 124–5). It is no good 'teaching' ethics or character in the same way as one might teach a technical skill:

> Only in his whole being, in all his spontaneity can the educator truly affect the whole being of his pupil. For educating characters you do not need a moral genius, but you do need a man who is wholly alive and able to communicate himself directly to his fellow beings. His aliveness streams out to them and affects them most strongly and purely when he has not thought of affecting them. (Buber 2002a, p. 125)

It would be tempting to see Buber as recommending schooling as involving nothing more than a general teaching of character, without any further description needed of curriculum. However, the sense in which pupils meet the 'image of man . . . in the material [the teacher] presents' (Friedman in Buber 2002a, p. xviii, quoted above) already gives a clue to the sense of the curriculum as that which the teacher 'stands behind'. This is illustrated by Buber through the significance of teaching about 'important issues'. In his first lesson, the account goes, a newly qualified teacher simply asks 'What did you talk about last in geography? The Dead Sea? Well, what about the Dead Sea?' (Buber 2002a, p. 134). The question is addressed at a particular pupil, one whom the teacher has seen as curious about what the teacher is to bring to him, and the boy 'begins to *tell a story*', describing his visit to the Dead Sea. The boy finishes his story, saying 'And everything looked to me as if it had been created a day before the rest of creation' (Buber 2002a, p. 134). This 'surprise' in the conversation suggests to Buber that the teacher had correctly understood the curiosity of that pupil, and in so doing had given him the opportunity to surprise. The class falls silent and listens.

Dialogue beyond the school, for Buber, therefore builds on the dialogue within the school. Such dialogue may be with the families of pupils and with other members of local or wider communities, and may be over time, for example with the writers of literary, sacred and other 'canonical' and historic texts (as with the otherwise uncomfortably elitist Leavis, described above). Dewey has a straightforward view of school learning, as needing to 'be continuous with that out of school', so as to avoid a monastic isolation that would make 'school knowledge inapplicable to life and so infertile in character' (Dewey 1916, pp. 358–9). This is put in a spiritual context by Watson, for whom '[s]pirituality escapes the institutional; just as a truly free person may escape her education, once she has one' (Watson in Ota and Chater 2007, p. 122). For Buber, the dialogue beyond the school is more profound, in connecting to the world (all that is not the isolated individual), and in this way transcending the individual, in meeting, and thereby connecting to God. It is a religious approach to schooling, which nevertheless objects to the 'religious' being a separate sphere.

Since experiencing his own failure, as a young man, to listen to a friend who visited him, Buber said 'I have given up the "religious" which is nothing but the exception, extraction, exaltation, ecstasy; or it has given me up', adding that 'I possess nothing but the everyday out of which I am never taken' (Buber 2002a, p. 16). The everyday connection has the world, the world as it is in all its ambiguity and with all its conflict, as its immediate context. Buber writes for a conference for Jewish teachers in Palestine in 1939 about the need to address 'difficult questions' about contemporary and historic Arab–Jewish issues (Buber 2002a, p. 129), concluding that 'the test of the educator lies in conflict with his pupil' (Buber 2002a, p. 130). The teacher 'has to face this conflict and, whatever turn it may take, he has to find the way through it into life, into a life, I must add, where confidence continues unshaken – more, is even mysteriously strengthened' (Buber 2002a, p. 130).

Connection beyond the school is also typically made through art, as 'all art is from its origin essentially of the nature of dialogue' (Buber 2002a, p. 30):

All music calls to an ear not the musician's own, all sculpture to an eye not the sculptor's, architecture in addition calls to the step as it walks in the building. They all say, to him who receives them, something (not a 'feeling' but a perceived mystery) that can be said only in this one language. (Buber 2002a, p. 30, and see Buber 1998, Chapter 7, for a full account of his aesthetics)

Himself translating and retelling sacred and other religious narratives (e.g. Buber 1965), the dialogic opportunities for schools in religious texts and music and architecture are clear (see for example Stern 2004 for illustrations of the use of religious music). Architect Sverre Fehn describes a museum as 'a dance around dead things' (in Yvenes and Madshus 2008, p. 29). Dialogue with the dead, through their art, their 'bit[s] of "frozen" potential communication' (Taylor 1989, p. 526, quoted in Chapter 1), allows also extension to dialogue with those dead known to the pupils and teachers. Klass works with the bereaved, and explicitly connects his work to Buber's philosophy:

[O]ur spiritual life cannot be lived alone. If we feel at one with the divine and in touch with the basic order of the universe, but the experience does not bring us into communion with at least some of our fellow human beings, we have the symptoms, says James Hillman . . . , of paranoia. We are living in a pseudo community, that is, a community of people who are only in our imagination. Without community, the spiritual life is Buber's *I* without the *Thou.* (Klass 1999, p. 27)

Klass's work emphasises the 'continuing bonds' with the dead (Klass et al. 1996), and this is a form of what he calls 'spirituality' that cannot be fully captured by phrases such as 'school ethos' (as in MacBeath et al. 1992) or 'every child matters' (DfES 2004a, but see also Stern 2007b). It is this complex, rich, and spiritual approach to dialogue that distinguishes Buber's philosophy from most other accounts of educational dialogue, and that provides a basis for the analysis of schooling today.

The spirit of the schools

Buber's account of dialogue and schooling is investigated directly, in the *Spirit of the School* project, in an attempt to uncover some of the 'hidden' real dialogue (Buber 2002a, p. 22) that may be present in schools. Research tools include ways of describing 'what is typically said' in classrooms, and the interview questions asking 'tell me about a time in school when you talked about something important to you' and asking for a description of what would be said to a person going through a bad time. However, the entire research process and all its questions and activities were an attempt to generate dialogue, and examples of dialogue or the lack of dialogue in schools came from across the research.

Dialogue within the school: silence and being there

One of the simplest ways in which pupils recognise the value of dialogue is in the value of silence. For Buber, dialogue is possible without words, through the 'glances which strangers exchange in a busy street as they pass one another with unchanging pace' (Buber 2002a, p. 5). 'Dialogue can be silence', Buber writes, but the dialogic silence is not the same as the silence when someone is 'shut', as when a person suffers from schizophrenia or paranoia:

> It is sometimes very difficult to talk to a schizophrenic . . . I can talk to a schizophrenic as far as he is willing to let me into his particular world that is his own . . . But in the moment when he shuts himself, I cannot go on. And the same, only in a terrible, terrifyingly strong manner, is the case with a paranoiac. He does not open himself and does not shut himself. He *is* shut. There is something else being done to him that shuts him. (Buber 1998, p. 165)

A pupil in Afton, a Church of England primary school (UK), described times the school made her feel good about herself, saying:

> I was teaching [name] how to be good [Interviewer: . . . he's the naughty boy . . .] yes, I was helping him to be good and . . . said [name] if you can't say anything nice don't say anything at all, and now he's being really good and nice.

The lesson for the 'naughty boy' appeared to be a lesson in inclusion as well as in 'being good', and this is stressed in some of the other responses to the question about what would be said to someone who was going through a bad time. Amy (aged 11) stresses the active nature of inclusion, while also allowing for the person to have time alone:

> I would just try and cheer them up and get them to come and join in a game, but if they don't want to, then just let them be for a couple of minutes and then come back again and see if they've changed.

It is less clear whether the conversation described by the younger Angie (aged 6) is an example of monologue or dialogue, as it describes discussion with the pupil's imaginary friend:

> my imaginary friend called Penelope is going through a bad time, because she's going to hospital [Interviewer: what would you say?] to make her feel better, I would say 'I hope you get better soon'.

Many responses to this exercise involved questions: 'what's the matter?' or 'I'd go and ask his friends if they could play with him'. Here, Angie is simply saying what her hope is, and in consequence she seems to be reaching towards dialogue rather than engaging in dialogue. This is probably appropriate for a child talking about her imaginary friend.

Good, silent, listening can make what is said that much more important. In Richardson primary school (UK), Mark, aged 8, is asked about 'a time in school when you talked about something that was really important to you', and responds 'When, when you, when the teacher is listening to you'. He explains this as working in both directions, with either the pupil or the teacher doing the listening: 'When he's asked a question and you're listening and when you, then they're listening when they're making eye contact.' It seems that Mark realises that the act of listening makes what is said 'really important', irrespective of the content of what is said. Teachers in Richardson thought in the same way, with one teacher saying 'that they're not on their own and there's always somebody here to help and that we'll find the time to listen'. Help itself may be valued, of course, but listening and 'being with' someone seem to dominate the descriptions. 'When I was diagnosed of being quite seriously ill . . . everybody offered to help', one teacher says, and another teacher whose house was flooded said 'I've had people offer me nice help to do my washing . . . and people have offered me help, and asked me, asked me they've been continuously asking me how I was doing as well which has been really nice.' The headteacher explains how 'being there' to listen comes before active help:

> I would like to say something about being able to support them in any way that we could, obviously depending on the problem whether that was just an informal, someone to chat to, to let off steam to, a shoulder to cry on or can the school as an organisation . . . help you . . . if you need to go somewhere having an afternoon off or if you are really ill . . . time for appointments, I would hope that the school either formally or informally would support them and help them through it.

A similar account is given by the headteacher at Long Barrow (a Church of England primary school, UK), who says 'I would invite them to come and talk to me and I would ask how can I help . . . what can we do to help you through this?' He continues by saying 'we do have very good relationships with each other and I try to be as flexible with people as I possibly can be because I know through my own life, and through my own children things happen at home that . . . you are not in control of'. This openness and flexibility suggests a genuine, real, dialogue is what is expected in times of trouble.

Silence can be good in a rather less obvious way. Nine-year-old Jack, in Richardson school, describes a time when there was talk about something important to him, and responded 'when I don't get my name on the board [a 'warning' system used in the school], and Mrs Swiss rings my mum up and tells my mum that I haven't got my name on the board and my mum is really proud of me'. The absence of being named seems a little sad, and is made sadder because the boy is so pleased that the teacher has told his mother that he has not got into trouble. Perhaps there will also be opportunities for him to be actively praised for what he has done. In Long Barrow primary school, a teacher notes the pleasure of a mother, when called about her child, precisely because it was a positive engagement: 'I've had quite a few new children in the class . . . and . . . there's one in particular after about a couple of weeks . . . seemed quite down, and I called her mother up and she was really grateful, she's never been contacted by a school before in such a positive way.'

When people are troubled, the conversations described can help clarify forms of dialogue. One pupil in Richardson suggests saying, simply, 'it's alright', and another expands on this, suggesting saying 'I'll help you, you're not alone . . . I'll keep you company'. A third pupil adds 'ask them what, what's wrong with them and help them', while a fourth pupil is more concerned with resolving conflict, suggesting saying 'tell them to go and say sorry to the other person who they've been arguing with'. Pupils are sensitive to insincerity, with the eight-year-old Mark suggesting people 'try making you happy and stop you thinking about what . . . was wrong with you and why you was upset and those things', followed by ten-year-old Charlotte interrupting with 'people . . . pretend that they're all real nice to you but then they are real nasty, you tell them and they go like sprag it [i.e. tell other people about it]'.

One of the ways in which Richardson encourages dialogue on important issues is to have a 'feelings chart' in every room. This is derived from the school's involvement in a 'restorative justice' project (as in Hopkins 2004, West-Burnham and Huws Jones 2007, pp. 87–8). Each pupil and teacher puts their name label next to a list of feelings. One teacher says 'I've noticed, I think the fact when the children come in they share how they are feeling, they alert us, so we can be more sensitive . . . but I've noticed that since I've gone round the class that the children are asking each other "Oh why you are sad today?", so they're actually beginning to recognise different . . . people's emotions and empathise and want to know why and can they help, and that's something that definitely I feel a move in the right direction.' This appears to be an important stimulant to real dialogue, albeit needing the pupil Charlotte's warning that people might end up *spragging* – insincerely collecting sensitive information and passing it on to others. Interestingly, the pupils in Richardson are also allowed to indicate what their teacher's feelings are, and this is seen by teachers as valuable: they say that pupils 'are much more aware now'. The dialogue is not restricted to pupils, and teachers themselves value opportunities to talk to each other about their lives outside school, as 'there are so few times now in school where we are all together'. Teachers get together in circles, with topics such as 'have you got an unfulfilled ambition in life?', 'what's your favourite film?' or 'who would you most like to have dinner with?'

Another systematic stimulus to dialogue was described by the headteacher of Long Barrow as the traditional process of registration at the start of the day. He shares the process with another teacher:

I actually register them one morning a week and Sarah registers them on the other four mornings . . . and she'd introduced a personal registration system where the children came and they had to put their name, it was a magnetic one . . . on to the board and the children had to put their names in certain places . . . and it was . . . probably good for the children to do that but it doesn't work all the time because the children are late for school or they've gone out to do flute or other guitar activities, you look at the register to do it and you can't complete it, so then you end up going round the class to find the ones that have missed. . . . So, I think much to Sarah's annoyance really, I said I was going to continue with the traditional way and I've always felt that registration was the one time in the day when you could make certain that you actually spoke to every child and . . . that was really why I wanted to keep it going, and we say good morning, we speak to every child, ask them what their lunch time arrangements are, have you got anything to send into the office, we have a little discussion, who's not brought that slip back, who needs to bring this back and I feel the traditional registration has, has a lot going for it. We did have a student teacher last year and we'd actually put it up on the smart

board and the students used to come in and move their names
around on the smart board and it was a lovely whizzy system but I felt
that the personal side of it had disappeared really.

Although the content of the discussions seems like 'technical dialogue',
in Buber's terms (i.e. exchanges of information), the process as a personal process is what is being stressed by the headteacher, and it therefore
appears to be structured in such a way as to stimulate 'real' dialogue. One
of the pupils at St Bede's, a boy aged 13, describes the role of the personal
tutor, in a similar way. There is a formal relationship, based on academic
progress, but dialogue with the tutor was made more 'real' by the tutor's
interest in the pupil's life outside school:

> My golf outside the school, he always, he always asks me . . . how is
> the golf going, . . . he always makes you feel like at home . . . he
> always like tutors me and talks about your, like academic levels and
> . . . how are things going at home and everything

Dialogue beyond the school: dead hamsters

In the BBC religious education training video, *Eggshells and Thunderbolts*
(Stone 1994), the process of 'implicit' RE is criticised by John Logan.
Implicit RE, he says, often involves no more than looking after the class's
pet hamster, which is hardly appropriate RE. However, he continues, 'at
least if the hamster died, you might be able to do some good RE'. Logan
is right to point out the value of dialogue on such important topics, and
dead hamsters are also mentioned in a recent textbook on spiritual development in schools (West-Burnham and Huws Jones 2007, p. 122). To one
ten-year-old in the *Spirit of the School* research, talking about her dead pet
hamster was indeed the most important talk she could describe. Others
talked about visits and visitors, family members and celebrations, health
and hobbies: all ways in which dialogue within the school transcended the
school.

Visitors are important to many children, and seem more important
than is recognised in the literature. To make the school more of a community, Desmond, aged 10, at Richardson primary school, wanted to draw
people in to the school and some art: 'Just put famous pictures on the
walls, . . . get some . . . people from the world to come and visit us sometimes.' It is worth noting his phrasing ('people from the world'), which
suggests the school is a somewhat unworldly place, to be made more
worldly by visitors from that planet. For Lizzie, aged 7, visitors are there to

listen. She responds to the question about a time when you talked about something that was really important to you with the response 'When special visitors come'. The interviewer asks what was talked about, and Lizzie says 'We talked about different things, like what we're doing in lessons'. Talking to visitors, to 'special visitors', makes the talk itself important. Whereas for Lizzie, the listening seemed more important than the topic, for others, the topic itself was important. Jack, aged 9, says that he talked about something that was important to him: 'my family . . . and my pets', to which Charlotte, aged 10, adds 'my hamster . . . when it died, Miss'. This at least confirms Logan's view of opportunities for engaging religious education. Jack, aged 9, suggests that talking about his puppy, 'my baby, a little puppy, . . . called Shep', is important, and nine-year-old William mentions 'when I talk about my pit dog'. As well as the listeners and the topic making a conversation important, the context of the conversation can also make it more significant. Desmond refers to 'school councillors' as being important. He is himself a school councillor, and the talk in the school council is clearly engaging. Visits were not only important to pupils. The headteacher of Richardson was asked what she would spend her time on, if given a term off to do something educational. She said 'I'd probably go round visiting other schools and finding out what makes them successful and then bring it back to here if I thought it would help or benefit us'.

The need for dialogue with other schools was also emphasised by the headteacher at Long Barrow, who said that if given a term to study education, 'I would like to go and work in an Italian school for a while and . . . have a look at their systems, I'd really like to go to the United States as well, . . . I think I'd like to go and study primary education in one or two other countries really'. This would not be a one-way communication, as the headteacher is confident in his own ability to influence other headteachers, saying 'there are lots of times . . . that I feel good about the school, . . . when we had a head teachers' meeting last week of some of the smaller school heads and a couple of them came here and it's some time since they've been and one or two were asking questions as to "Where did you get that?" "How did you, who did you do that with?" and it just gives you that inner glow that colleagues are wanting to do the same'. Similarly, the head of St Bede's said that if given a term off, he would visit other schools as part of a project to reformulate and implement the vision for the school:

I would want to spend some time reading, to help me formulate and reformulate and re-express a compelling vision for the school

beyond the sound bites which we . . . all . . . need to do sometimes
and the second thing I want to do is to go around and see what
people are doing because the vision is one thing but making it
happen is the other thing.

Health is mentioned a number of times as an important topic, and at
Richardson there had recently been a health-themed day in the school,
which the headteacher had 'started . . . by bringing lots of things from
home and talking what's important healthwise in our house'. Desmond
refers to a time he talked in school about the event four years previously:

> I was about six years old, Miss, and somebody from work put a stick
> in the back, in the front of my wheel, I fell over the handlebars, and
> I thought I was going to have a load of stitches and actually had only
> twelve.

As well as health, family events that were important in school included
prospective births, as Mark, aged 8, gets excited about 'when, when my
mum, my mum had a baby', corrected by another pupil who reminds him
that she has not yet had a baby. 'She's having a baby in . . . the end of
December or January', he continues, 'it's . . . a boy and it's called [name]
she's got loads of clothes already, she goes to Mothercare, she's ordered
the pram from Mothercare and it comes on Wednesday'. A teacher also
talks about her own child, saying that 'I was working in year five, and we
were looking at . . . baptism and . . . I was telling the children how important my son's christening was to myself, actually sharing a . . . personal
experience and I got a lovely response'. The response was said to be all
the more powerful because of the photographs she brought in, and the
discussion that followed about making decisions for the child: 'we were
looking at the fact that the decisions are made for a young child by christening a young child . . . and they were really interested and I think with
having the photographs because it was . . . personal to me and . . . I think
they liked that'. A teacher at Long Barrow provides an even more
powerful example of how she talked about a personal event, related to the
work the children were completing.

> We . . . were about to do some work on, on road safety, . . . we were
> talking about road safety in general and when . . . is a good time to
> cross the road and . . . I was saying to the children that . . . road
> safety it is very important to me because I lost my friend when I was
> sixteen . . . due to somebody being silly on the road and . . . they

really thought about that, it was something that kept being mentioned . . . and . . . I said it's . . . a very sad bit, . . . I didn't want them
to be frightened but it was somebody else's mistake . . . so . . . they
kept not bringing it up but talking about how, they were really
sensible, giving some really sensible ideas because they could
obviously see it was something that's quite close to my heart.

At Ruislip primary school, there were four different kinds of evidence
of dialogue of Buber's kind: discussion of important things, dialogue
involved in designing a stained glass window, dialogue involving 'show
and tell', and dialogic engagements with visitors. Some of these issues
have been discussed above, in Chapter 3, but it is worth considering
certain of these four items once more. The first was the discussion of
'important things' in circle time. Lucia said 'once in circle time we talked
about, I think it was in English I think, and we talked about good changes
in our life and bad changes', and it is difficult to see how that could have
avoided important issues. The principles of circle time (as in Mosley 1993,
1996) focus on listening and avoiding making judgements, in a way that
should promote dialogue, although if dialogue is restricted to circle time,
the rest of the school day would end up entirely monologic. When the
Ruislip pupils talked about circle time, the conversation went on to
describe a second kind of dialogue, as Terence expanded on Lucia's
account of a circle time discussion of changes, saying 'I were talking about
like something about changes in assembly and how our halls are changing
out there'. This in turn led to talk of the pupils' involvement in designing
a stained glass window for the new hall. There was dialogue with the
manufacturer of the stained glass window, and a kind of dialogue across
time with the designers of the York Minster stained glass windows in a
detailed description of a visit to the church to investigate its windows.
    After this part of the conversation, circle time is introduced again, and a
third example of dialogue was given by Jonathan's description of 'show and
tell': 'we like, sometime somebody gives, brings some stuff to show and we
have to sit in a circle and we pass 'em all along . . . and we have to, like, and
look at it'. Terence expands: 'we're like talking about something saying like
what's happened that's good in your life and you're like we've, somebody
like bring in something and when you get the thing, then you say something that's like important . . . and nobody else can talk'. It may seem
strange that a situation in which 'nobody else can talk' should be described
as dialogue. However, pupils in schools have extensive experience of
people – teachers or pupils – interrupting them or continuing an apparent
conversation without really having listened, so that an experience of not

being interrupted, or others not talking and making judgements immediately after something has been said, is likely to be interpreted as dialogue.
It suggests the absence of 'the hinderer', or Satan himself. As Fines says:

> I have in the course of my teaching career learned many hard things
> but the hardest of all has been to shut up. The instinct to lecture
> children is profound and we have to chain it, and to learn to listen.
> (Fines and Nichol 1997, p. 231)

A fourth kind of dialogue described by Ruislip pupils is the dialogue
with visitors, particularly talk with visiting musicians and with visitors from
different religious groups. It is not clear how dialogic the meetings were,
but as the talking was sufficiently memorable to be mentioned, it may well
be that real dialogue took place.

Conclusion for persons

The school-based research completed in the early stages of the *Spirit of the
School* provides significant evidence of dialogue, and it provides a model
for what has been described as a form of 'action philosophy', that is, an
attempt to understand, philosophically, where that understanding
informs and is informed by professional activity in schools (Stern 2007c
and 2007a, pp. 1–2). The purpose of this chapter has therefore been to
indicate some of the ways in which Buber's philosophy of dialogue has
relevance to and may be complemented by listening to what is happening
in modern schooling. By describing some of the responses to a number of
research questions, it is also hoped that the process of research can itself
help teachers and pupils enter into a dialogue that could make their
schools more creative, more inclusive, more real. The philosophy underpinning the *Spirit of the School* project is one that makes clear that people
do not have an existence outside their relationships. Relationships, made
through dialogue, are not helpful additional benefits to individual
people: they are what make people. It is the distinction between 'individuals' and 'people' that is at the core of this philosophy. In his discussion
with the psychotherapist Carl Rogers, Buber's final words are telling: 'if I
may say expressly Yes and No to certain phenomena, I'm *against* individuals and *for* persons' (Buber 1998, p. 174, and quoted above in Chapter 1,
with a fuller account in Anderson and Cissna 1997, pp. 103–4). Here,
Buber stresses what is important to him, and what is important to the
process of schooling. Schools can be learning communities of particular
kinds, and it is dialogue that will make them 'real'.

Chapter 5

'Great-souled' schooling and the spirit of the leader

I'm not a lonely person.

(George W Bush, *Harper's Magazine* 2004)

Introduction

There has been a long if specialised tradition of more ethical and personal rather than technicist research on school leadership, including the work of Greenfield (e.g. Greenfield and Ribbins 1993) who writes of 'humane' leadership, and Bottery (1992, especially Chapter 12), who writes of management or leadership in a 'moral community'. Work on the spirituality of school leadership is even narrower, with significant work by Bhindi and Duignan (1997) and West-Burnham (Bowring-Carr and West-Burnham 1997, pp. 129–30) and more recently Woods (2007, also referring to Houston and Sokolow 2006). From the school-based research with school leaders, in the *Spirit of the School* project, emerged several themes that are represented in the current chapter, even though the results of that research are used as illustrations of arguments initially presented from academic literature. As the voices of the school leaders become more dominant, through the chapter, it is hoped that their influence on this structure is made even clearer. Even within the more ethical research on school leadership, a number of the emerging themes did not seem to have been fully explored in the previous literature, leaving some of the most important experiences of school leaders untheorised. These experiences included the loneliness and isolation of the job, the pleasure in and value of performance or 'acting' skills that can be developed in the job, and the need, somehow, to be 'above it all' without becoming arrogant. By presenting research under those three headings, a single argument is made, related to spirituality as conceived throughout the book. Relational, dialogic, spirituality is distinctively possible in schools as Macmurrian communities, and school leadership is in turn distinctively theorised within that context.

It is helpful to start with a very simple question: should leadership involve loneliness? Many leaders, including school leaders, find the job a lonely one, so it is a little surprising to hear of the then US President George W Bush able to say that he was not a lonely person. One of the models of sad, lonely leadership is Shakespeare's troubled and banished leader, Coriolanus. He talks of his aloneness, 'Like to a lonely Dragon'. Although referring to his banishment, Coriolanus seems just as lonely when returning to power. Some leaders seem to want to cultivate this kind of loneliness, exploiting their 'lonely dragon' status, 'fear'd and talk'd of more than seen' (*Coriolanus*, Act IV, Scene 1). Does loneliness have a value, or an inevitability, for leaders? In an article entitled *Lonely Leaders*, two London headteachers talked about their isolation. One said that '[a]t first I found it difficult to cope with the fact that there was no one after me – I was in charge', while another said that '[t]he isolation and loneliness is the most difficult thing . . . [as] I underestimated the pressures from all the different audiences you have to respond to' (TES 1996). The headteacher of Afton (a Church of England primary school, UK) said in the *Spirit of the School* research, 'it is quite a lonely job at times'. There is something refreshing about such statements, an honest appraisal of how difficult it can be to lead a school. A contrast, perhaps, to those leaders who are too embarrassed to admit to such loneliness. Although not known for his sensitivity, George W Bush's rejection of loneliness may be an example of just such embarrassment. The American songwriter Randy Newman wrote *Lonely At The Top*, and apparently offered the song to Frank Sinatra and to Barbara Streisand. Both of them rejected the song, reportedly because 'people wouldn't see the irony' (www.answers.com/topic/randy-newman?cat=entertainment, accessed 24 October 2008).

This chapter investigates leadership, and attempts to show why many leaders are lonely, and why those leaders need not be lonely, even if, instead of loneliness, they nevertheless need some privacy and solitude. Loneliness is a distinctively modern emotion, used roughly in its present sense only from the late sixteenth century, with 'sadness' as a part of the meaning only from the early nineteenth century (SOED 2007). It is associated by a number of authors with modernist individualism. Hay writes eloquently about 'the lonely European' (Hay 2007, p. 43). He identifies this emerging loneliness in the philosophy of Hobbes (Hay 2007, pp. 64–7, and see also Wood 1959, p. 653), in the apparently lonely life of the individualist anarchist philosopher Stirner (Hay 2007, p. 47), and through to the loneliness he sees as inherent in Calvinism, as illustrated by Hogg's *Confessions of a Justified Sinner* (Hogg 1978, Hay 2007, p. 63). Building on Hay's account, this chapter on the spirit of the leader starts with a consideration of the loneliness, isolation, solitude, and privacy of leaders. This is not an attempt to separate leaders from others in schools, as that might itself exacerbate loneliness, but is an exemplification of the risks of unconnected loneliness in education. It builds a positive picture of the possibility of self-realisation, in situations where headteachers can be isolated, and can have solitude and privacy, while not needing to be lonely. The Olympic swimmer Michael Phelps, interviewed on television after his successes, was asked whether he had a girlfriend. 'I have a private life', he replied, sensibly. It is an answer that more people in the public eye might reasonably give. Asserting a private life is needed even for, especially for, those in publicly exposed positions. Within a school, it is the headteacher who fulfils the most public of roles, the most public of figures within the school community. Headteachers are open to requests from and responsible for supporting every member of that community, and are also exposed to the gaze of the school's governing body, public bodies and politicians responsible for education, and the news media. Any scandal or tragedy, and the head will be asked to make a public statement. Privacy and solitude are needed precisely by those most open to such public scrutiny.

A school leader who does achieve self-realisation is unlikely to see that as enough: school leaders would want to achieve much more. Leading a school is a creative, constructive, activity, just as teaching and learning are creative, constructive, activities. School leadership is therefore described here as being something of a craft, like acting or musical performance. It is a craft exercised by people placed at the top of a hierarchy within schools, and hierarchies are all too rarely admitted in educational cultures striving, for good reasons, to be democratic. Aristotle was comfortable with hierarchies, and he described leadership in terms of magnanimity, *megalopsuchia* or, more literally, being 'great-souled'. This he described as the 'crown of the virtues' (Aristotle 1976, p. 154, also analysed in Stern 2002). Current debates too often stress democracy while leaving less democratic organisations morally adrift. Understanding hierarchical organisations therefore means understanding the morality of hierarchy. The theme has been taken up more recently by Sennett (2003) in his account of 'respect in a world of inequality'. It is a concern to understand how leaders contribute to the spirit of the school, while fulfilling a role at the top of a hierarchy of power, that underpins this account of the possibility of great-souled school leadership.

Avoiding loneliness

It takes two to be lonely. People can be alone, but loneliness is not the same as aloneness. To be lonely requires a sense of rejection by, or a failure to be connected to, other people. It has become a literary cliché to talk of the loneliness of crowds, with characteristic accounts given of people moving from close-knit and small communities into cities, and finding loneliness in the very places where there are most people. Cities are not *necessarily* lonely places, but loneliness did seem to increase as cities grew. The urbanisation of the nineteenth and twentieth centuries coincided with social and industrial changes, especially the separation of family life from the life of paid employment. This is described as leading to two different kinds of separation or loneliness: alienation and anomie.

The industrial processes and the economic relationship of employee to employer was said by Marx to lead to 'alienation', the active separation of people from their own essence as 'creating' beings, from the products of their work, and from other people through competition. It is a 'transformation, through the division of labour, of personal powers (relationships) into material powers' (Marx and Engels 1970, p. 83), and these changes 'are no product of nature, but of history' (Marx 1973, p. 162). Whereas '[i]n a real community the individuals obtain their freedom in and through their association' (Marx and Engels 1970, p. 83), in a money-dominated system, there is what Trilling calls a 'transformation of the self into what is not human' as '[m]oney . . . is the principle of the inauthentic in human existence' (Trilling 1972, pp. 123–4). Quoting Marx in the *Economic Manuscripts*, Trilling notes the shock that it was felt necessary to state '[l]et us assume *man* to be *man*, and his relation to the world a human one' (Trilling 1972, p. 123). The money system separated each person from '*real individual* life' (Trilling 1972, p. 124, original emphasis). Marx was writing in a tradition well developed in the late eighteenth and early nineteenth centuries. Schiller had written in the 1790s of modern society having become a sort of 'clock-work mechanism – a mechanical kind of collective life' in which '[e]verlastingly chained to a single little fragment of the Whole, man himself develops into nothing but a fragment; . . . he never develops the harmony of his being, and instead of putting the stamp of humanity upon his own nature, he becomes nothing more than the imprint of his occupation or of his specialized knowledge' (Schiller 1967, sixth letter). Schiller sees the need to 'restore by means of a higher Art the totality of our nature which the arts themselves have destroyed' (Schiller 1967, sixth letter). That is, recovery is possible through the transformation of society that itself caused the alienation in the first place.

Within schooling, alienation has been described in many ways. Billington says that by 'acknowledging and focusing upon alienation', and using the insights generated to develop a 'science of relationships', it would be possible to 'resist the separating and excluding which currently characterize our practices with children – practices which are too often subservient to political discourses of (dis)ability, gender, race and social class' (Billington 2000, p. 88 and p. 119). Alienation is described in a more personal way in a biography by Seldon of UK Prime Minister John Major, who says that he 'didn't like the shepherding together of lesser beings who were told that they had to be subservient to and respect these greater beings who happened to be the schoolmasters', and that '[t]he reason I didn't work at school was my sense of alienation from this particular school' (quoted in Chitty 2002, p. 42). He continues: 'If you had the sort of difficulties we faced at home at the time, you were alienated. I wasn't interested in school. I wasn't stupid at school. I just didn't work. I couldn't work' (quoted in Chitty 2002, p. 42).

Combining the theorising of Marx or Trilling with personal, school-based, research, Salmon writes of how '[f]or a minority, the "kings of the school", the gang represents a context of personal recognition' while for 'young people who feel alone and vulnerable in the heaving numbers in the playground or the lunch hall' there is a 'lonely crowd [which] bestows no sense of collective belonging, but only anonymity and alienation' (Salmon 1998, p. 32). This is not a 'playground problem' alone. It is created by the forms of schooling in which learning is individualised and cooperative work is generally disallowed as cheating. 'As institutions, schools are not merely asocial places in which to be; they are, in some senses, positively anti-social', as they 'do not set out to foster the development of mutual appreciation and respect between pupils' but 'to some extent they actually undermine such development' (Salmon 1998, p. 34). For Grey, there is a need to 're-enchant' childhood, by going beyond the 'business model of life' (Grey in Ota and Chater 2007, p. 12) to 'turn again to the earth, to recover the lost connections' as 'our alienation has made us refuse limits to growth, and led us to exploit resources like oil and water, even to the extremes of fighting wars' (Grey in Ota and Chater 2007, p. 16). Both Salmon and Grey note the need for pupils and teachers to avoid alienation, and give the prime responsibility for this to teachers. The alienated adult is a lonely figure, shockingly described in this passage from Buber:

At times the man, shuddering at the alienation between the *I* and the world, comes to reflect that something is to be done. As when in

the grave night-hour you lie, racked by waking dream – bulwarks
have fallen away and the abyss is screaming – and note amid your
torment: there is still life, if only I got through to it – but how, how?;
so is this man in the hours of reflection, shuddering, and aimlessly
considering this and that. (Buber 1958, p. 94)

Sadly, many teachers and school leaders would recognise such nights,
with their combination of alienation and puzzle as to how to overcome
alienation. For Buber, it is through relations that alienation is overcome,
or more specifically through the realisation that 'the extended lines of
relations meet in the eternal *Thou*' (Buber 1958, p. 99). This religious
denouement of Buber's argument, in 'the eternal *Thou*', is a reminder of
the religious meanings of alienation, as separation from God, and the
route to alienation through sin. It is repeated in Macmurray's account of
alienation in which '[e]ach of us stands, in unescapable isolation, over
against the whole universe in its infinite otherness', which can only be
overcome if 'we . . . somehow pass beyond ourselves and enter into
fellowship with the world' (Macmurray 2004, p. 161). 'Through the love
of men and women our individual selves reach out to fellowship with the
whole infinite otherness of the world which is not us', he continues, and
'the infinity that stands over against us must needs be a personal God'
because 'God is the postulate of our own being; and our self-realization is
the realization of God' (Macmurray 2004, p. 162).

Alienation can be described as a result of economic or social competi-
tiveness or as a result of sin. In both cases, it is associated with being rule-
bound: either 'swallowed up' by inhuman rules, or breaking divine rules.
Anomie, in contrast, is a description of the absence of rules, of floating
without rules, and the great theorist of anomie is Durkheim. If Marx saw
the economic division of labour as the cause of alienation, Durkheim said
that 'the ideal of human fraternity can be realized only in proportion to
the progress of the division of labor' (Durkheim 1973, p. 143). It is the loss
of a role in the division of labour that leads to anomie, and is the cause, for
example, of anomic suicides. The loss of role can be the result of positive
rejection from a role (Durkheim mentions divorce and retirement as
examples of this) or can be the result of a loosening of roles so that they
disintegrate (as in Yeats' prelude to the Second Coming: 'Things fall apart;
the centre cannot hold' and 'The best lack all conviction', Yeats 2002,
p. 60). The lack of conviction, the lack of certainty, is characteristic of post-
modernity, and is prefigured in the writings of near-contemporaries Yeats
and Buber. It is traced by Macpherson in the degeneration of ideologies
of liberalism, from the strongly normative utilitarianism of James Mill and

the active work-centred humanist theory of John Stuart Mill, through to
the emptied-out formalistic choice-system of the twentieth-century plural-
ist political theory of Schumpeter and Dahl, in which '[d]emocracy is
reduced from a humanist aspiration to a market equilibrium system'
(Macpherson 1973, p. 79). The absence of beliefs or convictions in such
forms of liberal democracy (which might better be described as individualist libertarianism), the absence of a sense of truth or, in post-modernist
terms, 'meta-narrative', is a cause of anomic weightlessness and, inevitably,
loneliness. According to Trilling, this is the end-point prefigured by
Goethe's description of Young Werther's suicide. Honesty is not enough
without conviction: a 'distintegrated consciousness, he [Young Werther]
had persisted in clinging to the simplicity of the honest soul' (Trilling
1972, p. 52).

The contrast between alienation and anomie is therefore between the
problem of rules and the problem of the absence of rules. Both lead to
loneliness, the sense of being with people but rejected by or unconnected
to them. The solution to anomie (the lack of being connected through a
system of rules) is not simply to have rules: that might lead to alienation or
to forms of fanaticism. 'The fanatic', as Noddings describes the term, 'is
perpetually incomplete and insecure' and 'cannot generate self-assurance
out of his individual resources – out of his rejected self – but finds it only by
clinging passionately to whatever support he happens to embrace'
(Noddings 2003a, p. 223). Fanaticism involves holding to a single view
without any flexibility, and without any dialogue. The fanatic is single-
voiced or 'monoglotal', in contrast to those who are 'heteroglotal', involved
in active dialogue (see Stern 2007a, pp. 26–8). The solution to anomie is
not simply the presence of rules, then. In the same way, the solution to
alienation (being caught up in a rule-bound system that appears to act
against you) is not simply to take away the rules: that would lead to anomie
or to the looseness of relativist forms of post-modernity. What is needed is a
dialogic form of relationship that allows connectedness, a system of rules
that is more human or humane. Loneliness, whether alienated or anomic,
corrupts a person. People in positions of power who are pushed into loneliness are particularly liable to corruption, as the corruption of power exac-
erbates the corruption of loneliness. Power can corrupt through making
the powerful feel that power makes them better people, and therefore
unable to have mutual relationships with the less powerful. It can also
corrupt by making the powerful feel they have a privileged access to the
truth, making dialogue with the less powerful unnecessary. Meanwhile,
loneliness can corrupt through making the lonely progressively incapable
of making any kind of relationship that would overcome loneliness.

Headteachers themselves describe the possibility of loneliness of both the anomic and the alienated kinds. The headteacher of St Bede's (a UK secondary school with a Roman Catholic foundation) was asked to complete the circles of importance exercise. A slightly edited version of the transcript is given here, followed by analysis.

Interviewer 1:	What do you belong to in school, what membership, to what do you belong?
Headteacher:	In many senses, I don't belong to very much at all . . .
Interviewer 2:	In what sense?
Headteacher:	I think because you can't as a head and in the sense which you, you have to be removed, that's one of the costs of it you have to, you can't belong as you might have done as a, as a teacher or as a head of department or as a student or as even as a deputy, . . .
Interviewer 2:	Does that feel isolating?
Headteacher:	Yeah it does yeah but I think that's, that's the way it is, . . . there are as I say it's, as I said to you before it's a fantastic job and I wouldn't swap it for the world but it's like everything, it has its cost
Interviewer 1:	So, can I ask you when you, when do you feel most included in school? . . .
Headteacher:	On a human level, probably when I'm working closely with other people, when I'm working as a team, . . . but I think in some senses my job is also to, to be the one that's ensuring that people are included . . .
Interviewer 1:	But not always yourself?
Headteacher:	Not always . . . and I think, yeah . . . I think there's also a sense that your, rightly or wrongly, your contribution is only a passing one, is, . . . is only a passing one . . . I think as a headteacher and perhaps in particular for everybody . . . all of us are, er, dispensable
Interviewer 1:	'Indispensable' or 'dispensable'?
Headteacher:	Well, I wouldn't say, you know, people are dispensable, I wouldn't use that language, . . . but we are, I am not indispensable, . . . the school will not stand or fall by [name of the interviewee] . . . and I like to think I have a contribution to make at this moment in time
Interviewer 2:	And this is sustainability as you as well as the degree to which you feel that although you are in transit or if you are potentially, do you feel that if you suddenly left that

Headteacher:

some of the issues that you've put, you know, some of those or most of them are sustainable?

I hope so, . . . I do hope so because you know leadership across the school is really very important and my primary purpose or one of my primary purposes is to develop that leadership capacity, so for example, the school is still running when I'm not in school when I'm out at various meetings sometimes for an extended period of time and I've no doubt that's you know, a healthy senior team will have very significant leaders within it.

Starting with the lack of 'belonging', and the consequent reluctance to fill in the 'belonging' circles of importance, there is evidence here of anomie specific to headship. As a headteacher 'you have to be removed', and this is a 'cost' of the job that is not shared by other staff or pupils. The headteacher agrees that this is 'isolating', and answers the following question, about when he feels most included, by saying it is 'when I'm working closely with other people, when I'm working as a team'. Yet even this teamwork is limited, as the follow-up starts with 'but' – a sign that the preceding statement is rejected. His job is to 'ensur[e] that people are included', but not always himself as his 'contribution is only a passing one'. After seeming to say that he is dispensable, the headteacher is asked by the interviewer whether he said 'dispensable' or 'indispensable'. Reluctant to agree that he did indeed say 'dispensable', he clarifies by saying 'we are', then corrected to 'I am not indispensable'. It is the combination of uniquely 'not belonging' with being uniquely 'not indispensable' that suggests a somewhat anomic position. However, the recovery from anomie is hinted at in the following exchange. The headteacher would 'like to think' he has 'a contribution to make', at least 'at this moment in time', and this is framed in terms of an apprenticeship model of leadership. He sees one of his primary purposes as developing the 'leadership capacity' of other staff in the school, so that his absence is not missed. There is therefore a sense of anomie, with two possible routes out of anomie, one being teamwork and the other being creating his successors (even though this makes him redundant). Teamwork had been mentioned earlier in the interview, in response to the circles of importance exercise on 'who are the people closest to you?' On that exercise, the headteacher had said that 'on one level . . . it would be probably quite a traditional hierarchy', but that this can be overcome. 'I think the, the trick is, . . . to have a hierarchy without being obvious as a hierarchy, it needs to be more fluid and more human and that and I think that if an institution hides behind a hierarchy . . . then it, then it fails . . . so, I suppose part of my role is to, to value everybody equally'. Even if escaping from the corruptive power of leadership is described as a 'trick', it is a value-rich trick, of valuing everybody equally. Anomie may in these ways be overcome.

The same exercise with the headteacher of Richardson (a UK primary school) produced quite a different response. To the same question ('to what do I belong in school?'), the headteacher interprets 'belonging' as a noun rather than as a verb, 'a belonging' rather than 'a member of a group'. She says 'I've got pupils, parents and teachers in the middle because, I think I belong to the pupils', adding with passion 'oh I hope I do, I hope I do'. With slightly less enthusiasm, she continues that 'I also think I belong to the parents . . . I definitely think that some parents think I belong to them', 'and I also feel I belong to the teachers because they, for different reasons, . . . demand things'. The sense of being a belonging sounds as though it is an account of Marxist alienation, a person who is alienated from herself through becoming an object belonging to others. However, the account is moderated as the interview continues. The interviewer says of the word, 'belonging: that sounds like sort of possession, that they possess you . . . [Headteacher: 'yes'] rather than belonging like it's a group you are a member of'. The head replies 'it's, it's both . . . both sides of that'. She feels that she 'saw it from their point of view that I'm not one of them, . . . but I'm one of their belongings . . . because . . . they need me and I need them'. It is not a simple alienated existence as 'a belonging', as 'it's a two-way process, . . . and you can't separate it, . . . as much as they belong to me, I belong to them . . . because we all need each other . . . to make the school work'. A partial cure for being an alienated 'belonging' is therefore to understand the mutuality of belonging. Complementing this is the additional cure provided by whole-school events. Due to 'the nature of the job' she sometimes 'feel[s] excluded', especially 'when the staff are having a moan about whatever' or when 'as a head you are giving difficult messages'. However, she feels most included in the school in 'things like assemblies and celebrations when the school is together'.

If the headteacher of Richardson avoids alienation, to an extent, through a positive sense of togetherness and a consciousness of the mutuality of dependency, the headteacher of North Humber School (a UK secondary school) is fighting, with some success, the alienation of commercialisation (Ball 2007). The school has successfully won bids for various statuses. 'We are a training school', the headteacher says, 'we're a specialist school and we are a Sports Partnership school.'

Headteacher: The unique thing about the school that people seem to keep coming about is that they see us as being very entrepreneurial and so we actually have lots of little businesses running and lots of little fingers in all sorts of pies, so we run a training business, a catering business, a sports business, a consultancy business . . . and because of that we actually financially are relatively buoyant compared with a lot of other [local] schools, but equally we are financially buoyant because we had to do the restructuring as well, so again a lot of schools avoided that but if you didn't do the restructuring obviously your budget was always going to be a problem . . .

Interviewer 1:   . . . from what you have said it sounds like you derive enormous satisfaction from having lots of different activities generating new ideas, producing new things for the kids to do and keeping your staff energised . . . and that is entrepreneurial, not in some nasty capitalist way, because lots of the things are entrepreneurial, would you say that is your greatest satisfaction, is that the thing that really gives you a buzz when you come into school in the morning?

With all this 'entrepreneurial' success, the headteacher is very clear that she is open to accusations that it is commerce that motivates her. 'If my parents are going to be critical', she says, 'if they are writing a letter to complain to the chair of governors, . . . that will be the thing they will slate me on, they will say, "you are more interested in money and entrepreneurial approaches than you are interested in education and children", and in some ways they know my Achilles' heel because that one sends me into the next stratosphere.' Fighting this description, she also recognises the risk of indeed being caught up in the commercialisation: the accusation is her 'Achilles' heel'. This is also well described by her account of the ambiguities of a 'Women of Achievement' prize. She refers to it as 'naff' (i.e. somewhat tasteless), but is clearly proud of having won the award, and emphasises how the people at the ceremony 'were selling this business about what drives you'. Explaining what drives her, even at the risk of being thought commercially driven, she continues:

all these people are all business women and what have you and I said at the end of the day, you know at the end of the day you have still got your roots that it's about kids and education and about them getting life chances . . . the danger is the more successful you are at bringing in resources and money, the more it looks like that's what is driving you and it's not because, I mean at this school every class-room has got a computer, every classroom has got a whiteboard, not interactive but you know has a projector and a lot of them have got interactive whiteboards and that is something we decided we needed to actually really change the way we were teaching . . . now you had to go out and you had to get that, it's no good me sitting here and saying well that will come from the LA [local authority], it won't come . . . so that is the thing, if you really want to put your finger through me and burst my bubble, that will be the thing you can do.

This is a good account of the risks of alienated loneliness, as the head-teacher is successful in her commercial activities, and this is seen by some as taking her away from a concern for the education of the pupils. It may also seem to take a headteacher away from the teaching activity, working directly with pupils, that had been the basis of the prior professional career. Teachers can lose their sense of being members of the teaching profession when promoted to headship. The loneliness of the head-teacher may be created by being among people who were professional peers, and perhaps friends too, but by being seen as separate from them. The head of Richardson compensated for missing teaching through her enjoyment of whole-school celebrations, while the head of North Humber reinforces her own sense of 'child-drivenness' during lunchtime at the school:

I will tell you what the biggest satisfaction is for me . . . I go out on dinnertime duty every day . . . now when I first started doing that four years ago the behaviour was poor at lunchtime in fact it was awful, and there was no response from the kids as you walked round, when I walk around now every child talks to me and every child has a conversation and they are ongoing conversations with children, . . . there is one little boy that every day asks me for the time and it's his way of coming to talk to you, he hasn't got the communication skills to do anything else he always asks me about the time and there is this one who always goes 'respect' and that's every day, he does 'respect' to you and I think if you said about satisfaction probably that's the biggest satisfaction I have on a day-to-day basis is the response of the kids and that's the one that is important, the staff might . . . not like the fact that you have . . . changed the contracts and whatever . . . , but if that means they are operating more successfully in the classroom, I can ride that, that doesn't impinge. If when I walked round at a lunchtime the kids ignored me, or when they saw me they carried on misbehaving or you know whatever that would be really upsetting for me so ultimately there is that child-drivenness that other people probably think isn't there.

The need for, and successful achievement of, dialogue with pupils is a helpful example of how to avoid the potential loneliness of school leadership.

Solitude and privacy for school leaders

Although 'our spiritual life cannot be lived alone' (Klass 1999, p. 27, writing about bereavement and quoted in Chapter 4), there may be times, when bereaved or when in school, when aloneness is valued. In the film *Gregory's Girl* (Forsyth 1981), the headteacher, played by comedian Chic Murray, is shown, filmed through a door, playing the piano entirely for his own amusement. The headteacher is interrupted by pupils looking at him through the door. 'Off you go, you small boys', he says, and continues playing the piano. This small account of a headteacher achieving solitude in the midst of a busy school is a good description of what headteachers may need in school: a time of solitude. Chapter 3, above, provides an account of those pupils who said they felt most included in school when left alone (Hatfield 2004). As the introduction to the current chapter explains, headteachers are so publicly exposed that they are particularly in need of times of privacy and solitude. This sense of privacy and solitude is, of course, just as socially framed as the various forms of loneliness. According to the historical accounts of Webb (2007) and Vernon (2005), the idea of a need for privacy and the value of solitude emerged in Northern Europe between the twelfth and seventeenth centuries, starting from monastic theories and developing later in the period to a broad social change that separated the 'private' from the 'civic' or 'public'. Whereas there had been biblical warnings against the moral dangers of being alone ('Woe to him who is alone, for there is none to pick him up if he should fall', Ecclesiastes 4:10, quoted in Webb 2007, p. viii), positively framed solitude, and the privacy of individuals or small groups such as families, developed in medieval Europe.

Bernard (1090–1153, later St Bernard) wrote of the value of solitude for monks: 'remain alone, so as to preserve thyself for him alone, whom thou has chosen to thyself from among all others' (Bernard, in Webb 2007, p. 64). There is a need for solitude even when in company, as '[t]he essentially interior meaning of solitude is further elaborated for the benefit of men who in fact lived in a closely packed community' (Webb 2007, p. 64). This may be Bernard's 'solitude of mind and spirit', developed through 'avoid[ing] disputes', '[o]therwise you are not really alone, though there be no one with you' (Bernard, in Webb 2007, pp. 64–5). In an interesting two-part statement, Bernard concludes '[h]owever large be the throng of men in which you find yourself, you are alone if only you take care not to listen eagerly to the conversation around you, nor to judge of it rashly' (Bernard, in Webb 2007, p. 65). It is the refusal to judge things rashly that makes this statement particularly interesting, suggesting a slow consideration of issues to be vital to making a positive use of being alone. Webb suggests a modern version of this might be those who read books in the company of members of their family, carefully considering the book and in that sense being 'alone', though in company.

How families work is central to the account given by Vernon of the English development of a new division between the civic and the private, which he suggests happened in the second half of the seventeenth century. Before this period, a number of everyday activities, including eating, toileting and sleeping, were broadly 'public' activities taking place in a 'household' (a building where these activities happened, and not what would later become a 'family home'), among family, friends, allies, and colleagues. Hence '[t]he physical intimacies of kissing and eating and sleeping together were symbolic of what we might call social capital; Francis Bacon called it "countenance" and others "honour"' (Vernon 2005, p. 109). In seventeenth-century England, there was a shrinking of what took place in such social spaces: eating, toileting and sleeping 'started taking place within the much narrower confines of what we now call the marital space' (Vernon 2005, p. 111), and lost their wider social meanings. Colleagues and friends were no longer literal 'bedfellows', in the sense of sleeping together: the term became figurative. As Vernon says, 'the public institution of the household was replaced by the private institution of the family' (Vernon 2005, p. 111). Accompanying the changing boundaries is a change in descriptions of sexuality. A more ambiguous sense of sexuality was restricted to the home and family, and increasingly 'fixed' into the categories regarded as 'normal' and 'abnormal', as 'bodily intimacy ceased to be an instrument that could be used to carry wider social meanings, including friendship, and came to be associated primarily with the more limited concerns of married couples' (Vernon 2005, p. 111). That is how the public 'household' became the private 'family'.

It is as though the valuable solitude and privacy described by Webb was finally institutionalised in homes. How do schools fit in with these developments? Although Vernon describes families and homes as they developed a sense of privacy, it should be mentioned that there was a continuation of the earlier forms of 'household', that is, places where eating, toileting and sleeping took place among family, friends, allies, and colleagues. The social institutions continuing such forms included religious communities (monasteries and convents), the armed services, prisons, and boarding (residential) schools. Later institutions added to the list might include communes and kibbutzim, both political developments from the twentieth century. (The practices of social networking sites in the early twenty-first century also blur the public/private boundaries, and may be seen as extensions of 'household' models in some ways, although this social formation is probably too recent to be properly understood.) Setting aside the armed forces and prisons, both of which have clear externally directed functions, what all the other institutions have in common with families is their exemplification of Macmurray's meaning of a 'community'. All are organisations in which people can be expected to treat each other as ends in themselves rather than as means to ends. Vernon's thesis of the late seventeenth-century emergence of a split between the 'private' and the 'civic' is significant. However, it belies the continuation of a third type of 'place', that is, the community as understood by Macmurray. There remains a sharing of, for example, eating, toileting and sleeping, and in many of the places there is a more ambiguous sexuality, too.

Schools and other Macmurrian communities belie a simple 'private vs public' division, or rather overcome that dualism described by Buber (in Chapter 1, above), between 'the separated *It* of institutions . . . and the separated *I* of feelings' (Buber 1958, p. 63). In some of his writing on schools, Macmurray concentrates on boarding schools, to emphasise the principles of education 'under conditions where children and teachers are continuously together for considerable periods, and where every aspect of the educational process has to be provided by the school' (Macmurray 1968, p. 31b). It is not that boarding schools are the only communal schools, but rather that boarding schools can illustrate the fullness of the relationships that are also characteristic of non-boarding schools. In such communities, the kind of solitude and privacy needed by headteachers, or any of the staff or pupils, is likely to be of a different kind from that needed in 'societies' – externally directed organisations. The model of monastic communities in which 'solitude of mind and spirit' can be developed through 'avoid[ing] disputes' (Bernard, in Webb 2007, pp. 64–5, quoted above), is an interesting approach, given the opportunities for headteachers to be involved in disputes. What is recommended, though, is not ignoring any dispute, but making sure that you do not 'judge of it rashly' (Bernard, in Webb 2007, p. 65). That sense of being above or beyond the disputes within school is also a good description of magnanimity, and this theme is developed further, below. The description by Bernard of achieving solitude in a busy and full community, through careful consideration and reflection, is in modern terms an encouragement for headteachers to engage in reading and research. It is the power of the research process, involving headteachers in reflecting on their own views, that stimulates the 'portrait methodology' of Bottery (exemplified in Bottery 2007). That approach to leadership research was used as the basis of the distinctive headteacher-directed questions in the *Spirit of the School* project.

One headteacher, interviewed simultaneously for Bottery's portraiture project and the *Spirit of the School* project, described some of the external pressures on, or intrusions into, the school in terms of interference with the toileting and eating and drinking 'household' qualities of the school. She notes that the earlier inspection system of Ofsted was 'hugely stressful': 'everybody was stressed, it was five full days, they went into every toilet if they wanted to' (Headteacher, North Humber secondary school, UK). Legislation on healthy eating was also a potential intrusion:

> I mean I remember when the whole thing about food came in, . . . and we weren't allowed to sell all sorts of things and then they tightened it up again and you had to, certain nutrients in every meal and then you had to do this and that, we all agreed with the healthy eating and everything but then it was beginning to feel like it was a thing around your neck, it was almost like 'have you checked the children's sandwich box?', you know and I'm like, 'no I am not going to stand there and check a child's sandwich box', and some of the primary heads were actually doing that because they thought that the legislation was making them do it and I think you have just got to keep going forward the legislation you try and get round it. (Headteacher, North Humber secondary school, UK)

The headteacher of a Church of England primary school led the school during and after the school was flooded. When teachers were interviewed, one of the times the school made them feel good about themselves was when the headteacher gave a bottle of wine to each member of staff, as a 'thank you'. Some time later, the staff reciprocated, as the headteacher explains:

I have turned forty-five recently and the staff made quite a fuss . . .
much to my huge embarrassment, I don't like having, having a fuss
made at all and I preferred, preferred they hadn't but . . . I felt you
know very special and included and, and I suppose went away and
thinking 'Well they, they must have quite liked me or they wouldn't,
kind of wouldn't have gone to that'.

This is a school that is clear about its communal aims, as described by
Macmurray, having written into its 'statement of values', that '[w]hen we
leave this place we will always be able to call it home'. Teachers in Northcliffe (a UK secondary school) said that one of the ways the school,
consistently identified as having a long way to go to become more of a
community, could become more communal would be through agreeing
to the 'draconian measure to ban all tea and coffee machines in individual departments'. This would 'make people come down to one staff room
and make everyone sit together'. Such household/home characteristics
are particularly important for headteachers, not only in achieving their
own solitude-without-loneliness, but also in helping develop the spirit of
the school.

Being able to retain a place for solitude is vital for reflection, even if
the self-knowledge that results can be uncomfortable. Webb provides
accounts from the period of the fourth to the eleventh centuries of the
'pioneers of solitude'. Living a busy life without solitude can hide a
person's self-understanding, as 'anyone who lives in a crowd: because of
the turbulence he does not see his sins; but when he has been quiet,
above all in solitude, then he recognizes his own faults' (Webb 2007,
p. 28). This is not only relevant to headteachers, but the 'corruptions' of
leadership, described above, make the need for solitude, and the chance
to realise limitations or even 'sins', all the greater. It will always be true
that headteachers will need this flexibility, as described by Matoes: 'He
who dwells with brethren . . . must not be square, but round, so as to turn
himself towards all' (Matoes, quoted in Webb 2007, p. 26). Having investigated loneliness and how it can be overcome, it is the activities completed
with others, the 'turning towards all', that are investigated in the next
section.

Crafty leadership

When social class definitions are considered, job categories are typically
described as manual and working class or non-manual and middle class.
One of the puzzles of these categories is why some jobs that are patently

'manual', such as being a concert pianist or a medical surgeon (from the Greek *kheirourgia*, a handworker), are grouped with the non-manual jobs. The training for those jobs, involving a long period in universities gaining qualifications, and their pay and status, all justify them being grouped with other professional jobs. But the jobs themselves are still manual, they are still crafts based on manual dexterity. Professional workers tend to regard 'crafts' as beneath them, socially. Sennett has written widely on the sociology of work, and has recently investigated the craft-qualities that are missing from, or needing to be celebrated in, modern education and working life. He blames Aristotle for initiating a downplaying of craft-workers, as those described as 'public[ly] productive' (Sennett 2008, p. 22) become known as mere 'handworkers'. Aristotle 'abandons the old word for the craftsman, *demioergos*, and uses instead *cheirotechnon*, which means simply handworker [i.e. the word that became 'surgeon']' (Sennett 2008, p. 23). Modern education and modern society copy Aristotle and look down on crafts and their techniques. Schools may even reject craftwork altogether: '[a]fraid of boring children, avid to present ever-different stimulation, the enlightened teacher may avoid routine – but thus deprives children of the experience of studying their own ingrained practice and modulating it from within' (Sennett 2008, p. 38). Technique, he continues, 'has a bad name; it can seem soulless' (Sennett 2008, p. 149), which is of particular significance for research on spirituality. Some, occasionally, recognise its significance, as Kant is said to have 'casually remarked', '[t]he hand is the window on to the mind' (Sennett 2008, p. 149). There is a sense in which being a headteacher is a craft, a technique that is 'publicly productive' and that is refined through practice, and in which being a headteacher copies the social systems of craft trades, such as apprenticeship models of learning. And there is a sense in which being a headteacher is *like* craftwork, and a comparison will be given, here, with the craft-related profession of music.

Being a headteacher is a craft. It is an activity requiring technique refined through repetitive practice, it is a productive activity and the 'products' of the craft (pupils, staff and the school community) are themselves regarded as the measure of the job done. And in one crucial respect, headteachers along with other teachers in many countries mirror the traditional craftworker responsibility as *in loco parentis*, in the place of the parents, of the apprentices/pupils (University of Bristol 1998, p. 11, with a more sceptical view in Myers 2005, p. 77). The school leader is someone who is building school communities and developing young people and school staff. It is reasonable to point out that the activities of headteachers include a considerable quantity of repeated and routinised activity, such as daily welcoming of pupils and staff, assemblies, telling-off and congratulating pupils and staff, weekly staff meetings, weekly or termly awards ceremonies and governing body meetings, annual introductions to new pupils, and leaving ceremonies for pupils and staff at the end of their time in the school. Such activities involve complex skills that are practised and refined to such an extent that headteachers are rarely aware of the skills, but instead are sensitive to the impact of the activities and how that can be improved. Like the carpenters more conscious of the wood and the product being made than of their own activities and tools, experienced headteachers become more conscious of the staff and pupil reactions than of their own rhetoric.

Suggesting that headteachers develop a routinised craft of performing in such situations is a contentious claim. Ball talks eloquently of the era of 'performativity', when what he refers to as '[a] kind of *values schizophrenia* is experienced by individual teachers where commitment, judgement and authenticity within practice are sacrificed for impression and performance' (Ball 2003, p. 221). He sees this as a threat to the teacher's 'soul' (Ball 2003, p. 215). '[W]hile we may not be expected to care about each other we are expected to 'care' *about* performances' (Ball 2003, p. 224), and if this were the choice, Ball would be right about the loss of soul. However, the argument focuses on figures more than on care, and misses the possibility of combining caring and performance. '[T]he more figures we use, the more the great truths seem to slip through our fingers', and '[d]espite all that numerical control, we feel as ignorant of the answers to the big questions as ever' (Ball 2003, p. 215). It is the numbers that Ball is concerned with, as the 'performance' he describes is the meeting of quantitative targets, but his point is a more general one, about the 'set of dualisms or tensions' between the measures by which their 'impression and performance' are valued and 'authentic and purposeful relationships' (Ball 2003, p. 223). Ball makes this general point about performativity, illustrated with reference to performance directed towards measurable and quantifiable targets. This is not unreasonable, in a policy context dominated by such targets, yet something can be lost. There is a need for a sense of performance as valuable and as integral to the role of the headteacher. What needs to be analysed is the purpose of the performance itself. In musical terms, is the headteacher performing for the audience of pupils and staff and the wider school community, or for inspection agencies and local or national government agencies? Ball's contrast between performativity and 'authentic and purposeful relationships' might be clarified by allowing for a contrast between performativity directed towards pupils and staff, and performativity directed towards

inspectors or government agencies. Furthermore, if headteachers are skil-
fully performing for the former group, then they may indeed combine
performativity and authenticity. In an extreme form, this can be justified
in Oscar Wilde's terms, as he recommends artificiality and mask-wearing
as necessary for truthfulness (Trilling 1972, pp. 118–21, explored below in
Chapter 6). The rejection of the craft-like performance of headteachers,
by writers such as Ball, can alienate the very headteachers who might wish
to join Ball in rejecting external and commercially driven targets.

The craft of leading a school is worthy of analysis, and this includes the
nature of the performance of the headteacher. A metaphor used in a guide
for new teachers of history (Stern 1999), is of the teacher as an orchestral
conductor. Two implications of the metaphor are that, first, the orchestra
contains many different instruments, just as a school contains many different people: an encouragement to differentiation. Secondly, the teacher as
conductor of an orchestra of pupils clearly indicates that the performances
of the pupils matter: they are 'players' and not 'audience'. In other words,
rather than rejecting performativity, the term can be extended to all school
staff and to school pupils. People who are new to orchestral music are often
puzzled by the role of the conductor, as it appears as though the sound
comes from the players and not the conductor, making the conductor
unnecessary. Orchestras can, in fact, perform without a conductor: the
purpose of the conductor is to help the orchestra perform better, not
simply to make it perform. Pupils, too, can learn without teachers, but can,
it is hoped, perform even better with teachers. The second point, that
pupils are performers rather than audience, is an important counter-
balance to a popular view of teachers as soloists performing to the audience
of pupils, captured for example in literary depictions such as Muriel
Spark's *The Prime of Miss Jean Brodie* (Spark 2000), and Christopher Rush's
even harsher though rather less well known *Last Lesson of the Afternoon: A
Satire* (Rush 1994). Teachers and headteachers who are soloists are necessarily trying to perfect a performance, and are not trying to develop the
pupils and teachers and school.

An example can be given from the *Spirit of the School* research, of the
impact on a pupil of a headteacher's routine performance. One of the
teachers at Afton primary school (Church of England, UK), when asked
to describe the times from her own schooling when the school made her
feel good about herself, gave an emotional account of a ceremony from
when she was aged 11 or 12.

> I was once given a book, a needlework book, and it was given to me in
> front of the whole school, and it was my first year of senior school, and

I'd come top in every single subject. I really had worked hard, and I was determined that I going to do so well in this school, and I didn't know they were going to do this 'cos I was new to this school, and they had on the last day a prize-giving ceremony and it was a big comprehensive school, and I had to walk up in front of 14 or 15 hundred other people, you know, and receive this book. And just at that moment where it was put into my hand and the head looked at me and he just said 'well done', and he knew my name, it was 'well done [Name]'. And I've still got the book, I still fill up when I look at it now, it was just that 'well done' that worked.

The teacher was indeed tearful when she described the incident. What is striking is that this must have been a much-repeated routine by the headteacher. He had probably given dozens or even hundreds of such prizes, and may have made the same comment to each prize-winner. It is not that he rejected performativity, but that he performed well, and achieved a moment of true dialogue, a touching moment remembered with emotion several decades later. During a typical day, a headteacher might have had to tell off a pupil for some misbehaviour in the classroom, reported to rather than witnessed by the headteacher, discuss school policies with a challenging and difficult parent of a pupil, demonstrate to a local authority official or the chair of the governing body why the funding policy should be adjusted to enable the school to repair the central heating boiler, and give out prizes at an end of year ceremony. The ability to perform in ways suited to each of those situations, and to perform with sincerity, is a carefully-practised craft. Some academic writers objected to Marland's work on the 'craft of the classroom' (Marland 1993, title), both because it referred to a 'craft' rather than a 'profession', and because it was subtitled 'a survival guide' rather than a guide to flourishing. The second criticism is fair if misguided, as survival (i.e. the retention of teachers in the workforce) is an increasingly important priority for schools, even if it is not appropriate as their main priority. The first criticism misses the point, that performance and sincerity or authenticity are not alternates, but should be combined in the person of the teacher and especially the headteacher – as headteachers typically have so many, contrasting, performances and performing contexts. And it is not just headteachers and teachers who must perform. In a striking analysis of pupils on their first day in school, Willes explains how these four-year-olds are already expected to know how to 'bid' for attention, and how some pupils are disadvantaged by their failure to come to school with these performance skills in place (Willes 1983). Willes' criticism is not of the need for young pupils to perform, but of the expectation that they know how to perform without all having been given an opportunity to learn the appropriate performance skills.

To the extent that headteachers are performing, it may be worth considering their attitude to the 'script' being performed. In schools, the scripts may be the school and government policy documents, curriculum guidance, laws and administrative regulations, and social and cultural expectations. Sennett comments that, although '[e]very actor and musician has a text upon which to base his art', the room for manoeuvre 'lies in how much the performer believes his own work can be "notated"' (Sennett 1978, p. 197). Hence, a musician who believes that the script cannot be a complete account of what should be performed, will expect to 'find what is missing from the printed page', just as the actor can 'treat the text . . . as a set of suggestions for a character in Shakespeare's or Ibsen's mind, suggestions which cannot be ignored, but leave him much freedom', or can in contrast 'treat the text as a bible which, once understood, will tell him how to act' (Sennett 1978, p. 197). The reference to treating the text 'as a bible' is somewhat problematic. Within religious communities, bibles are treated in many different ways, and relatively rarely as a strict instruction manual. There is therefore a continuum from those prioritising text and therefore the scriptwriter to those prioritising the freedom of the performance and therefore the 'presence of the performer's personality' (Sennett 1978, p. 198), but in all cases there is a dialogue between writer and the performer of the text. The development of the more 'free' approach in musical and theatrical performance, according to Sennett, happened through the nineteenth century. European classical music derives from religious traditions and from popular folk and dance music. In the former, members of the 'audience' are genuine participants in the sacred ceremonies rather than mere 'listeners', and in the latter, members of the 'audience' are also typically participants in the chorus and in the dancing. What emerged in nineteenth-century music was the increasing independence of the performer from both the composer and the audience, such that the pianist Liszt could announce that '[t]he concert is – myself' (quoted in Sennett 1978, p. 199).

A return to a greater balance, and a clearer sense of the dialogue between scriptwriter, performer, and audience/participants, came with the twentieth-century rejection of some of the extremes of Lisztian virtuosity. This is best signified by the American composer Cage, who wrote *Four Minutes and Thirty-three Seconds* (1952), a piece in which the performer sits silently at the piano for the time indicated. It is not that the piece is one of silence: it is one where the 'incidental noises from the audience' (Rosen 2002, p. 127), their coughing or shuffling or sniffing, and the noises of the room in which the performance takes place, become the focus of the performance. The piece 'amuses the audiences and embarrasses the serious music-lovers' (Hutcheson 1975, p. 392); it also mocks the hubris, the excessive pride, of Liszt and all those soloists who believe that *they* are the performance. Liszt himself was aware of the dangers of charismatic virtuosity, as demonstrated in what he wrote in a notice of the violin virtuoso Paganini's death. Paganini, according to Sennett, is 'unlike them [the audience], as are all charismatic figures, but he is also permanently isolated from anyone he arouses' (Sennett 1978, p. 202). As Liszt said:

> [T]his man, who created so much enthusiasm, could make no friends among his fellowmen. No one guessed what was going on in his heart; his own richly blessed life never made another happy. . . . Paganini's god . . . was never any other than his own gloomy, sad 'I.' (Sennett 1978, p. 202, ellipses in the original)

Liszt was aware of his own charismatic and self-promoting style of performance, and therefore he seemed to be more able to achieve successful relationships. He even managed to understand what he described as his 'charlatan' qualities. A contemporary of Liszt, who enjoyed the music of Bach, accused the pianist of charlatanry, and asked him to play some Bach. Liszt asked how he wanted it played, and was told 'the way it ought to be played'. The pianist proceeded to play the piece three times, once 'as the author must have understood it', a second time 'as I feel it, with . . . a more modern style', and finally 'the way I would play it for the public – to astonish, as a charlatan' (Rosen 1995, p. 510):

> And, lighting a cigar which passed at moments from between his lips to his fingers, executing with his ten fingers the part written for the organ pedals, and indulging in other *tours de force* and prestidigitation, he was prodigious, incredible, fabulous, and received gratefully with enthusiasm. (Rosen 1995, pp. 510–11)

Having that range of performances open to him, it is hoped that Liszt was able to be in dialogue with Bach and with the sophisticated 'authentic' Bach-lover and with listeners who would be impressed by prestidigitation. He was less at risk of having for his 'god' merely 'his own gloomy, sad "I"'. As Spender rightly said, '[a]n "I" can never be Great Man' and will finally 'long for "We dying"' (quoted in Yeats 1936, p. 433). The sad, unconnected and perhaps lonely, virtuoso Paganini is portrayed as something like Buber's golem: the 'animated clod without soul'; the self-aware, enthusiastically sociable, and nuanced virtuoso Liszt lies just on this side of the line between pride and hubris, and may be said to be more spirited than the violinist. Headteachers may stray towards the performing approach of Liszt, they may indulge in prodigious *tours de force*, but if they go further and lose their connection to others in the school, they will lose their own ability to flourish, and the rest of the school community will lose their own possibility of being related to the headteacher. As Sennett said of the audiences of self-absorbed virtuosi of the nineteenth century, '[t]he people who were witnesses to these performers saw their powers at a comfortable elevation', but 'it would be a great mistake to think therefore of the silent spectator as a comfortable man', as '[h]is silence was the sign of a profound self-doubt' (Sennett 1978, p. 205).

The Lisztian virtuosic style of school leadership is certainly not a universal model, and was not even the only style available to Liszt, as described of his playing of Bach. Headteachers have the choice across a wide continuum, from the proper pride (but not excessively arrogant pride) of the cigar-smoking pianist Liszt to the humility (but not excessively pusillanimous humility) of the silent pianist Cage. Other staff and pupils are also, in more spirited schools, best able to develop when they are in a relationship with, a dialogue with, the headteacher. Headteachers may be given 'scripts', such as policies and legislation, but they are at best in a kind of dialogue with the authors of those scripts – with the script authors and the headteachers at different times having the greater influence. Early nineteenth-century classical music saw the rise of performers who were able through their virtuosity to have priority over composers, but the dialogue was not entirely lost, and the dialogue with witnesses to the performances was also maintained. The opportunity for virtuosity is linked, here, to the need for a relational approach to school leadership, exhibiting virtues such as pride and humility. It is the virtues, rather than virtuosity, of the headteacher that therefore conclude this chapter on the spirit of school leadership. As Trilling explains, copying Aristotle's gender-specificity,

> Aristotle's virtuous man in his highest development quite precisely sees himself: he whose virtue is such that it wears the crowning perfection of *megalopsychia*, 'great-souledness' or 'aristocratic pride', is to be recognized by the way he comports himself, by his slow gait, his low-pitched voice, his measured diction, his conscious irony in dealing with inferiors – the virtuous man is an actor. (Trilling 1972, p. 86)

From virtuosity to virtue: magnanimity and humility

The current chapter has argued that school leaders can avoid alienated or anomic loneliness, in part through maintaining relationships within the school community and in part through their ability to achieve some solitude in the peculiarly private-public 'household' that is the school community. It has also argued that being a school leader may involve deeply personal relationships with members of the school community, without rejecting the possibility of following 'scripts' written by those outside the school, and without rejecting the craft-like performative qualities of the job. Pressures to 'perform' are often seen as acting against the possibility of ethical leadership, as in Ball's entirely proper concern for the 'teacher's soul'. This account allows for a carefully crafted performance, yet there is still a need to address the ethical dimension more explicitly. It is the virtues of school leadership that are considered in this final section, and especially the distinctively Aristotelian virtue of magnanimity and the supposedly contrasting virtue of humility that is often attributed to the Jewish and Christian traditions.

'Magnanimity' is the term used to translate Aristotle's *megalopsuchia*, described by one editor as 'magnanimity, proper pride, self-respect – there is no real English equivalent for this very upper-class Greek virtue' (Aristotle 1976, p. 153). Of course there is the term 'magnanimity' itself, but as the editor was aware, that term had by the twentieth century lost its pride. An earlier definition of the term described magnanimity as a '[w]ell-founded high regard for oneself manifesting as generosity of spirit and equanimity in the face of trouble etc.; loftiness of thought or purpose; grandeur or nobility of designs or ambition' (SOED 2007). In later uses of the word, pride is lost, although the other qualities are still largely present. The more current usage is said to be '[s]uperiority to petty resentment or jealousy, generous disregard of slights' (SOED 2007) or 'loftiness of spirit enabling one to bear trouble calmly, to disdain meanness and pettiness, and to display a noble generosity' (Encyclopædia Britannica 2008). What is described as 'upper class' in Aristotle's usage is the presence of pride, and pride specifically in the art of leadership itself. In other words, as well as being 'above' petty conflicts, the magnanimous person is in a position to be this when, and only when, they are conscious of themselves as being good leaders in every other way. As Aristotle says, it is a form of self-respect based on true worth: a person is magnanimous 'if he thinks that he is worthy of great things, provided that he *is* worthy of them' (Aristotle 1976, p. 153). It is not necessarily an 'upper class' virtue, but it is a virtue therefore of someone in a position within a hierarchy,

when considering people lower down the hierarchy. Perhaps 'worthy of
greater things' would be better than 'worthy of great things', as 'great'
implies an absolute position of power, rather than a relative one.

How does this Aristotelian magnanimity (that is, the modern magnanimity with added pride) suit school leadership? There are many ways in
which the pride-free version of magnanimity might be expected of school
leaders, and of others in school when dealing with people lower in the
hierarchy – such as teachers dealing with pupils. A simple example of how
to 'bear trouble calmly' was given by the headteacher of St Bede's secondary school (Roman Catholic, UK). When asked to describe a time when
the school made him feel good about himself (itself a disguised elicitation
of the rather un-English 'pride'), he said:

> I think this morning, in reflecting with my senior team on an
> incident yesterday afternoon involving a young man who had just
> lost his temper really, lost the plot, and I was reflecting on our expe-
> rience this morning with the senior team and explaining how I was,
> ordinarily I wouldn't be in the thick of the action so to speak, I was
> yesterday and it became very clear to me how hard people work to
> make things, the simple things happen, so it was apparent to me, for
> example, how efficient the system seemed to be, how calm people
> were, how well people worked as a team and, and obviously I felt
> pleased to be, to be in some way responsible for that and very much
> to be part of that. So, that's, that's, . . . so it was, was an institution I
> was trying to say this, it doesn't happen very often at St Bede's, you
> know it would rank as a critical incident, a young man losing the plot
> and a little bit violent, threats of violence, foul language, very
> unusual but I think it showed, it showed the school at its best in
> crisis. [Interviewer: You felt it personally?] Absolutely.

The pleasure for the headteacher was in the way staff, himself included,
were calm and systematic in dealing with the violent and emotional pupil.
As a school with few such incidents, this was dealt with generously, with
the pupil's behaviour framed as unusual for that pupil, as well as for the
school. There was no evidence of staff becoming angry themselves, or
vindictive, in the face of this pupil's anger. It is a clear description of magnanimity in the modern sense, and the headteacher's presentation of the
case as one that made him feel good about himself suggests, further, that
this is also a description of Aristotelian magnanimity. The headteacher
was proud of what he and his colleagues did in this critical circumstance,
and understood that his pride was not simply related to this incident, but

was related to the leadership of the school or 'how efficient the system seemed to be'. It is an example of proper pride and of consciousness of being worthy.

One of the school leaders described a kind of Aristotelian magnanimity displayed by pupils, and implied that it was, in turn, a source of his own pride. The principal of School 1 (a secondary school in Hong Kong, with a Protestant foundation) described how 'more and more visual art works of our students are displayed around the campus', as a response to being questioned about how the school made him feel good about himself.

> So many of our students took visual arts so we need to open up the subject in F.6 and 7. This is our first year in A level now. Their works are excellent and they won many prizes in competitions. They also got good grades in public exams. Apart from getting good grade in academic subjects, they have also made great achievement in this aspect. I am so happy about this. Who say that our students cannot learn under our way of teaching? Not only they have learnt well, their talents in many other aspects are also developed. They are also proud to be a part of this school.

Pupils have good reasons to be proud of their work, as evidenced in their grades and prizes, and this is described more broadly as their being proud 'to be part of this school'. It is a 'proper pride', that is, they are indeed worthy, and it is how they manage the range of their work in a school context that systematically encourages such work: pupils 'might start off having low self-confidence or self-esteem, but we would help them to build themselves up, with the hope that they would find the objectives of their lives and establish their own sets of values'. The pupils are 'leading' their own learning, and their pride can in this way be described as close to magnanimity. It is the same principal who described his refusal to be drawn into conflict with a pupil's parents, and the careful leadership shown in these circumstances:

> We received some applications from controversial students. . . . For example, [Name] who always hit the headline a few years ago. My colleagues dared not to take her because her parents made a lot of troubles and had been complaining fiercely about every school she was in. But after we interviewed her, we saw that she had a lot of potential. We thought that she shouldn't be punished because of her parents. So I decided to take her but I did it in a low key so that, firstly, she would not hit the headline again and we're free from the

harassment of the news reporters. Then she could concentrate on
her work and development. Secondly, I had very good communication with my colleagues to help them to treat her as an ordinary
student. I had especially counselled them on dealing with problems
from the parents. Thirdly, before I decided to take her, I had discussed with the girl's parents and had agreed on some terms. One of
the parents was actually not very suitable to be a guardian. So I made
a bold step. Apart from asking the other parent to be her guardian,
I also asked them to have their family social worker to replace the
complaining parent, to make communication between us easier. . . .
We also explained to the parents and the social worker how we were
going to teach the child. They trusted us and signed a letter of
consent. The student has been with us for more than two years now
and she learns well and had great personal growth.

This is an important example of magnanimous school leadership,
being actively determined not to let conflict distract him from his educational goal, and being prepared to provide some 'leadership' even to
the family/care system beyond the school, in order to enable the school
to educate the pupil without inappropriate interference. By describing
this as how he had overcome difficulties generated by legislative require-
ments (presumably, in this case, the care roles of parents and social
workers), the principal, in his fourth year as principal in this school
following five years as principal in another school, is also clearly aware of
his own 'worth' and the need for the courage to be 'bold'.

Pride may need to be 'teased out' of respondents who are, understandably, reluctant to appear arrogant or vain. Yet it can be found in these
examples and many more, not only in research with headteachers, but
also in research with teachers and pupils. When combined with the
modern version of magnanimity, that is, calmness in the face of difficulties, the Aristotelian conception of magnanimity re-emerges, as being
'great-souled' (the translation given in Stern-Gillet 1995, p. 110) or
having a 'loftiness of spirit' (Encyclopædia Britannica 2008) in a
somewhat more literal sense than the dictionary writers might have
intended. For many, this kind of magnanimity is in stark contrast to the
virtue of humility, yet it is not clear whether these are binary opposites, so
much as 'upper' and 'lower' limits to a proper sense of oneself, rather as
it has been argued that Liszt and Cage represent, in certain circumstances, upper and lower limits to the dominance of the pianist-
performer. The real contrast is between on the one hand vanity, conceit-
edness or arrogance (the person 'who thinks that he is worthy of great

things although he is not worthy of them is conceited', Aristotle 1976, p. 153), and on the other hand excessive humility or 'pusillanimity' (those who do not think they are worthy of great things but are worthy of them, Aristotle 1976, p. 105). A single leader may, at different times, exhibit both magnanimity and humility, just as a single leader may exhibit both arrogance and pusillanimity. These are virtues related to hierarchical positions, and the range of virtues appropriate to leaders reflects the fact that all leaders are likely also to be followers: all hierarchies are embedded in larger hierarchies, so a magnanimous leader may inevitably be also a humble follower, and a leader tempted to vanity may at other times be tempted to pusillanimity.

The ability to combine magnanimity and humility can be further explained with reference to religious views of humility, especially as humility is itself described as a distinctively 'Christian virtue' in contrast to the ancient virtue of pride. For Macmurray, Jesus is a democrat, as he taught people 'to base their relationships upon the mutual service of equals and to condemn and exclude the desire for power' (Macmurray 1996, p. 181).

'He that would be greatest among you,' he said, 'let him be the servant of all.' Explicitly he contrasts with this principle of democratic community the practice of the kings of the nations who exercise authority over their subjects. In particular he insists upon economic democracy. (Macmurray 1996, p. 181)

It is not clear whether Jesus can so easily be interpreted as a democratic, or what exactly is the nature of 'service' described here and at several points in biblical texts. The biblical quotation supporting Macmurray's argument is from Matthew 23:11–12: 'he that is greatest among you shall be your servant / And whosoever shall exalt himself shall be abased; and he that shall humble himself shall be exalted'. This is certainly a promotion of humility, but it refers, as do all the biblical references to humility, to humility in the face of God. That quotation is preceded by 'And call no man your father upon the earth: for one is your Father, which is in heaven' (Matthew 23:9). The positive uses of humility in the biblical texts are either examples of how God will lift up those who are low (as in Job 22:29: 'When men are cast down, then thou shalt say, There is lifting up; and he shall save the humble person'), or of how God is greater than all and therefore not to be approached with arrogance or vanity (as in Psalm 2:1–3: 'Why do the heathen rage, and the people imagine a vain thing? / The kings of the earth set themselves, and the rulers take counsel together, against the Lord, and against his anointed, saying, / Let us break their bands asunder, and cast away their cords from us'). Humility in the face of a greater power, indicated in these texts, is not the same as humility in all circumstances; the absence of vanity in the face of greater power does not imply the inappropriateness of all pride. Even in Proverbs, where 'Pride goeth before destruction, and an haughty spirit before a fall / Better it is to be of an humble spirit with the lowly, than to divide the spoil with the proud' (Proverbs 16:18–19), this is in the context of the presence of God, who is described as hating the arrogant version of pride (i.e. excessive pride), in Proverbs 8:13: 'The fear of the Lord is to hate evil: pride, and arrogancy, and the evil way, and the froward mouth, do I hate'.

An interesting example of humility, explicitly framed in Christian terms, can be taken from the *Spirit of the School* research. The principal of School 4 (primary school, Protestant, Hong Kong) was asked 'of all the issues and difficulties that face you as a principal, which would you say is the most persistent and troubling?' He responds by describing the challenges provided by the school having 'taken in' both pupils and staff from other schools that had closed, and the dangers of unjustified pride – pride based on having been an experienced school leader, when he started in the school, but not appreciating the different context.

> The toughest task was to deal with a staff member who should have been terminated 11 years ago. He/she was not terminated but promoted to senior position. If this has become a norm, nobody would work hard. If somebody makes a mistake, he would think that he would say, '[Name] can get away, why can't I?'. It was an unforgettably dangerous experience when I had to terminate the employment of this colleague. He/she had a poor record on his/her file. The chairman of the school management committee called to show his strong support. It was also when I experience the love of my God as I remember the words from the Bible 'My grace is sufficient for you, for my power is made perfect in weakness' [2 Corinthians 12:9]. When I was about to leave my previous school, my pastor told me to pack light and go. I didn't understand it at all. I felt heavy on my shoulders. But then I came to understand that I shouldn't have lived myself in my previous experiences. The achievements I had in the past shouldn't be brought forward to this school. I'm no longer a leader but just a manager. I shouldn't have lived in my past success and ignoring the new context where the old experience may not be applicable. Pride knocked me down. I was not willing to do what a

manager do: to have confrontation with colleagues and watch students coming to the school on time. God reminded me that I was coming to this school to learn, but I was proud of my 11-year experience in my previous school. So it was a good learning opportunity for me, not only for my being a manager or a leader, but also for my soul.

To 'pack light and go' is interesting advice, suggesting that achievements as a leader in one school may appropriately lead to pride, but that such achievements are not necessarily transferable to other schools. If the person carries their 'pride', then it will become unwarranted, and mere arrogance. The principal in this case seemed to have forgotten the hard work and the need to build systems and confidence, the 'management' tasks, needed to be in a position to be a 'leader'. He had a 'good learning opportunity', in this challenging new school. He says, significantly, that 'whenever I'm asked about this, I feel I should be thankful to God: without those difficult experiences, I won't feel that I'm now in "heaven"'. Humility, in this example, is needed in order to regain a position in which the principal may be properly proud and, because he has developed the 'management' of the school and would therefore be conscious of his own worth as a leader, magnanimity.

A second example of humility can be given from St Bede's, a Roman Catholic secondary school in the UK, whose headteacher has already been cited as an example of magnanimity.

The way the staff come together in their, in staff briefing, so each member of staff if they are invited to, they can opt out, would lead staff prayer or you know kind of a thought for the day I suppose and there's, there's a temptation to control that, hang on you're controlling the story here, now you want to control the story, the chief story teller you can tell the values, you know, give the, the orthodox interpretation and I think it's healthy to, to say yeah, what have you got to say to us, what's your affection and your experience as a teacher at St Bede's College? What have you got to offer for us whether it's faith-based or otherwise. . . . Now I think that's very, very powerful.

This is an intentional giving up of power, a power to 'control' that is given him as the headteacher, but one which he is prepared to give to teachers. It is the same headteacher who referred to himself as 'dispensable' (quoted earlier in this chapter), also an example of humility in the face of history or mortality. He also warns of the dangers of excessive humility, of sacrificing oneself to the job. When asked what would lead him to leave the job of headteacher before retirement, he says:

> I think it would be health, that's what I worry about . . . I think it is, it is surprisingly physically demanding, obviously emotionally demanding, it is my life, it goes back to the question you were asking about, about a sense of isolation, part of the cost of this job is to be in some sense alone here and not have the time to engage with other people outside of the job because . . . it demands so much energy, if you've got, you won't have time for your immediate wife and family. So, I'm a sad old case in other words.

Roseneil notes how common it is for those in 'caring' professions to be 'excessively humble', or what she refers to as 'over-caring' or 'debasing oneself to care', so often expected of mothers or parents. This sub-servience in the carer is likely, according to Roseneil and attributed by her to Aristotle, to produce selfishness in the cared-for (Roseneil 2004). Having sufficient humility to realise the limits of one's influence, but not so much as to be tempted to sacrifice one's health and oneself to the cared-for, is also illustrated by Lawrence-Lightfoot, who describes a teacher who has become a parent:

> I felt humbled by the realization that no matter how much affection I had for my students, I probably had only a fleeting influence. I know – and am now ashamed that I never understood it before – that my students' parents loved their kids far, far more than I ever would, and that I was not at the very center of their reality. (Lawrence-Lightfoot 2003, p. 188)

School leaders can exhibit an Aristotelian magnanimity and a biblical humility, as leaders aware of their own qualities, as leaders sensitive to the contexts in which they work and the relationships they have with other staff and pupils, and as leaders sensitive to the wider hierarchies of history or society (including families) or politics proving that they are not god-like 'absolute' leaders. These are the virtues illustrated here, and they also form the starting point for this chapter's conclusion.

Conclusion

The spirit of school leaders requires magnanimity, a proper well-founded pride, a pride in leadership qualities themselves, and a pride that grants others the freedom to develop themselves. Those qualities should be matched by, and imply, a form of humility, a letting others be, and a groundedness in the face of situations that are not entirely controllable. To become sufficiently self-aware to realise these qualities, school leaders need enough solitude to be able to consider their own situation within a close-knit Macmurrian community. Achieving all these qualities, it is not surprising that Aristotle refers to magnanimity as the 'crown of the virtues' (Aristotle 1976, p. 154), only available in circumstances where the leader is able to demonstrate the other virtues. Although this suggests a somewhat exceptional quality, it is an exceptionalism that school leaders themselves referred to in interviews. The headteacher of Richardson (primary school, UK) describes the need to explain to parents of pupils 'that what we are providing for their children is exceptional, not just good but exceptional'. She is particularly proud of having recently been told that the school is 'in the top one percent of schools for improvement in literacy at key stage two in the country', a genuinely exceptional achievement. It may be that schools strive to be exceptional, and that school leaders who achieve a wide range of leadership virtues crowned by magnanimity are themselves somewhat exceptional, but the spirituality described in this chapter remains a mundane and grounded spirituality. It is the overcoming of dualisms, described in Chapter 1 and throughout the book, that is most important to school leaders. Groundedness is explicitly – if somewhat dogmatically – described by the principal of School 3 (secondary, Hong Kong) in terms of his view of the need for emotional stability:

> A principal must have a stable family life before he could be motivated and be emotionally and mentally stable to carry out complicated daily tasks. This is a value which I dearly uphold. This is because I can set aside more effort to take part in school tasks and education-related matters only if I have a stable personal and family life.

This can also be likened to Riley's description of what she calls *'spiritual consciousness*, or what others might label as a *robust moral* or *ethical foundation'*, which 'can help school leaders weather the physical, the social and the emotional storms' (Riley 2007, pp. 12–13). The overcoming of dualism is, in turn, particularly well described by the headteacher of Lythley primary school (Church of England, UK).

When I first came it was very, there was a very 'us and them' . . . mindset covering every aspect of this school, there were the parents out there and us in here, . . . there was the teaching staff and the support staff, . . . there was the children . . . there was no cohesiveness . . . and it was . . . that fight or flight mentality . . . and because there were so many issues it was always somebody else's fault . . . and that's what we had to stop . . .

That September I came in, I had to stop . . . and then we had a clean slate with all the staff together and it, that first year made a huge impact, . . . and for, for those staff that were there then and are still here now, to go through that made them really strong team players I think and for the children that could feel the difference . . . you open the door and you let your parents . . . in all of a sudden . . . and that makes such a difference . . . for, for everybody.

Having a headteacher describe some of the ways of overcoming divisions within the school is a good conclusion to a chapter that tries to describe the position of the school leader who is conscious of the responsibility of the position at the top of the school's hierarchy, able to connect herself with members of the school community and able to help all the different groups within that community work better together. It seems to be both a magnanimous and a more spirited approach to school leadership than those focused entirely on the meeting of external targets. That virtuosic headteacher seems to demonstrate virtue, too. Spirited leadership is the mundane answer to loneliness in leadership, although that is not why it is important. Spirituality involves the humanising of scripted, performative, and crafty school leadership, so great-souled schooling reaches beyond the headteacher, allowing for magnanimity also among the rest of the school staff and pupils.

Chapter 6

Conclusion: understanding and promoting the spirit of the school

I believe that the language of architecture is not a question of a specific style. Every building is built for a specific use in a specific place and for a specific society. My buildings try to answer the questions that emerge from these simple facts as precisely and critically as they can.

(Zumthor 2006, p. 27)

Introduction

The spirit of this or that school will be different. This book has attempted to steer a path between, on the one hand, universalist or standardised approaches to schooling and, on the other hand, post-modern relativism. It has done so by promoting the dialogic and communal nature of personhood, with people becoming human in specific places, and the way in which communities can grow and overlap, horizons broadening and overlapping. For this concluding chapter, there are several important sets of issues still to be addressed. One is the set of issues around research methodology. Educational research is caught up in all the debates on social scientific and philosophical research, and has some additional characteristics consequent on the embeddedness of research in the very processes of education itself. Research is what educational institutions do; it is of their essence. Here, an attempt to describe the distinctive qualities of educational research in general, and research on the spirit of the school in particular, is made in terms of the *virtue* and the *value* of that research, especially the value of sincerity in research. Sincerity has had a bad press in recent years, hence the much-repeated joke of Jean Giraudoux from early in the twentieth century: 'The secret of success is sincerity: if you can fake that, you've got it made' (www.quotationspage.com/quote/481.html, accessed 24 October 2008). Indeed, for Oscar Wilde,

The first duty in life is to be as artificial as possible. What the second duty is no one has yet discovered. (Quoted in Trilling 1972, p. 118)

However, sincerity is still of value: Wilde is, as Trilling suggests, teasing respectable Philistine qualities (Trilling 1972, p. 119). Sincerity is a personal virtue with a long track record in cultural as well as educational contexts.

If educational research is to be of value, there are implications for schooling. Schooling, or at least mass schooling, is a relatively recent invention, little more than a century old, so its future is by no means secure. Yet those working in schools over the last century, all too often, find that what happens to schooling is rarely the result of systematic policy-making and planning, but rather the result of classroom events, created by teachers and pupils and local communities. It is hubris to believe anything very different: the same hubris that leads television weather forecasters to report that 'the weather didn't go as planned, yesterday, but the rain eventually came towards evening'. Forecasters predict, rather than plan, the weather, and the weather is not something that could be planned, anyway. Schooling is a little more predictable, a little more subject to planning, but not much. The good and bad qualities of schools are rather stubborn, and educational research must understand those 'stubborn particulars' (Cherry 1995), if it is to have any influence on the future of schooling. Understanding schooling is the necessary precursor to understanding and promoting spirituality, and it is by returning to definitions of, and ways of promoting, spirituality that this chapter concludes.

The virtue and value of research

Empirical research on spirituality and religion in schools raises a number of important methodological issues, one of which is the notion of the importance of sincerity in education research (Stern 2006b, Chapter 8, Stern 2007a, Chapter 14). Sincerity is promoted, here, as a *virtue* in education research. It sits alongside other possible virtues, such as trust, courage, kindness, modesty, humility, truthfulness, openness to criticism, and respect (Pring 2004, pp. 257–61). Without wanting to raise the debates over the distinction between ethics and virtue, the social research literature appears to treat research ethics as a technical set of rules to be followed, and rarely discusses the personal qualities – what shall, here, be described as virtues – of the researchers themselves. It is understandable that researchers should look at rules governing their work as necessary, without spending so much time considering their personal qualities, but of course the two approaches to research complement each other. Social researchers, 'when they carry out research, enter into personal and moral relationships with those they study' (BSA 2004, p. 2). Is it enough to state this, alongside statements about appropriate degrees of confidentiality and limits to the harm done by research, without looking positively at the value of the research and what qualities a 'good researcher' might exhibit? Or are virtues to be promoted simply as a form of risk management, because researchers cannot be monitored all the time, as implied by Pring's justification of virtue because 'not every detail of the researcher's work can be checked' (Pring 2004, p. 258)? Within school contexts, the Elton Report (DES 1989) was prompted by public concerns over 'disobedience' in schools, but concluded by recommending a move away from a set of school rules describing what should not be done, towards behaviour policies that describe what should, positively, be done. It helped change the culture of schooling, although that culture is always under threat from those who feel a simple set of negative behavioural rules is all that is needed. The same could be said for social research. There is a need for positive descriptions of virtuous research, to help complement the guides to research ethics that concentrate on restricting particular types of activities.

Sincerity is one of the virtues promoted here, as it has a very specific relevance to the characteristics of creative, dialogic, teaching and learning in schools, to spirituality as conceived in this project, and to a wide range of research methodologies. Research virtues are also imbricated with a set of research values, and all contribute to an understanding of the value of research itself – notably, its educational value. This chapter therefore explores the nature of sincerity and its relation to other virtues in education research, and the value of research, with special reference to research on spirituality. It sits alongside Chapter 1, which provides the starting points of the philosophical approach to researching spirituality, and the Appendix, which provides the fine details of the procedures used for the empirical research used in the *Spirit of the School* project.

Vicious research, stealing or ignoring souls

The whole range of social research can be more or less virtuous or vicious. It may help explain the need for virtue, therefore, to start from some of the possibilities of viciousness in educational research. Of all the ways in which people can hurt each other, research is not the worst offender. There are, however, some ways of researching that are damaging, and these form a good starting point for developing a sense of the positive research virtues. Finding out, exposing, making public, can always be damaging, and this is recognised by the ethical codes developed to control research, which note, for example, that 'social research intrudes into the lives of those studied', and 'the experience may be disturbing' (BSA 2004, p. 4). 'Even if not harmed', that guidance continues, 'those studied may feel wronged by aspects of the research process', especially 'if they perceive apparent intrusions into their private and personal worlds, or where research gives rise to false hopes, uncalled for self-knowledge, or unnecessary anxiety' (BSA 2004, p. 4). This is not a matter of truthfulness: the intrusion and the making public may be damaging, whether or not what is made public is true. Indeed, the truth may be more damaging than a falsehood: it is easier to deny a falsehood than it is to withdraw a truth.

The simplest form of 'making public' has been recognised as sensitive by cultural and religious traditions throughout history. This is exemplified by rules on clothing to cover bodies or restrictions on the use of mirrors or other images. Turning mirrors to the wall when someone has died (as in the Jewish tradition, Encyclopaedia Judaica 1971, 5:1426) was explained by Frazer in terms of the soul being projected out of the person in the shape of the reflection in the mirror, at risk of being 'carried off by the ghost of the departed' (Frazer 1922, p. 197). He goes on to report the fear of souls being stolen by portraiture, up to the very specific objection to photography, including in his day (writing in the late nineteenth and early twentieth centuries) in Greece and the West of Scotland (Frazer 1922, pp. 198–9). The embarrassment or offence caused by creating an image is recognised by most people, at least in terms of their sense of a need to prepare to be photographed or to look in a mirror, so as to protect their sense of themselves. The shock of looking in a mirror unexpectedly, and seeing this strange – perhaps older, less attractive, more miserable-looking – person, is damaging enough. It is likely to make people realise that how they are portrayed by such mechanical devices, never mind by researchers, contributes to their self-concept. Research is like photography. It can be a form of soul-stealing, or it can try to avoid this, and enrich people's lives. If you approach a mirror knowing it is there, you can use it to construct yourself, and if you pose for a photograph, you can help make your future memories.

Research on spirituality can raise issues that might be uncomfortably revealing for the participants. It might give rise to 'false hopes', as warned against in ethics guidance, or bring out 'uncalled for self-knowledge' (BSA 2004). It may simply reveal what could be or become uncomfortable. An illustration from the *Spirit of the School* research provides an example of that risk, and the publishing of this example might itself increase the risk. (The risk is mitigated by the opportunity the interviewee was given to check the transcript and to cut out any statements that were not to be used.) One of the headteachers of a school with a church foundation said of himself that he was 'not a practising Christian', and was someone with 'a secular viewpoint'. The school's statement of values was discussed, including the sentence 'As a community our best will only ever be good enough; the best we can be, the best we can do and the best we can offer to God'. The interview proceeded in this way:

Interviewer:	Is it [the statement of values] different to what you would have written on your own?
Headteacher:	Possibly but the, in spirit, no, I mean I
Interviewer:	Well, is it what you ended up thinking anyway because you had those discussions [mentioned earlier in the interview]?
Headteacher:	I, I think it's just, well, I am but one, I keep saying that and
Interviewer:	Yeah
Headteacher:	it, it, it is just a statement of what the, all the stakeholders
Interviewer:	Yeah
Headteacher:	could, could buy up to it, so it's rather like
Interviewer:	You didn't sign up for it
Headteacher:	it's, it's rather the protocol that, that all the countries in the EU might have to sign up to it, it's not going to be perfect for any one country but the thrust of it certainly you know, that the God bit is, is there and that's not really there for me but, but the rest of it . . . [At this point, the headteacher goes on to talk about the parts of the statement of values that he likes.]

It would be hard to script a better account of discomfort than the initial response of the interviewee, in this exchange, of 'possibly but the, in spirit, no, I mean I'. When challenged as to whether he was persuaded of the statement as a result of discussions with staff, governors, children and their families, he responds with a statement of humility or membership of a larger group: 'I am but one'. This is followed up with the statement that 'it is just a statement of what . . . all the stakeholders could buy up to', and when this is further challenged, the agreement is described as like that of an international organisation such as the European Union. 'It's not going to be perfect for any one country', that is, for himself as 'but one' person, yet 'the thrust . . . is there'. Furthermore, there are other parts of the statement he is very happy with, notably the references to 'home'.

The response of the interviewee in this case clearly suggests that the headteacher had considered the principles carefully before supporting the statement of values, and before describing this support in the interview. It is important that an interviewee is allowed a degree of flexibility in response, as here, seeming to be answering 'yes', 'no' and 'possibly' to a single question. The ambiguity of the response is not simply accepted and ignored, but challenged, in order to clarify the issues. As the architect Zumthor says of objects, and as is surely even more applicable to people, 'richness and multiplicity emanate from the things themselves if we observe them attentively and give them their due' (Zumthor 2006, p. 31). Requiring a single answer (of either 'yes', 'no' or 'possibly') would have been either damaging to the person, in pushing the respondent to an uncomfortable certainty, or damaging to the research, in pushing the respondent to give a less meaningful answer and thereby potentially reducing the seriousness of other responses. Here, it is hoped that the more open questioning, and the challenging of the responses by the interviewer, encouraged a less damaging response. Evidence for the continued seriousness of the interviewee can be found later in the transcript. At one point, the headteacher said that he was 'absolutely, diametrically opposed in any way to any kind of selection on the basis of, you know, social background or culture or faith or skin tone or socio-economic, . . . profile or, or indeed level of attainment'. Later, he mentioned his own background as having been to a selective grammar school as a child. The transcript continues (in a slightly edited version) with the first response being the best example in the whole project of a genuinely ambiguous response combining 'yes', 'no' and 'possibly':

Interviewer: You mentioned . . . going to the grammar school was the thing that made you, my feeling is from what you've said that you might not be in favour of creating grammar schools, as you've said you reject selection for this, that or the other

Headteacher: No, no, yeah you are right but it is . . . there's clearly a slight contradiction there yeah, thank you for picking it up

Interviewer: Sorry

Headteacher: No, it is, it is and, I suppose hand on heart there's, there's, it's, it's easy to sit here and pontificate about values and vision and what's right for a community of the size of this school, when it comes down to oneself and in particular one's own children, sometimes one's values go out of the window.

At this point, the interviewee talks about whether he might send his own child to a private school. Although he 'believe[s] in children being taught with their, the people they grow up with in their local communities', adding 'I, I honestly believe and I don't just say it because I want more children in the school, it's not self-serving', he justifies going against that principle by reference to principles of inclusion:

> I suppose going back to that same set of similar principles if we talk about community cohesion as being accepting . . . without you know being sort of lily-livered about it saying 'Well you can never, you can never disagree with anything then you know' it will be too open-minded I suppose but grammar, grammar school suited me and . . . the grammars or the, or the high-performing private schools that, that will suit a certain kind of child who is very, very motivated and it's naïve to think that society doesn't need these high, high-flyers but, but there should be an alternative that is in many ways just as good but just better suits the, the skills of the other children.

This part of the interview is concluded with an admission of the complexity of the situation, recognisable by many educationists:

> I, I have my own internal conflicts on that, it's easy to paint a vision but the reality is that if we are being truly inclusive, I think, I think they have to, that they are you know, provide you know a range of provision to suit, to suit all sorts.

The self-awareness and moral complexity of the views of this respondent are presented here both as an example of the complexity of education in general, and, more specifically, the dangers posed by researching education. There are dangers to self-understanding and to relationships between people: research that fails to allow for such nuanced and complex responses may itself damage the respondents and the research process.

It would have been easier to have avoided such sensitive topics, or to have accepted the first responses rather than challenging them. However, such an approach is likely to ignore, if not 'steal', the souls of the respondents. Research may therefore ignore souls, or ignore the spiritual nature of humanity. Two psychoanalysts write of their refusal to accept a mechanistic view of humanity. Their book 'is indebted neither to the behaviourism of a B F Skinner nor to the positivism of a Karl Popper but to the methodology of psychoanalysis', as 'it does not seem justified to trim the

human stature to fit measurements derived from experimental psychology' (Mitscherlich and Mitscherlich 1975, p. xv).

> Rather, we are at pains to use man's [*sic*] understanding of himself in
> all his facets as our point of departure and, in our factual descriptions,
> to avoid as far as possible any isolating distance from the human
> subject. Indeed, in our opinion, the way human self-understanding
> comes about is extraordinarily complex; hence, any attempt to trace
> the portrait of man using the methods of natural science ultimately
> produces more nearly the effect of a caricature. (Mitscherlich and
> Mitscherlich 1975, p. xv.)

That their work is a study of Germans unable properly to mourn the
loss of their erstwhile hero and father-figure, Hitler, makes this insistence
on a portrayal that is close to, rather than distanced from, the subject,
even more powerful.

Stealing or ignoring 'souls', as described here, suggests that in relational terms, research may damage or break relationships between people
and between groups, or may exacerbate dualisms. That is the lesson of the
Mitscherlichs, and the relationship between the analyst and the patient
may be likened to that between researcher and researched. Even in film-
making, a film director may have a positive, dialogic, relationship with
actors, as in the description of Kaurismäki's 'empathy and respect for his
characters', in which he 'does not keep his actors on a leash; he does not
exploit them to express a concept, but rather shows them in a light that
lets us sense their dignity, and their secrets' (Zumthor 2006, p. 53). The
implication of that description is that many film directors would fail to be
empathetic or respectful, and might use actors to express the director's
concept, denying the actors' dignity. It may be hard to maintain everyone's dignity in the artificial world of film-making. It is even harder in the
wider world riven by social divisions, into which social researchers must
step.

After the research is finished, researchers 'should be aware that they
have some responsibility for the use to which their data may be put and
for how the research is to be disseminated', which 'may on occasion be
difficult, especially in situations of social conflict, competing social interests or where there is unanticipated misuse of the research by third
parties' (BSA 2004, p. 2). An example of such misuse was provided in
Stern 2001a, when two research reports were presented to the headteacher and staff of a school, several months apart. The research presented relatively straightforward school development planning data,

based on the approach of Dalin (Dalin and Rust 1983, Dalin with Rolff 1993). It surveyed and reported on 'gaps' between the views of staff on the present school, and on an 'ideal' version of the present school. In this case, gaps were reported between staff views on the school's ethos or sense of community, and their views on an 'ideal' ethos or sense of community. On presenting the first, preliminary, report the headteacher and several staff expressed their thanks for a 'positive' and 'supportive' document. Later in that academic year, after the research had been completed, a second report was presented to the headteacher. Although he expressed his thanks for the report, on this occasion he seemed to be alone in his gratitude, with no positive comments to the researcher by any other staff. This might be explained by his remarks, recorded as part of an interview for the ongoing research, that the report provided him with clear evidence of the destructive effects on the school of teacher trade unionism: 'the unions destroyed this school'. The headteacher explained that:

> [In nineteen] eighty six [eight years prior to the date of the interview] we had superb exam results and we were going somewhere – wallop we got hit by the NUT [National Union of Teachers], and they destroyed us, they literally destroyed this school . . . there was nothing of joy in the school . . . it was a very sour and bitterly fought battle between me and the NUT . . . it destroyed the relationship between the Head and the staff which has still not come back in many senses. (Stern 2001a, pp. 94–5)

In distributing copies of this report to all staff, the headteacher apparently introduced the report with that same interpretation. Such an unlikely interpretation, and the response to it by staff other than the headteacher, illustrated the unpredictability of the misinterpretation and consequent misuse of research results. As McDonald says, when 'outsiders' attempt to contribute to school development, they must believe that change is possible, but must also

> have a sense of the immense complexities and staggering ambiguities of life on the inside and of how all outside interventions of policy, curriculum, and method are transformed by inside culture.
>
> Outsiders who have the right attitude play a role that is interpretive and catalytic, and they play it with patience. . . . Their efforts are powerful only insofar as they spur efforts by the true insiders. (McDonald 1989, p. 207)

Research on the school ethos, like research on the broader spirit of the school, is clearly in need of careful management, yet it will never be possible to avoid altogether the misuse of such research – as described here.

Bad poetry

One response to the need to avoid vicious research might be a simple and naïve form of sincerity, as expressed in the phrase 'honesty is the best policy'. According to the literary critic Trilling, nineteenth-century English novelists 'belonged to an earlier historical development, in which Spirit manifests itself as the "honest soul" whose relation to society is one of "obedient service" and "inner reverence" . . . [with] sincerity as its essence' (Trilling 1972, p. 114). He goes on to make the political claim that these novelists 'appear to be in agreement that the person who accepts his class situation, whatever it may be, as a given and necessary condition of his life will be sincere beyond question' (Trilling 1972, p. 115). Americans in the nineteenth century, and the English in the twentieth century, had moved on to a period of '"disintegrated" or "alienated" consciousness' (Trilling 1972, p. 114). Simple, politically or socially conservative, sincerity was no longer meaningful in literature or in society more generally. The prophets of the new age, he says, included Oscar Wilde, for whom 'all bad poetry springs from genuine feeling' (quoted in Trilling 1972, p. 119). That is, writing what you think and feel, a naïve honesty, does not necessarily illuminate the world. Wilde's attack on bourgeois respectability, of which this forms a part, led him to promote the idea that masks reveal, rather than hide: '[m]an is least himself . . . when he talks in his own person . . . [: g]ive him a mask and he will tell you the truth' (quoted in Trilling 1972, p. 119). Wilde may be attacking a naïve sincerity, but he was not rejecting the search for truth, and his truths were as emotional, sentimental even, as any of the earlier nineteenth-century English writers. He knew that sincerity could easily be distorted, or used to excuse bad poetry.

An even more robust enemy of poetry was Plato. Rejecting many things from his city, at the climax of *Republic*, Plato proudly describes his 'refusal to admit all imitative [*mimetic*] poetry . . . [as] all such things seem to pollute the understanding of those who hear them, unless they possess a knowledge of their real nature' (Plato 1908, p. 336). A mirror image or photograph can be intrusive, as has already been described by anthropologists, above. Plato pre-empted this position by noting that a person can 'make' all the things on earth, 'in a manner': 'It is most easily done perhaps if you take a mirror and turn it round to all sides' (Plato 1908, p. 338). This imitative 'making', characteristic of poets and artists, is no substitute for knowing things 'as they are in truth': it is 'the user of each thing' who knows the truth of the thing, and the physical manufacturer of the object who should be guided by that knowledge (Plato 1908, p. 338). The mere artistic imitator comes a poor third. This criticism of poetry was the starting point of Auerbach's magisterial review of the history of mimesis: portrayals of 'reality' in literature. The turning point in literary history, the starting point of modern literature, was the *Divine Comedy*, in which Dante claims 'he presented true reality' (Auerbach 2003, p. 554). Poetry may be rejected by Plato, as mere imitation, but from Dante onwards, poetry and the rest of literature might once again be suited to the Republic. Literature as itself, a manufactured, created, world of its own, was all the more real for that sense of its own creativity rather than mere mimesis.

Research on any education topic, and most especially on spirituality and religion, should likewise avoid the temptation to imitation, to reporting what has been seen or heard without any additional creativity in the reporting. Research that is 'bad poetry' in Wilde's sense, or mimesis in Plato's sense, includes a significant amount of quantitative research that reports data generated by questions requiring simple unambiguous responses. The value of ambiguity, or rather the value of research that elicits the levels of ambiguity that are characteristic of human beliefs and actions, has been described above, and is explored further in Hoyle and Wallace 2005. A moment of insight from the *Spirit of the School* research can be described, where 'bad poetry' might have resulted from taking the first, no doubt honest, response at face value and failing to follow it up. The pupils aged 8 and 9 in Ruislip (a UK Church of England primary school) were discussing 'important times in your school'. Jonathan (aged 8) suggests 'Worship, worship to God and Jesus'. The transcript continues:

Interviewer: Why is that special then Jonathan?
Jonathan: Because God is, he made everything and if you don't like appreciate him you, you're not nice because he, he built everything in the world
Interviewer: That's good
Terence: Some, that's what Christians believe
Interviewer: Yeah, you're right. You're right Terence. Christians do believe that. Do you believe that?
Terence: Yeah

Interviewer:	You do
Terence:	Yeah
Interviewer:	Jonathan do you believe what you've just told me? That's good. How about you Lucia?
Lucia:	Yeah
Jonathan:	I'm not Christian but I still believe
Interviewer:	Do you?
Jonathan:	Yeah
Interviewer:	That's interesting. That's good. So what else, who else do you learn about? Do you just learn about Christians here because it's a Christian school?
Jonathan:	No
Terence:	No, we learn about Jewish
Jonathan:	yeah about Jewish and
Interviewer:	A Jewish lady came?
Terence:	Yeah
Jonathan:	Yeah and we were, what is the other kind of language?
Lucia:	Hindi
Terence:	Buddhism. We learned a bit about that
Lucia:	Yeah
Jonathan:	Yeah, we learn about Jewish and I can't remember the rest what we've learned about.

Jonathan describes 'worship to God and Jesus' as special, and the statement is subtly modulated by Terence who explains 'that's what Christians believe'. That adjustment would be a model of good practice for an adult, and is exceptionally subtle for a pupil, and leads eventually to the enigmatic statement of Jonathan, 'I'm not Christian but I still believe'. Jonathan may follow another religion such as Judaism, given that this is the only religion he goes on to mention in the subsequent conversation, while the other pupils talk of Buddhism and 'Hindi'. Perhaps he is not religious, and the statement 'but I still believe' is an affirmation of the ability to believe outside religion. The word 'but' is particularly interesting, as it suggests an awareness of the challenge he presents to a 'Christian school': belief is possible *despite* being other than Christian. It is a more confident position than the rather sad statement beautifully analysed by Rudge, and providing the title for her article: 'I am nothing: does it matter?' (Rudge 1998). The assertive statement 'I'm not a Christian but I still believe' is therefore presented here as an example of 'good poetry'. Such an exchange provides helpful evidence also that the school is following the Church of England's own guidance on religious education in church schools, which says that pupils should 'reflect critically on the truth claims of Christian belief' (Hall and Taylor 2005, p. 6), rather than accept such claims uncritically. That is, religious education should be relatively weakly framed, in Bernstein's terminology (as discussed in Chapter 3, and the Appendix).

Virtuous research

Describing various forms of vicious research necessarily outlines the possibilities for more virtuous research. One of the central virtues for researchers is that of sincerity, and this sits alongside a range of virtues such as trust, courage, kindness, modesty, humility, truthfulness, openness to criticism, and respect (Pring 2004, pp. 257–61). These virtues will be discussed in turn, each being related to research in spirituality. It is certainly not an attempt at a comprehensive account of research virtues: that would be a book in itself. Rather, there are indications of possible ways of considering the virtues that might be helpful in planning, carrying out and evaluating educational research, and illustrations of some of the implications of a more virtuous approach to such research. If the themes developed in the account of vicious research were 'stealing souls', 'ignoring souls' and 'bad poetry', their opposites could be framed as 'longing for souls', 'soulful research' and 'creative research'. However, the framing is instead managed in terms of particular virtues, with the other themes having been already addressed, to an extent, in the more vicious section of this chapter.

The virtue of sincerity

Sincerity is, according to Trilling, 'an essential condition of virtue' (Trilling 1972, p. 3), at least in certain historical and cultural circumstances, with a 'very considerable originative power', albeit somewhat eclipsed in recent years by 'authenticity' (Trilling 1972, p. 12). The 'originative power' of research, and of learning more broadly, encourages the promotion of sincerity as a research virtue. Research is a form of learning, of finding out, and as Hanks correctly describes it, 'learning is a way of being in the social world, not a way of knowing about it' (in Lave and Wenger 1991, p. 24, also quoted in Chapter 3, above). Research is similarly embedded in the everyday work of schools, and must be sensitive to the relationships and the ways of life that make up the whole school community. Sincerity is a valuable principle that can help research, schools and religions through to a better future, a future of more than

not lying (as described in Stern 2007a, Chapter 14). Research methods
that follow orthodox social scientific methodologies are likely to focus on
questioning in a way that avoids confusing (over-complex or unclear) or
leading questions. By avoiding misleading questions, it is thought that
lying will be avoided and truth will emerge. Those involved in spiritual
and religious issues will understand how limited is 'avoiding lying' as an
approach to research, and how much more is required for meaningful
dialogue. Reaching towards the truth requires more than not lying. The
'more' that is required is sincerity. Sincerity is barely addressed in mainstream methodology textbooks, but it is supported by philosophic heavy-
weights such as Wittgenstein and Macmurray. Wittgenstein contrasts
'truthfulness' and 'sincerity', so that 'A dog cannot be a hypocrite, but
neither can he be sincere' (Wittgenstein 1958, p. 229e): people and dogs
can be truthful and can lie, but only people can be sincere. Macmurray
contrasts 'negative untruthfulness' (i.e. lying) and sincerity, with sincerity
being 'much more than' avoiding lying. Sincerity 'is positively expressing
what you do think and believe', and '[t]o refrain from expressing what
you think or believe or know to someone, if it is to his advantage or to
someone else's advantage that he should know it, is positive dishonesty',
that is, 'dissimulation – the suppression of the truth' (Macmurray 1995,
p. 76). Researchers should therefore exhibit, and should try to elicit from
respondents, sincerity.

There is a straightforward link that can be made between sincerity in
research and phenomenological approaches to research. Phenomenological research focuses on 'meaning-making', with the meaning often being
seen as made by individuals, and in some circumstances by the researcher
and the respondent together (Pring 2000). Research methods used
include participant observation when the researcher joins the group to be
studied, the close analysis of conversations or texts, and in-depth interviews sometimes modelled on psychotherapeutic interviewing techniques
(Silverman 1997, and McCutcheon 1999 for religious research). Moustakas describes heuristic research as an open investigation or discovery,
sometimes by trial and error, and 'refers to a process of internal search
through which one discovers the nature and meaning of experience and
develops methods and procedures for further investigation and analysis'
(Moustakas 1994, p. 17). In this model of research, '[t]he self of the
researcher is present throughout the process and, while understanding
the phenomenon with increasing depth, the researcher also experiences
growing self-awareness and self-knowledge', so '[h]euristic processes
incorporate creative self-processes and self-discoveries' (Moustakas 1994,
p. 17). Researchers should be 'immersed' in the world being researched,

and should pause and consider the meaning of their own lives, as 'knowledge does not end with moments of connectedness, understanding, and meaning' (Moustakas 1994, p. 65). 'No scientific discovery is ever complete . . . [and t]his is the beauty of knowledge and discovery . . . [that i]t keeps us forever awake, alive, and connected with what is and with what matters in life' (Moustakas 1994, p. 65). The sincerity of the researcher, and of those being researched, is easily integrated into this approach.

The danger in heuristic research of encouraging the virtue of the researcher to be the main aim of the research, rather than a helpful contributor to the research, is pointed out by Silverman, who stresses the need 'to broaden our conception of qualitative research beyond issues of subjective "meaning" and towards issues of language, representation and social organization' (Silverman 1997, p. 1). Moustakas himself refers back to Buber's 'explorations of dialogue and mutuality' (Moustakas 1994, p. 17), and it is the dialogic and communal, rather than exclusively self-exploratory, dimensions of research that are needed in research on the spirit of the school. The mutuality of relationships in community is underpinned by Macmurray's concern with schools as communities, affirming the humanity and integrity of pupils and teachers alike. Integrity, here, is likened to sincerity, and older people in schools have, often enough, 'betrayed the personal integrity of our childhood in becoming conformed to the fashion of this world' (Macmurray 1968, p. 18). In order to 'recover our integrity, we have to become as little children', and '[f]rom this perspective the task of the teacher appears no longer as an effort to achieve an integrity of character that is absent in the young animal; but rather to preserve the integrity of childhood through the process of its growth and maturity' (Macmurray 1968, p. 18). If integrity and, it is suggested, sincerity are central to teaching and learning in school, they are just as central to research in these contexts.

Of all the approaches used in phenomenological research, ethnographic research is particularly likely to exhibit such sincerity, as it helps bring people together, based on an attempt to understand what things mean to people in communal and social groups. People, in this approach, matter. That what people say matters is also the basis of sincerity. The immersive fieldwork in a community typical of ethnography is 'that kind of research which takes seriously the perspectives and the interactions of the members of the social groups being studied', 'based on the premise that social reality cannot be understood except through the rules which structure the relations between members of the group and which make it possible for each to interpret the actions, gestures and words of others'

(Pring 2000, p. 104). Sincerity may in these ways be exhibited in phenomenological, especially heuristic and ethnographic, research. It can
also be a virtue in other kinds of social research: the appropriateness of
sincerity in more positivistic research is described in Chapter 14 of Stern
2007a. As the *Spirit of the School* project follows the more phenomenological methodology, it is less important here to follow up the implications
for positivistic approaches. Instead, a range of other research virtues is
worth considering.

The virtues of humility, modesty and openness to criticism

There are three related virtues of humility, which can mean relatively low
self-regard but also groundedness, modesty, which implies mildness and
self-control, and openness to criticism. All can be seen as informing and
justifying the academic research practice of peer review, and the evaluative dimension of creativity as embedded in education policy. To start with
peer review, complex and influential systems of such review have been
developed in academic research, notably within publishing (chiefly with
respect to academic journals), within networks of conferences and colloquia, and within research audits such as the UK's Research Assessment
Exercise (RAE) and Research Excellence Framework (REF). The
processes of scholarly peer reviewing are well described in Hefce's (2005)
RAE guidance, and that also highlights the hierarchy of peer reviewing,
related for example to how research will be more highly regarded if the
peers acknowledging it are 'international' rather than 'national'. Although
there is controversy related to the processes, especially with respect to the
likelihood of peer groups being biased towards already-established 'insider'
research and against more truly innovative research, the process of peer
review itself is broadly welcomed by academics and is seen as worth defend-
ing when other ways of judging research (such as statistical measures of
citations or numbers of research students) are at risk of having a larger role
(Times Higher Education 2008).

Those completing school-based research may have their research peer
reviewed in this way; many will also have their research peer reviewed in
other ways, with the process of professional and public recognition being
of this broader kind. For example, whether research is commissioned by
or used by professional bodies or government departments or agencies
may be an indication of review by peers outside the 'academic peer
review' community of practice, but clearly within a distinct 'professional
educator' or 'education policy' community of practice (Furlong and
Oancea 2005). As well as academic peer review, and peer review by other

professional or policy communities, some school-based research processes can be recognised in other ways. Engagement in research may be said to have an impact on other aspects of work in education, and the professional recognition by peers may not be directly of the research itself, but of the person who has engaged in research. Hence, school staff who have completed research (for example, through having completed a research degree such as a doctorate) may be advantaged in the job market, simply through the recognition of the value to the profession of having completed research. The nature and extent of this kind of recognition is likely to vary from school to school, and from country to country. In some countries, for example, a doctorate or other higher degrees may be rewarded with higher pay or a smaller teaching commitment (as in Sweden), or in other benefits such as different pension rights (as in the Irish Republic). There is a role for further comparative analysis of such processes: their importance, here, is in illustrating various ways in which researchers may need the virtues of humility, modesty and openness to criticism. As Kipling had it: 'If you can talk with crowds and keep your virtue . . .'

All who have engaged in these forms of peer review are likely to have experienced the humbling effects of such review, when the review indicates revision or rejection, as well as the proper pride in eventual peer acceptance. The academic structures that require such openness to criticism encourage a modesty in academics, a virtue that may not always come easily to experienced professionals, but one which can help maintain an appropriate level of self-regard. In the absence of those virtues, peer review is likely to be seen as an unwelcome intrusion. The research generated by those without such virtues is in turn likely to be less convincing (i.e. it will not be written in order to 'convince' peers), and more self-serving (i.e. promoting the researcher rather than voicing those researched), intellectually brittle (i.e. more likely to be undermined by a simple counter-argument), or stereotyped (i.e. avoiding more nuanced accounts of society). Describing the virtues in this way makes for a straightforward connection to spirituality as conceived in the *Spirit of the School* project. An attitude to oneself, in the form of proper humility (and therefore proper pride), a wish to relate to others dialogically (being 'open to criticism', for example), and a modesty or mildness in communicating (rather than attempting to dominate or to be entirely subservient), are all appropriate to the spirit of the school, and research on spirituality more generally. These same virtues are expected of school pupils, as described in some policies on creativity. DfEE (1999) describes the creativity expected of even the youngest pupils in terms of originality, purpose, imagination, and value (i.e. evaluation), in contrast to the routine, the passive and the non-evaluated (as addressed in more detail by Chapter 3, above). Pupils, teachers, and academic researchers are all expected to be original and to be both self-evaluative and open to evaluation by others. If someone is 'finding out' in a way that is original, careful and systematic, and that is placed in a systematically constructed 'theory', then that person may well be completing research. Research is, in this sense, something quite ordinary or mundane, something with which teachers and pupils are regularly involved. It is also a practice that encourages, and is enhanced by, particular virtues.

The virtues of respect, courage and trust

Highlighting the quiet virtues of humility and modesty might give an impression of research being carried out by rather scared people who dare not speak up. Addressing courage as a research virtue may help counter any such impression. Courage is, here, grouped with respect and trust. All three are exemplified by the researcher who attempts to be innovative and to change practice, their own and that of their peers. Starting with the courage that it takes to change one's own practice, through research, Salmon describes a piece of research with alcoholics, in which they were asked to rank a set of photographs according to 'their apparent similarity or dissimilarity to themselves as people, as well as to their personal ideal' (Salmon 1980, p. 3). A puzzle emerged, that the respondents 'nearly always seemed to choose, for the person they would prefer to be, the face which was most like their own', as judged by others (Salmon 1980, p. 3), yet they did not do this when choosing the picture closest to how they actually were. 'My test results suggested that when people make comparisons between themselves and others, they tend to distance themselves from that part of their experience which is directional, striving, evaluative', or '[a]t least, they distance themselves from it to the extent that the perceived ideal self is usually very different from the perceived actual self' (Salmon 1980, p. 3). In other words, other people might recognise the more ideal self-aspects of a person, even when the person does not recognise their own ideal self-aspects.

> As I thought about it, I realized that my own experience of myself was very much like that. The person who was really me lived in constant awareness of another sort of person, who was always there with me, but was not me. That person continually made comments on me and my life, often being critical and sometimes inspiring. In this inner relationship, however, I was always subservient. The peculiar findings I had noticed in my research enabled me, for the first time in my life, to question this situation. I began to see that my

values, my moral strictures, my hopes for myself, were every bit as much me as – the rest of me. . . . The same must be true of the way other people experienced me; the person they knew encompassed the ideal self who to me had been a kind of separate person living with me. This realization was very liberating. It became possible to feel a personal ownership of things that had always seemed outside and beyond me. (Salmon 1980, pp. 3–4)

The courage to understand oneself, and to use that understanding to change, is fundamental to action research, as promoted over many years within education research (Biott and Storey 1986, Bottery 1997, McNiff with Whitehead 2000, O'Hanlon 2003, Whitehead and McNiff 2006). It is the pain associated with much self-learning that requires courage to endure. Salmon uses Kelly's interpretation of the biblical narrative of Adam and Eve to explain. Adam and Eve come to a knowledge of good and evil, and 'this is fateful knowledge', as '[t]hrough seeing moral possibilities where none existed before, we lose our simple delight in the way things are . . . [and w]e now possess, for better or worse "the awful responsibility for distinguishing good from evil"' (Salmon 1995, p. 19, with the quotation from Kelly). Education does not end with knowing, as knowing has consequences: 'knowledge is not the end of the story, but rather the beginning of a new, qualitatively different chapter . . . involving the transformation of the protagonist' (Salmon 1995, p. 19). That is, 'like Adam, we may find that we must buy our knowledge dearly', and '[w]hat we know may make us lonely in our social worlds' and 'may impose responsibilities we would far rather not possess' (Salmon 1995, p. 20).

Courage is needed by researchers, but it is not enough; there is also the need to be trusting. In the world in which complete knowledge is impossible, researchers need to trust in others and in the future. If teaching and learning does not deal in 'final answers' but in answers that generate new questions, then '[t]he understanding which teachers offer is necessarily provisional – for the time being only', and 'for all that school knowledge has high social consensus and is grounded in the whole cultural heritage, it is also indelibly personal' (Salmon 1995, p. 22). The trust in oneself, in others in community, is characteristic of a Macmurrian community, a community allowing for the possibility of friendship. Teachers who do not trust themselves will be likely to hide behind syllabuses and textbooks; teachers who do not trust their colleagues and their pupils are likely to hide behind their own subjects or qualifications. The same can be said of researchers. It is a common piece of advice given to new researchers, that if they find out what they expect to find out, there is a good chance that the research is flawed. Most research undermines at least some of the researcher's previous understanding of the world. Real research, like Buber's real lesson, 'develops in mutual surprises' (Buber 2002a, p. 241, further explicated in Chapter 4, above).

Trusting others is not a matter of trusting them to have particular characteristics. They must be trusted 'as they are', or *respected*. The UK Nursing and Midwifery Council's draft advice that practitioners should 'promote and protect the interests and dignity of patients and clients, irrespective of gender, age, race, ability, sexuality, economic status, lifestyle, culture and religious or political beliefs' (NMC 2004, p. 5), suggests respect for people stripped of their qualities, the qualities of gender, age, race, ability, sexuality, and so on (addressed in Chapter 4, above). Respect therefore accompanies trust, with trust being a virtue needed both in schooling (as described in Bryk and Schneider 2002) and in research (as in the almost apologetic advice that 'research relationships should be characterised, *whenever possible*, by trust', BSA 2004, p. 3, emphasis added). It is respect that Lawrence-Lightfoot (2000) describes as the virtue underpinning professional practice across education, health, photography, and especially her own field of education research.

In its more assertive forms, trust and respect, as well as courage, can be exhibited in research that 'voices' pupils and teachers alike. O'Hanlon describes the need for research to promote 'democratic or inclusive action research' (O'Hanlon 2003, p. 65), while Pring notes that 'it is difficult to see how good teaching can be separated from a research stance towards one's own teaching' (Pring 2000, p. 160) in order to 'help to transform the capacities of people to live a fuller and more distinctively human life' (Pring 2000, p. 17). The need to voice teachers underpinned much of the action research tradition, and in recent years this has been extended to the voicing of pupils. Flutter and Rudduck (2004) describes the role of pupil voice and pupils as researchers, in contrast to pupils as no more than recipients of knowledge. Trust and respect must also extend to others involved in the school community. Parents are voiced and given 'agency' in work such as that of Munn, Wolfendale, Vincent, and Lawrence-Lightfoot, as described in Chapter 3. The role of other school workers in school-based research has been the subject of less attention in the research literature, but some issues are addressed by Biott (1991) and Lacey (2001), with the specific work of educational psychologists addressed by Newton and Tarrant whose 'motto' is that 'Children learn – so can schools' (Newton and Tarrant 1992, p. 50). One of the senses of the word spirit is a courageous energy. This is the energy that suggests someone is *spirited*, or a team or a school has plenty of *spirit*. The need for this virtue, along with the related virtues of respect and trust, is therefore of special value in research on spirituality.

The virtues of kindness and truthfulness

The quiet and more inward-looking virtues of humility and modesty, and the louder and more outward-looking virtues of courage, respect and trust, may be able to be brought together in a researcher who is kind. Kindness implies an easiness and a gentleness with oneself and with others, and contrasts with both cruelty and rigidity. McDonald refers to the need for 'intimacy, empathy, and attention to the nuances of context that positivists strip away' (McDonald 1989, p. 207), and it would be difficult to describe kindness better than this. Much guidance on educational research presents contrasting and usually conflicting pairs: positivistic vs interpretive, quantitative vs qualitative, researcher vs object of research, objectivity vs subjectivity, mind vs body. Such contrasts can be helpful, but they emphasise dualisms by stressing these dichotomies. Spirituality as a way of overcoming dualisms therefore should encourage a more kindly approach. The so-called 'insider/outsider' problem in the study of religion (McCutcheon 1999, and see McDonald 1989 or Biott 1991 for other school-related versions of this problem) is solved not by entrenching oneself on one side or the other, but by bringing people together. In the same way, an imaginative leap to the reality of the other person can solve the loneliness characteristic of life in a competitive world whose economies are driven by individualism. Kindness can soften boundaries and can encourage researchers to be truthful, itself a virtue that brings the argument back to sincerity – the wish to exhibit more than not lying.

Kindness, trust, and the other virtues can be promoted by an institution. As Pring notes, for virtues to flourish in research, there is a need for 'a more democratic approach to the conduct of research – an approach based on certain principles but requiring shared dispositions if it is to be carried out' (Pring 2004, p. 260). He concludes that 'few institutions have such "dispositions", especially when educational programmes are increasingly directed to ends which are external to the deliberations of those communities and have not had to withstand scrutiny within them' (Pring 2004, p. 260). Not only this, but 'I [have] come to recognize my own vices', and 'that is why I am not a researcher': 'perhaps many others should not be either' (Pring 2004, p. 261). This is rather pessimistic. It certainly demonstrates the virtue of humility, or even what Aristotle criticises as 'undue' humility (Aristotle 1984, p. 1749). No one is perfect. A virtuous researcher can, at best, produce a report that is sincere and truthful, even though it cannot possibly be the final word or 'the whole truth' about the schools being studied. Research reports can be likened to architectural drawings, in the description by Zumthor:

> Architectural drawings try to express as accurately as possible the aura of the building in its intended place. But precisely the effort of the portrayal often serves to underline the absence of the actual object, and what then emerges is an awareness of the inadequacy of any kind of portrayal, curiosity about the reality it promises, and perhaps – if the promise has the power to move us – a longing for its presence. (Zumthor 2006, pp. 12–13)

Research on the spirit of the school may in this way have the power to create a longing for the presence of the schools studied. The more sincerity there is in research, and the more trust, courage, kindness, modesty, humility, truthfulness, openness to criticism, and respect there is in research, the more value that research is likely to have, in itself and for schools and the wider communities in which they are set.

Valuable research

Research has an educational value for pupils and for staff and others associated with schooling, an organisational value for school development, and a wider social value. Learning in schools can be valuable in various ways. Forms of learning that are merely technical learning can have an economic value, but a limited 'technological rationality' creates a society 'devoid of spirit, substantive values, emotion and authentic self-expression' (Samier et al. 2006, p. 83, quoted in Chapter 1, above). School learning can instead help 'make ourselves a little more real than we are' (Macmurray 1992, p. 143), through living beyond ourselves, as '[t]he more real our apprehension is of what is not ourselves, the more real we are in our own selfhood' (Macmurray 2004, p. 160). This 'becoming more real' is a creative learning process allowing for friendship. We learn, are creative, and become more human in schools, and we make community and friendship through dialogue. In more mundane terms, social research can be described as 'a valuable activity' that 'contributes to the well-being of society' (BSA 2004, p. 2). The *Spirit of the School* project is itself an attempt to enable learning that is valuable in these ways. Participants are asked to take part in activities that involve self-evaluation, forms of dialogue, and communal understanding.

The headteachers and principals who participated were asked this, as a final question: 'You are granted a one-term sabbatical from your duties to spend on things educational; what would you spend your time on?' It was a question that was enthusiastically answered, and it helps illustrate the value to practitioners of particular forms of research. Although schooling is inevitably future-oriented, even the most future-oriented staff may realise the 'present' value of research:

I want to do some research and make an orderly account of my own educational experience. It is a kind of self-reflection. Those who provide education shouldn't just be moving forward. Although I urge myself to reflect when I am alone or meeting with colleagues and parents, it can't be compared to a long period when you can put down your work and reflect in peace. This would improve the way I work, making it more effective and efficient, when I get back to my work. (Principal, School 1 secondary, Protestant, Hong Kong)

That is a useful starting point in describing the value of research on spirituality. The same respondent goes on to demonstrate a subtle view of the dialogic and communal value of research, along with the virtues of modesty, humility and trust:

Another thing is . . . I have had a lot of opportunities to share and exchange views with others. Sometimes I share my ideas with others, sometimes others share with me theirs. It is good both ways. But usually I don't have enough time to do so and you would always put matters in your school in first priority. If I got such a chance [for a sabbatical], I would attend such sharings, like I am going to school. It would be good if I could help others. Sometimes you just can't distinguish if you are helping others or yourself. If I was invited to share my views, it may turn out that I am the one who has learnt. These are the things I want to do. (Principal, School 1 secondary, Protestant, Hong Kong)

Most of the respondents included reference to visiting other schools. One prefaced this with a clear expression of the need to explore written sources of educational research. 'I would want to spend some time reading, to help me formulate and reformulate and re-express a compelling vision for the school beyond the sound bites which we can all . . . do', he says, and continues that 'I want to . . . go around [to other schools] and see what people are doing because the vision is one thing but making it happen is the other thing' (Headteacher, St Bede's secondary, UK, quoted above in

Chapter 4). The value of research may be described in terms of 'success', as in the headteacher who said 'I'd probably go round visiting other schools and finding out what makes them successful and then bring it back to here if I thought it would help or benefit us' (Headteacher, Richardson primary, UK). However, the same activity may be valuable in a much more personal way:

> I think I'd like to go and study primary education in one or two other countries really. [Interviewer: Why?] Well, perhaps, well perhaps it might be to reassure myself that I've been doing it right for the past thirty-odd years (laughs) perhaps I might have a big shock, I think it would be just to, to learn and hopefully come back and put some ideas into practice. (Headteacher, Long Barrow Church of England primary school, UK)

That wish for self-understanding, in order to develop practice, is sufficient illustration of the value of research. One headteacher saw the opportunity of a sabbatical as one that could involve other teachers, support staff and pupils, too:

> I would love to go somewhere else to make a difference, not abroad necessarily, to another school . . . to help to make a difference but I would also like to take some of my children and staff elsewhere because of where we are, they don't see always the bigger picture, the teaching staff do sometimes, with the support staff just to give them, this is what the world is like out here, in an inner city school say, . . . because we all work as hard as we can in whatever setting we are in and just to see what it's like on the other side of the fence, that, yeah would be of interest. (Headteacher, Lythley Church of England primary school, UK)

This is a fitting finale to an account of research virtues and values. Research in spirituality can provide a stimulus to learning and further research and the further promotion of the spirit of the school. In the US, there is a term used for a bump in the road that makes the people driving over it nod involuntarily. The bump in the road is called a 'thank-you-ma'am'. Research can also produce a 'thank-you', also at times involuntary and always somewhat bumpy.

Is it self-serving for an academic to say that the outcome of the research is that the best way of promoting the spirit of the school is to research it? Well, perhaps, but only if 'research' is narrowly defined. Academic research has become a very specialist field, measured and judged and influential for careers and for the funding of higher education. This has led to academic research being seen as separate from other kinds of research, a separation of 'Research' from 'research'. Within universities, there has been a further separation, with 'Research' often differentiated from 'scholarship', and in some cases scholarship in turn being differentiated and described as 'advanced scholarship' and mere 'scholarship'. Such separation serves many useful purposes. However, it can also mislead people, including researchers, into thinking that research (or Research) is something more than, and better than, other kinds of enquiry. What is argued here, starting in the Chapter 3 description of creativity, is that learning is how we are, not just what we do, and that pupils and teachers alike make sense in schools: they generate original ideas and practices and people. Because this is completed systematically, guided by curriculum principles and policies and regulations, and because it is required to have evaluation built in to it – evaluation by the 'creator' and by others, other pupils and staff – it has all the characteristics of the most refined levels of academic research. The only significant difference is the peer group or community that is in a position to evaluate the outcomes of creativity/research.

For school pupils, the evaluating group is made up of other children, teachers, and at some point examination boards. For teachers, the evaluating group is made up of other staff, inspection organisations, governing bodies, professional bodies, and, for those completing accredited programmes, the staff of accrediting bodies such as universities. University academic staff, working in education departments, may write textbooks and other materials for lecturers and students, teachers and pupils. This activity may well be described as 'scholarship', and the evaluating group is made up of colleagues teaching on similar courses to them, or professional colleagues in schools. When university academic staff write for 'academic peer-reviewed international journals', the evaluating group is made up of other senior academic staff across the world, and this activity will then be likely to be referred to as 'Research'. In other words, four-year-olds being creative in school, and senior professors completing 'Research', are doing the same thing, but are having their work evaluated by a different group of people. The *Spirit of the School* project is a 'big R' research project, working with senior academics in a number of countries and with preliminary findings evaluated at national and international conferences over two years. It is also a professional development tool for schools, with professional peer groups judging its worth, and a set of activities for pupils. Professional peer groups and pupils are able to evaluate and contribute to the use of the materials and the subsequent report for the school based on the outcomes of the research. The materials and their use in school is therefore recommended as a strategy for promoting the spirit of the school, and this is suggested because pupils and school staff, as well as academics, can make use of the work.

Hoping for the spirit of the school

Spirituality was described and variously defined in Chapter 1. Subsequent chapters have investigated various dimensions of spirituality, with the generation of the ideas on community or friendship or creativity in conversations with books and with people. It is an appropriate moment to define the spirit of the school, and to hope that it can be further promoted as a result of this definition and the research leading up to it. However influential this work is (and all authors would wish their work to be influential), there should still be a recognition of its place in broader developments. A need to define spirituality here and now, for the schooling systems of the early twenty-first century, will be the result of all kinds of political and social pressures, and no doubt all kinds of personal and professional interests of the people involved in the research. The book is recognised, therefore, as being situated. Zumthor describes this well, from his own perspective as an architect:

> I believe that the language of architecture is not a question of a specific style. Every building is built for a specific use in a specific place and for a specific society. My buildings try to answer the questions that emerge from these simple facts as precisely and critically as they can. (Zumthor 2006, p. 27)

Defining the spirit of the school

Here is a definition of a spirited school, based on the research already completed (including the definitions of spirituality in Chapter 1), and therefore forming a starting point for research still to come:

> The spirited school is an inclusive (bringing in from past times and local and distant places) community (people treating each other as ends in themselves) with magnanimous leadership (aiming for the good of the led) that enables (but does not insist on) friendship (by overcoming fear and loneliness and allowing for solitude) through dialogue (not monologue) in order to create and evaluate valuable

or beautiful meanings, valuable or beautiful things (including the environment), and good (real) people.

A shorter version, simply taking out the material in parentheses, would be as follows:

The spirited school is an inclusive community with magnanimous leadership that enables friendship through dialogue in order to create and evaluate valuable or beautiful meanings, valuable or beautiful things, and good people.

What more is needed to promote the spirit of the school?

To promote the spirit of the school, as defined here, requires a wide range of activities within schools, in local communities, in countries and internationally. The focus, here, has been on what happens in schools, and this has been for unashamedly Darwinian reasons (as described in Stern 2007a, Chapter 12). Darwin shocked the nineteenth-century establishment with his account of evolution by natural selection. The shock was not simply the implied absence of a need for a god-like creator of each plant and animal, but also, and more relevant to the spirit of the school, the implied absence of a need for large-scale centralised planning, to generate what appear to be coordinated and beautiful environments. It was Darwin's ability to model evolution as the result of the lives of plants and animals in their environments, living and dying and reproducing, with occasional random mutations, that upset the leaders and policy-makers of the time. What happens in schools is not quite 'evolutionary' in this sense. Schools are rarely battles of life and death, punctuated by attempts at reproduction. They do, however, have their own 'life'. Schools generate meanings (what evolutionary biologists tend to refer to as 'memes', Cavalli-Sforza and Feldman 1981), and they do generate people – at least in the sense that they contribute to the creation of the next generation. If there was one finding that was most surprising in the whole research, it was that current policy initiatives, the pressures to perform in terms of tests and examination results, the globalising influence of commercialisation, legislation and international conventions: all of these seemed to have little influence on what people in schools found meaningful. Even headteachers, those most susceptible to external political and social pressures, found children and teachers learning together, personal relationships, and the school community, the biggest influences, the most important pressures to continue their hard work, and the biggest rewards for that work.

If policy is to be generated with respect to the spirit of the school, then, it should be policy as seen as the formalised good practice of individual school communities. A history of the institution, in which the later stages of this research have been based, describes itself as 'a study of policy and its absence' (McGregor 1991, subtitle), and the foreword to the book is admiring of the author being 'unsparing in his criticism of the muddle, manipulation and vagaries which, from the receiving end, seem to have characterised government policy' (McGregor 1991, p. x). The *Spirit of the School* project has not as yet attempted a contemporary analysis, let alone an historical analysis, of policy on spirituality. If it did, then however muddled or vague the policies were, the spirit of the schools would be able to be promoted, as it were, in a Darwinian spirit. This is the hope for spirituality, and it is a hope that stretches into the future of schooling around the world.

The future is another place. English artist Antony Gormley has an installation currently on Crosby beach, in Lancashire, entitled Another Place (Gormley 1997). On the beach, he says, 'time is tested by tide, architecture by the elements, and the prevalence of sky seems to question the earth's substance', while 'human life is tested against planetary time' (Gormley 1997). Each sculpture is 'of a particular and peculiar body, no hero, no ideal, just the industrially-reproduced body of a middle-aged man trying to remain standing and trying to breathe, facing a horizon busy with ships moving materials and manufactured things around the planet' (Gormley 1997). We are all people, particular and peculiar, placed somewhere, and looking out to distant horizons, to another place, another time. Gormley stresses that the work 'was no exercise in romantic escapism' (Gormley 1997): a worthy aim. The author of the *Spirit of the School* book, also a middle-aged man trying to remain standing, facing a horizon busy with educational initiatives and policies, would like to join with Gormley in looking out to distant horizons. Our horizons are created by where and when we are, and although those horizons can be widened, we cannot lose the sense of horizon, without leaving the world: they are 'inescapable' (Taylor 1991, p. 31) even if they are sometimes 'fractured' (Taylor 1989, p. 305). Our horizons make us particular, and that particularity is not an imperfection. As Sacks says, in promoting the 'dignity of difference', we should fight against the dominant ideology that denigrates particularity:

I propose a revolutionary argument: that a certain paradigm that has dominated Western thought, religious *and* secular, since the days of Plato is mistaken and deeply dangerous. It is the idea that, as we search for truth or ultimate reality we progress from the particular to the universal. Particularities are imperfections, the source of error, parochialism and prejudice. Truth, by contrast, is abstract, timeless, universal, the same everywhere and for everyone. Particularities breed war; truth begets peace, for when everyone understands the truth, conflict dissolves. How could it be otherwise? Is not tribalism but another name for particularity? And has not tribalism been the source of conflict through the ages? (Sacks 2003, p. 19)

Schools are recognisable places, over many years. The *Spirit of the School* research indicated that pupils, teachers and headteachers were still dominated by the relational, personal, learning aspects of schooling. John Macmurray, one of the people whose work has most influenced the research, warned that 'The golden aim of education – to teach the children how to live, has vanished over the horizon – crowded out by a multiplicity of little aims . . . a bundle of more or less unpleasant tasks which are a weariness to the flesh, to be performed because they have to be performed, and that to escape from them is a blessed relief' (Macmurray 1968, p. 114). Happily, the *Spirit of the School* research did not indicate this: values appear to be intact. The work of schools inevitably involves reaching beyond the school, across space and across time. Again, this appears to be a constant, refreshingly evidenced by the research. Promoting the spirit of the school therefore includes holding on to the spirit of particular schools that already exist. This is the value of school-based research: to assure us of what we have, in the hope that this can be the basis of a better future.

Appendix

The *Spirit of the School* methodology and toolkit

I am not concerned with the pure; I am concerned with the turbid, the repressed, the pedestrian, with toil and dull contraryness – and with the break-through. With the break-through and not with perfection.

(Buber 2002a, p. 41)

Introduction

This appendix describes the guidance to participants on the purposes and procedures of the *Spirit of the School* project, and describes each of the research tools – the questions and activities – along with a description of the origin, significance, and methods of analysis appropriate to each item. The questions and activities changed during the project, so those presented here are the latest versions, responding to comments from participants and from other researchers. There were some small variations in the text of questions, to reflect national differences and changes over time, that are not all included here. 'Headteachers' may be referred to as 'principals', for example, and the names of school subjects varied. For the research in Hong Kong, the guidance and the research tools were translated into Cantonese, with the responses retranslated into English. The Cantonese text is not included here.

Those wishing to use the research tools in their own schools are very welcome to do so. It is hoped that the *Spirit of the School* project will lead to schools working together to support learning, across age and national boundaries. Therefore, people using these research tools are encouraged to let the author know of their work (by emailing j.stern@yorksj.ac.uk), and he will be able to coordinate and help with the work.

Guidance to participants

The initial guidance to schools was provided in a project toolkit, starting with the following text:

Welcome to the *Spirit of the School*. The purpose of the *Spirit of the School* project is to help understand and to help develop the spirit of the school. By using a 'toolkit', we can investigate what the spirit of the school is, what of the school promotes the spirit of the school, and what pupils and teachers and others do to contribute to the spirit of the school. The results of the investigation will provide a guide to the spirit of the school, and a guide to discovering the spirit of the school. Some schools have more spirit, some less: all schools can develop their spirit.

This booklet therefore describes the research tools to be used in the project, and provides a guide to using each of them and to analysing the data they generate.

Any school wanting to take part in the project is invited to discuss it with Julian Stern (j.stern@yorksj.ac.uk). A school taking part may want to use its own staff and pupils to run the exercises, or it may want to use 'outsiders' such as advisers, teacher trainers, researchers or Julian himself. However that is organised, the results of the exercise should be sent to Julian.

This research has been used in schools in the UK and in China, and is planned for use in the US, Australia, and several countries across Europe. Consent forms are included, for pupils and for their parents/carers, for teachers, and for headteachers (on their own behalf and on behalf of the school). These *must* be filled in if the work is to be completed by or sent to 'outsiders' (such as professional researchers), and it is a *good idea* if they are filled in even if the research tools are being used in lessons as part of the normal activities of the school. (If the tools are used by teachers in normal lessons, then it is useful but not essential to fill in the permissions, as consent to complete that work is given as part of the teachers' normal professional/institutional role.)

The research tools include the Salmon Line, the 'What is typically said?' exercise, the friendship, membership and thought concentric circles exercise, interspersed with interview questions. These are described in more detail in subsequent sections. The research tools are all complementary, so it is best if all are used. However, if just a selection of the tools or questions is used, it should still be possible to make use of the data generated.

It is recommended that for pupils, a set of six, or at most eight, pupils of different ages and interests be brought together to work through the activities: this should take about an hour. Similarly, for staff, a group of six to eight staff could be brought together, and the work will last about an hour. The headteacher will be working alone with the interviewer, and this may take 80 minutes. Using this pattern, and the suggested timings for completing all the activities, the research for a whole school could be completed in half a day – i.e. roughly three and a half hours.

The Salmon Line

This exercise is adapted from Salmon 1994 (and used in Stern 2006b, pp. 55–6 and Stern 2007a, pp. 7 and 76), which is in the tradition of personal construct psychology founded by George Kelly (Kelly 1955). The Salmon Line:

> seeks to draw forth something lively from below the waterline. Being essentially a line – no more than a line – it is infinitely flexible.
>
> The simple principle of this technique is that a line is used to represent some kind of psychological progression. The progression can be anything at all: a course of learning, a scale of competence, a dimension of preference, steps towards a goal – anything. And just as in the [repertory] grid [of Kelly], it is the subject who fleshes out what this line actually means psychologically. People do this by marking in points along the line which represent meaningful transitions. It is important, I think, that they mark in these points first, and only then begin to define what they are. As Kelly insisted, some of our most important constructs are not instantly available to verbalisation, but they may become so through realising them in use. (Salmon 1994, p. 2)

> [T]he Salmon Line stays close to the subject and does not at any stage remove his or her material for a different kind of processing. It allows, not just for the elicitation of meaning, but also for its development. (Salmon 1994, p. 3)

The exercise can be used with all participants, including pupils, teachers and headteachers.

Participants should consider their school as a community. For the first stage of the exercise, participants should, on their own, make two marks on a 'Salmon Line', a straight line with contrasting words or phrases at either end of the line:

Mark *Present* or *P* on the line where you think your school is at the moment.

Mark *Future* or *F* on the line where you would like your school to be in one year from now.

The school is a community	_____	The school is not a community

Figure 1: The Salmon Line

There is no precise 'scale' on this line – it simply involves making two marks, for the present and the future.

For the second and more important stage of the exercise, participants should discuss with each other how the school can get from the 'present' to where they would like it to be in the 'future'. This discussion can take place between pairs, or in groups of four or five. If discussion is difficult, the participant could write about how the school might get from one point to the other. The discussion should include what might be needed – including what the participant might need to do, but also what help might be needed, and what other things would need to change.

What is typically said?

What is typically said in science, in religious education, in English, in the playground? This exercise is derived from the work of Daniels, who asked 'what would your teacher like to hear you say?' (Daniels 2001, p. 159). It was further developed in the current form in Stern 2006b, pp. 71–3, and Stern 2007a, p. 100.

It is an exercise that asks what might typically be said in a classroom, in a number of subjects and situations in schools. In a school, it might be that a group of pupils could complete the activity for a number of subjects, a single subject might be researched in different age groups or gender groups, or the research might be used to compare classroom conversations to conversations in playgrounds or lunch halls.

In analysing responses, researchers will bear in mind the indications of 'classification' and 'framing'. Daniels (2001, and in Stern 2007a, p. 100) investigated the social constructivist approaches to schooling of Vygotsky. Stronger and weaker classification and framing refer to the divisions between subjects ('classification') and the degree to which pedagogy is teacher-centred rather than pupil-centred ('framing'). Stronger classification and framing are more likely in schools using more behaviourist approaches. Weaker classification and framing are more likely in schools using more constructivist approaches. Daniels illustrates the differences from art lessons in two schools. In the school with stronger classification and framing,

> the teacher read a story called 'Where the Wild Things Live' [*sic*]. She then told the children that they were going to 'make pictures of the wild things'. The teacher had prepared a number of different pieces of sugar paper and proceeded to assign children to these pieces of paper. Each piece of sugar paper had an outline of a 'Wild

Thing' on it and most of them had sections/areas of the paper marked off. Each section contained a code number and thus could be translated by a key at the bottom of the piece of paper. The children followed the key which dictated the material to be used to 'fill in' the sections/areas marked on the paper. The 'Wild Things' were thus constructed. The department head said of art lessons, 'We are interested in the results of art, of good productions rather than "experiencing" the materials'. (Daniels 2001, pp. 162–3)

In the school with weaker classification and framing,

the children were given different grades of paper, powder paint and a piece of foam rubber or sponge. The teacher then told the children to wet the paper and flick paint at it with the sponge. The children were encouraged to use different kinds of paper with different degrees of dampness. They were told to experiment with ways of applying the powder paint. (Daniels 2001, p. 163)

In this way, Daniels contrasts classrooms where 'you paint what you see' and those where 'you paint what the teacher sees' (Daniels 2001, p. 170). Indications of stronger or weaker classification will be seen in how different the descriptions are of different subjects, or how 'bounded' those subjects seem. Indications of stronger or weaker framing will be whether pupils are 'painting what the teacher sees' or 'painting what they see'. According to Daniels, weaker classification and framing are likely to be more inclusive, that is, more suited to classrooms where pupils have a wide range of educational needs. Discussion of the outcomes of this exercise – completed by teachers, as well as by pupils – suggests that there is a concern with the difference between the 'self-image' of religious education and how the subject works in classrooms. Pupils often see religious education in terms of 'right and wrong factual answers', and/or a confessionalist promotion of religious belief, with the former illustrated by a trainee teacher's description of what is typically said:

Teacher: Come on you still have all those questions to finish. You can finish colouring in that candle after you have done them

Pupil: But miss, you said to make it look nice!

Friendship, membership and thought circles

This activity involves filling in 'mattering' concentric circles, with respect to friendship, membership and thought. The choice of membership and thought as themes comes from Davie 1994 and others who have written about 'believing and belonging'. The choice of friendship comes from a concern with the nature of self and friendship, as described by Macmurray 1992 (see also Stern 2002). The concentric circles exercise has previously been used as a research tool in a number of studies such as Roseneil 2004 and Smith 2005, and is described in this form in Stern 2006b, pp. 38–9, and in Stern 2007b. Who is closest to you in school? To what do you belong, in school? What beliefs and ideas are most important to you?

For each of these ways of presenting yourself, a 'circles of importance' activity can be completed. This activity involves using a set of five concentric circles, putting 'me' in the middle, and the things closest to the 'self' in the inner circle, the next most important in the ring created by the next circle, and so on to the outer circles.

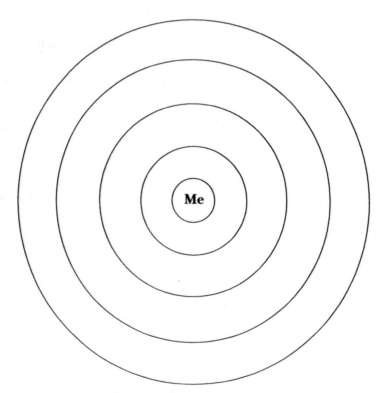

Figure 2: Circles of importance

For the 'friendship' version of circles of importance, the title will be 'me and the people closest to me'. Previous research using this technique indicates that at different ages and in different contexts, there may be a different balance of people in each of the circles. The use of this research tool is described in Smith (2005), with one quoted as saying 'I've put as closest God . . . because He is everywhere . . . [then] my mum, my dog, my baby sister', while another report indicated that 'the PS2 or Xbox was sometimes listed as a significant member of the household in network diagrams' (Smith 2005, p. 20 and p. 59, with more examples at mysite. wanadoo-members.co.uk/friendsfoodfaith/fffindex.htm). It should be noted that the question does not ask explicitly about 'friends' but about 'people closest to me'.

For the 'membership' version, the title will be 'to what do I belong?' Previous research suggests that the venue of the research itself affects the results: within a school, school membership is likely to be more 'central' than it would be for the same people completing the exercise in their homes.

For the 'thinking' version, the title will be 'what beliefs and ideas are most important to me?' Previous research suggests, as did the work on moral issues described above, that young people have very complex and sophisticated moral systems – just as older people do, of course.

Following each of the exercises, participants can discuss with each other why different people and memberships and ideas are so important.

Interview questions

The interview questions can be asked of individuals or of groups. There are three ways of completing the interviews: on their own, independent of any of the other exercises; after the end of completing some or all of the other exercises; or interspersed with the exercises. It is the third format that is recommended, and that is described in the schedule below. The questions can be expanded upon, as long as the expansions do not 'lead' the interviewees (i.e. guide them to particular types of response), and are directed to explaining and supporting and clarifying issues raised by the interviewees themselves. When interspersed with the other activities, the whole process should take about an hour for pupils and for teachers, and approximately 80 minutes for headteachers/principals. All interviews should be recorded using digital recorders (e.g. mp3 format).

It is the first of the questions that is likely to generate as much data as any other. This is the request to describe the three most recent or memorable times that the school 'made you feel good about yourself', and it is derived from Stern 2003a, p. 80, and also reported in Stern 2007b, p. 291. The question is intended to bring out the feelings of success, rather than listing what might be called 'objective' measures of success (such as test results or prizes), and to illuminate the distinctions made by Benjamin (2002) between discourses of 'normal success', 'consolation success' and 'really disabled success'.

> The dominant version of success relates to national benchmarks as enshrined in policy. But there has to be another version, in order for Newbrook to make sense of and for those students who are not going to be able to achieve according to this normative version. The answer is a deficit – consolation – version of academic success, where it is individual progress that is measured and counted as success. This version may look (and in many ways is) more humane than the dominant one. But the fact that it is deployed only in relation to students who are failing in normative terms means that it works mainly to shore up, and not to challenge or unsettle, the dominant discourse.
>
> The consolation version of success is one of individual, not purely normative, academic progress. But it does not account for all of Newbrook's students. . . . [There is] a further version, that of the 'really disabled student', in which it is personal and 'social', not academic, progress that is valued, measured and acclaimed. (Benjamin 2002, p. 138)

The idea that 'individual progress' (or ipsative assessment) is merely 'consolation' may be criticised, as much work on assessment for learning stresses the educational value of a focus on individual progress. Indeed, a focus on such ipsative assessment is likely to improve final examination results (Black 1998, Black and Wiliam 1998a, 1998b, Assessment Reform Group 1999, Wiliam 2005, and see Rudduck and Fielding 2006, p. 228 on the influence of such assessment on pupil 'voice'). At the level of school performance, too, there has been an increasing interest in 'value-added' measures:

> Value added is a way of measuring the progress a pupil makes between one stage of education and the next. The progress a school helps pupils to make compared to their different starting points allows comparison between groups of schools with different pupil intakes. (DfES 2005, p. 3)

However, the impact of 'raw' examination results on pupils is well described by Benjamin, with the pupils likely to be excluded from success in terms of the 'dominant discourse' (i.e. raw results, as the pupil quoted below 'is likely to get "E" and "F" grades at best', Benjamin 2002, p. 111) still prioritising the value – especially the employment value – of such a measure of success over any ipsative progress:

> Although many of the young women have come to realise that examination success within the terms of the dominant discourse is unavailable to them, they mostly continue to aspire, or continue wanting to aspire, to dominant versions of success. They recognize these versions as the ones that really count.
>
> *Hafsa:* C – it's – it's a grade where you can pass, really. It's a grade where you can get certain jobs if you get a C, you can get certain jobs. But with a D you've got – you can't – you can get *certain* jobs, depending on your other grades, you know, how you do well in science and English and maths – these three subjects are really, really important and any, like, I don't think D is a great, is a great show of achievement. (Benjamin 2002, pp. 110–11)

One of the philosophers whose work has underpinned this research, Macmurray, also described the problem of having examination success as the main aim of schooling, writing in the 1940s. For him, if 'the examination system frustrates your efforts to educate your pupils . . . [t]hen let's get rid of it' (Macmurray 1979, p. 13), and 'the major alteration required to make our method of education truly effective . . . [is] the abolition of the examination system' (Macmurray, 1968, p. 2, written in 1941). However, it is important to note that this did not indicate a disdain for examination results. His management of courses at Edinburgh University as Professor of Philosophy and as Dean suggested he was meticulous as a marker and monitor of examination scripts (Stern 2007a, p. 32). Examinations were clearly important to Macmurray, but they should not be the main *aim* of education. In the current research, the circumstances in which the school may be said to make people 'feel good' about themselves can illuminate the aims or communal nature of the school, and how these may be perceived in different ways by different pupils. Earlier research using the same research tool suggested that pupils at a young age responded in different ways depending on their academic achievements, with higher-achieving pupils more likely to describe learning-related circumstances, and lower-achieving pupils more likely to describe social circumstances (Hatfield 2004, working with pupils from 6 to 11). One pupil interviewed by Hatfield said, after having been in the school for three years, that the only circumstance in which school had helped to make her feel positive about herself was when 'I was . . . when I was starting to learn when I first came . . . I thought I could learn' (Hatfield 2004, also quoted in Stern 2007b, pp. 291–2).

Additional information for adult participants

This additional information for headteachers (on confidentiality, consent, child protection and disclosure policies) and for teachers (all other elements), is provided if the research involves those external to the school, as it has done for the research completed to date.

What happens to the information you give? Eventually we will be writing reports and books about our work. This will help those in and outside school understand more about life in school and the way they think. We will make sure that anything you tell us is confidential, which means that no-one who reads our report will be given your name or be able to work out which school you come from, as described in our confidentiality policy.

Confidentiality policy. In any published reports and papers personal and local identifiers will be removed. Individual interview and personal data will be confidential to the research team and tapes, transcripts, databases, etc., will be kept in secure locations. Participants will not be named or identifiable in any publication. All data collected will be deposited in a university archive with the condition that it will only be made freely available to other researchers for secondary analysis ten years after the end of the *Spirit of the School* project, or after three years for specific research proposals agreed in advance after negotiation with the original research team.

Consent policy. All participants, and the parents/carers of all young participants, will be informed about the research by letter. The letters will invite participants and parents/carers to give specific consent for themselves or their child to take part. All participants (of all ages) will be given the option to give or refuse their own consent to take part in the different stages of the research, based on as much information as can reasonably be given.

Child protection policy. Research staff who have contact with children in the UK will have completed the enhanced CRB (Criminal Records Bureau) disclosure procedure before they work with children, and the equivalent clearance in other countries. The general safety procedures of the schools in which we work will be applicable at all times. Any contact between a researcher and a child/children in the school setting will take place in publicly accessible and visible areas.

Disclosure policy. All conversations with children will be treated as confidential with the exception of matters which are obviously causing emotional distress to the child, and allegations of bullying, physical or sexual abuse. In both those cases the researcher will discuss with the child whether any other adult has been told about the situation and whether and whom the child thinks should be informed. In most such cases the researcher would ask permission to share the information with an appropriate teacher. Ultimately the researcher(s) will take a decision as to who, if anyone, should be informed informally or formally, even if this may be against the child's will.

Any questions? If you have any questions about the research please ask us. You don't need to take part in this project unless you are happy to do so, and there is no need to answer any question if you feel unhappy about it.

Permission. For you to take part in the research, we need to get your permission as an individual, and permission on behalf of the institution as a whole. As it says on the forms, you can withdraw your permission at any time, and you will get a chance to look at the interview transcript and edit out anything you have said that you do not wish to be included.

Who are we and what do we want to find out? We are a group of researchers working with Julian Stern. We want to investigate what is the spirit of the school, what of the school promotes the spirit of the school, and what do pupils and teachers and others do to contribute to the spirit of the school. We know that all people in the school work together in various ways, including learning about life by discussing important issues. The opinions of everyone in the school – young people and adults – are important to the school. Everyone has a right to be heard. We are not looking for 'right or wrong' answers to our questions. So please tell us honestly only what you want to say.

What are we going to do together in school? We'll be doing a number of different activities and we hope you will find all of them interesting and valuable. The whole set of activities should take about an hour.

Additional information for pupils

We think that you know about how this school works, and that you can help it work even better. This is your chance to take part in an interesting project, to tell us what you think and tell us about your life in school. You will be a co-researcher on the project. You will be helping the school become even better, too.

What happens to the information you give? Eventually we will be writing reports and books about our work. This will help those in and outside school understand more about life in school and the way they think. We will make sure that anything you tell us is confidential, which means that no one who reads our report will be given your name or be able to work out which school you come from.

Any questions? If you have any questions about the research please ask us. You don't need to take part in this project unless you are happy to do so, and there is no need to answer any question if you feel unhappy about it.

Permission letters. For you to take part in the research, we need to get your permission, and, if you are under 18, the permission of your parent or carer. The permission letters are included with this pack. If you are to take part in the project, please get this completed and give it in.

Who are we? What do we want to find out? We are a group of researchers working with Julian Stern. We want to investigate what is the spirit of the school, what of the school promotes the spirit of the school, and what do pupils and teachers and others do to contribute to the spirit of the school. We know that all people in the school work together in various ways, including learning about life by discussing important issues. The opinions of everyone in the school – young people and adults – are important to the school. Everyone has a right to be heard. We are not looking for 'right or wrong' answers to our questions. So please tell us honestly only what you want to say.

What are we going to do together in school? We'll be doing a number of different activities and we hope you will find all of them interesting and good fun. The whole set of activities should take about an hour.

- We'll be asking you some questions.
- We'll be having some discussions.
- We'll be asking you to do some worksheets.

Information about you: staff

Information about you [headteachers and teachers]

Your school: _____

Are you:

male ☐
female ☐

How old are you?
25 to 39 ☐
40 to 59 ☐
60+ ☐

Figure 3: Information about staff participants

Information about you: pupils

Information about you [pupils]

Your school: _____

Are you:

male ☐
female ☐

How old are you?

5 ☐		11 ☐	
6 ☐		12 ☐	
7 ☐		13 ☐	
8 ☐		14 ☐	
9 ☐		15 ☐	
10 ☐		16 ☐	
		17 or 18 ☐	
		19 to 24 ☐	

Figure 4: Information about pupil participants

Consent form for institutions/organisations

Consent Form for Institutions/Organisations

I, ... of ....

....

hereby give permission for this school to be involved in a research study being undertaken by Julian Stern and colleagues, and I understand that the purpose of the research is to investigate what is the spirit of the school, what of the school promotes the spirit of the school, and what do pupils and teachers and others do to contribute to the spirit of the school. The research involves written exercises and interviews. I understand that involvement for the institution means that it will be entitled to receive a report based the analysis of the data generated in this school, which can be used for the purposes of school development.

I understand that

1. the aims, methods, and anticipated benefits, and possible risks/hazards of the research study, have been explained to me;
2. I voluntarily and freely give my consent for the institution/organisation to participate in the above research study;
3. I am free to withdraw my consent at any time during the study, in which event participation in the research study will immediately cease and any information obtained through this institution/organisation will not be used if I so request;
4. aggregated results will be used for research purposes and may be reported in scientific and academic journals.

I agree that

5. the institution/organisation will not be named in research publications or other publicity without prior agreement;
6. I do/do not require an opportunity to check the factual accuracy of the research findings related to the institution/organisation.

Signature: .... Date: ....

The contact details of the lead researcher are:

The contact details of the secretary to the ethics committee are:

Figure 5: Consent form for institutions/organisations

Consent form for individual adults

Consent Form for Individual Adults

I, ... of ....

....

hereby agree to participate in this study to be undertaken by Julian Stern and colleagues, and I understand that the purpose of the research is to investigate what is the spirit of the school, what of the school promotes the spirit of the school, and what do pupils and teachers and others do to contribute to the spirit of the school. The research involves written exercises and interviews.

I understand that

1. upon receipt, any written material I produce will be coded and my name and address kept separately from it;
2. any information that I provide will not be made public in any form that could reveal my identity to an outside party, i.e. that I will remain fully anonymous;
3. aggregated results will be used for research purposes and may be reported in scientific and academic journals;
4. individual results will not be released to any person except at my request and on my authorisation, and extended quotations from an interview would be checked by me for accuracy;
5. I am free to withdraw my consent at any time during the study in which event my participation in the research study will immediately cease and any information obtained from me will not be used.

Signature: .... Date: ....

The contact details of the lead researcher are:

The contact details of the secretary to the ethics committee are:

Figure 6: Consent form for individual adults

Consent form for the parents/carers of individual young people

Consent Form for the Parents/Carers of Individual Young People

I, ... of ....

....

hereby give consent for my son/daughter/dependant

....

to be a participant in the study to be undertaken by a team led by Julian Stern, and I understand that the purpose of the research is to investigate what is the spirit of the school, what of the school promotes the spirit of the school, and what do pupils and teachers and others do to contribute to the spirit of the school. The research involves written exercises and interviews, all of which are educationally beneficial activities that could be completed as a normal part of the school curriculum.

I understand that

1. the aims, methods, and anticipated benefits, and possible hazards/risks of the research study, have been explained to me;
2. I voluntarily and freely give my consent to my child's/dependant's participation in such research study;
3. a report based on the results from all the children and adults across a number of schools, will be used for research purposes and may be published in journals or books, but no-one will be named or able to be identified in the book;
4. individual results will not be released to any person including medical practitioners;
5. I am free to withdraw my consent at any time, during the study in which event my child's/dependant's participation in the research study will immediately cease and any information obtained will not be used.

Signature: .... Date: ....

The contact details of the lead researcher are:

The contact details of the secretary to the ethics committee are:

Figure 7: Consent form for the parents/carers of individual young people

Consent form for individual young people

Consent Form for Individual Young People

I, ... of ....

....

hereby agree take part in a study being done by a team led by Julian Stern.

The research is trying to find out what is the spirit of the school. What about the school promotes the spirit of the school? What do pupils and teachers and others do to contribute to the spirit of the school?

The research involves written exercises and interviews. These are the kinds of activities that are completed in normal lessons, and should help children and the school to learn.

I understand that

1. I have been told what the research is about;
2. what I write or say will be anonymous: my name will be taken off any report, and I will not be able to be identified;
3. a report based on what all the children and adults write or say will be published in a book, but no-one will be named in the book;
4. I can say at any time that I want to stop taking part in the research, and if I do that, the researchers will stop straight away and what I have already said or written will not be used.

Signed: .... Date: ....

The main researcher is:

The contact details of the secretary to the ethics committee are:

Figure 8: Consent form for individual young people

Research schedule: questions and activities

(1a)   Please describe the three most recent or memorable times that the school made you feel good about yourself. Think about your answer first, and then talk about your answers. [All participants.]

(1b)   Could you cast your minds back to your own school days, describe the three most recent or memorable times when you were a pupil that the school made you feel good about yourself. [Teacher and headteacher/principal participants.]

(2)   Now, please complete the Salmon Line activity. [All participants.]

Mark *Present* or *P* on the line where you think your school is at the moment.

Mark *Future* or *F* on the line where you would like your school to be in one year from now.

The school is   _____   The school is not
a community   a community

When you have done that, discuss how the school can get from the 'present' to where you would like it to be in the 'future'. You can write what you think on this paper, as well as talking about it with other people. Then you can go on to question (3).

Figure 9: The Salmon Line activity

(3)   How can we make the school more of a community? [All participants.]

(4)   Please now complete each of the 'what is typically said?' sheets. You may also want to write about why you have written what you have written. [All participants.]

(4a) What is typically said in Science

We are in a Science lesson in a school. What do you think the teacher is saying, and what do you think the pupil is saying, in this picture?

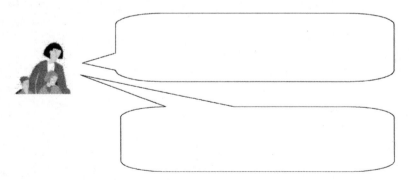

Figure 10: What is typically said in Science

(4b) What is typically said in RE

We are in an RE lesson in a school. What do you think the teacher is saying, and what do you think the pupil is saying, in this picture?

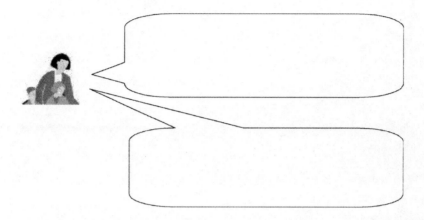

Figure 11: What is typically said in Religious Education

(4c) What is typically said in English/Literacy

We are in an English/Literacy lesson in a school. What do you think the teacher is saying, and what do you think the pupil is saying, in this picture?

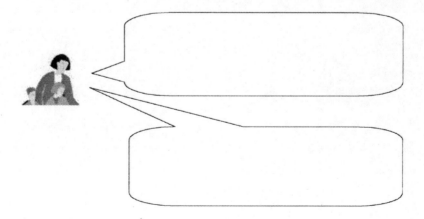

Figure 12: What is typically said in English/Literacy

(4d) What is typically said in Maths/Numeracy

We are in a Maths/Numeracy lesson in a school. What do you think the teacher is saying, and what do you think the pupil is saying, in this picture?

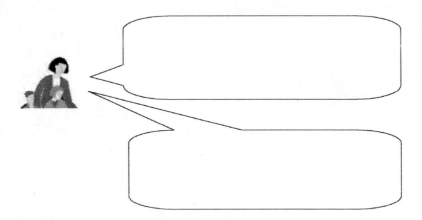

Figure 13: What is typically said in Maths/Numeracy

(4e) What is typically said in Art

We are in an Art lesson in a school. What do you think the teacher is saying, and what do you think the pupil is saying, in this picture?

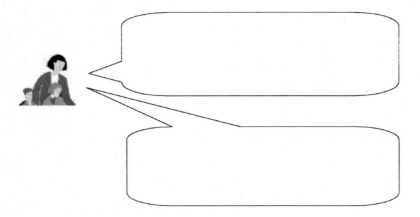

Figure 14: What is typically said in Art

(4f) What is typically said in Registration/Form Time/Tutor Time/Circle Time

We are in a registration/form time/tutor time in a school. What do you think the teacher is saying, and what do you think the pupil is saying, in this picture?

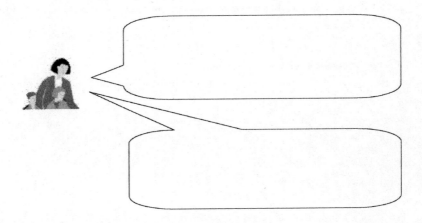

Figure 15: What is typically said in Registration/Form Time/Tutor Time/ Circle Time

(4g) What is typically said at Playtime or Breaktime

We have just finished a lesson in a school. What do you think the teacher is saying, and what do you think the pupil is saying, in this picture?

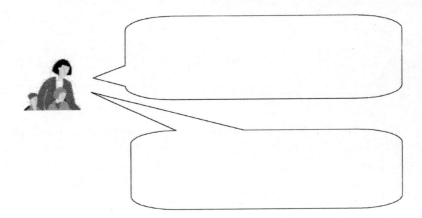

Figure 16: What is typically said at Playtime or Breaktime

(5) Now, please tell me about a time in school when you talked about something important to you. [All participants.]

(6) Please fill the first of the 'circles of importance' sheets, about the people closest to you in school. When you have done that, talk about why you have put people in the places you have put them. [All participants.]

Me and the people closest to me, in school.

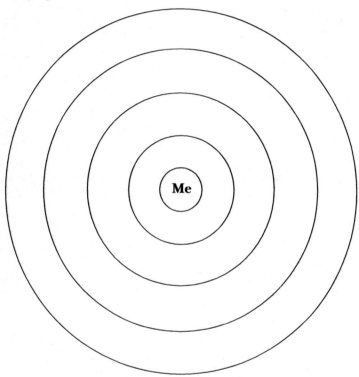

Figure 17: Me and the people closest to me

(7) Please fill the second of the 'circles of importance' sheets, about what you feel you belong to, in school. When you have done that, please talk about why you have put what you have put. [All participants.]

To what do I belong, in school?

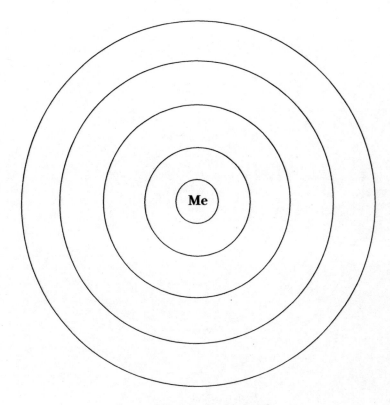

Figure 18: To what do I belong?

(8)   Now, please tell me, when do you feel most included in school? [All participants.]

(9)   Fill the third of the 'circles of importance' sheets, about what beliefs and ideas are most important to you, in school. When you have done that, talk about why you have put what you have put. [All participants.]

What beliefs and ideas are most important to me? What matters most to me?

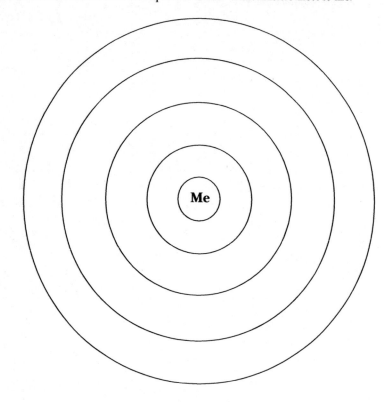

Me

Figure 19: Beliefs and ideas

(10) Now tell me what, from your life outside school, is something that is studied in school. [All participants.]

(11) Now, imagine a person (a pupil or a teacher) in the school is going through a bad time. What would you like to say to them? Describe the conversation you would like to have. [All participants.]

(12) There are now several questions that will only be asked of you as a headteacher/principal, starting with asking how long have you been a headteacher? [Headteacher/principal participants.]

(13) Why this school here? [Headteacher/principal participants.]

(14) Could you describe the school? [Headteacher/principal participants.]

(15) Could you describe the area around the school (the catchment area)? [Headteacher/principal participants.]

(16) Can you think of any problems or dilemmas you've faced where you wanted to make a decision that felt right but would have been difficult because of legislative consequences [or regulations, guidelines, ordinances]? [Headteacher/principal participants.]

(17) Can you think of any time when you wanted to go down a particular road but realized that this would have damaging market consequences for the school? [Headteacher/principal participants.]

(18) Can you think of a time when you wanted to make decisions which felt right but which would have been difficult to carry out because of the potential conflict with the school management committee? [Headteacher/principal participants.]

(19) Can you think of any time when you wanted to go down a particular road but felt it would be very difficult to do so through sheer lack of time/energy? [Headteacher/principal participants.]

(20) Of all the issues and difficulties that face you as a head/principal, which would you say is the most persistent and troubling? [Headteacher/principal participants.]

(21) What kind of thing would lead you to leave the job of principal before retirement? [Headteacher/principal participants.]

(22) What kind of values drive your determination to include an element of personal judgement in any of the decisions, dilemmas, issues you've described in the interview so far? [Headteacher/principal participants.]

(23) Where did those values come from for you? [Headteacher/principal participants.]

(24) Have you always had them? [Headteacher/principal participants.]

(25) You are granted a one-term sabbatical from your duties to spend on things educational, what would you spend your time on? [Headteacher/principal participants.]

That's the end of the activities. I would like to thank you for taking part in the *Spirit of the School* project. If you want to say anything else about the spirit of your school, do let me know.

Bibliography

How highly the marvellous power of books is to be estimated, when through them we perceive the boundaries of the world and of time, and contemplate both things which are and things which are not as if in an eternal mirror.

(Richard of Bury, 1287–1345, quoted in Webb 2007, p. 140)

Abbott, C (ed.) (2002) *Special Educational Needs and the Internet: Issues for the Inclusive Classroom*, London: RoutledgeFalmer.

Abbott, C (2007) *E-inclusion: Learning Difficulties and Digital Technologies*, Bristol: Futurelab (available at www.futurelab.org.uk/events/listing/digital_inclusion, accessed 24 October 2008).

Alexander, R J (2004) *Towards Dialogic Teaching: Rethinking Classroom Talk*, Thirsk: Dialogos.

Alexander, R J (2006) *Education as Dialogue: Moral and Pedagogical Choices for a Runaway World*, Thirsk: Hong Kong Institute of Education with Dialogos.

Alperson, P (ed.) (2002) *Diversity and Community: An Interdisciplinary Reader*, Oxford: Blackwell.

Anderson, R and Cissna, K N (1997) *The Martin Buber-Carl Rogers Dialogue: A New Transcript With Commentary*, Albany, NY: SUNY.

Aristotle (1962) *The Politics*, Harmondsworth: Penguin.

Aristotle (1976) *Nichomachean Ethics*, London: Penguin.

Aristotle (1984) *The Complete Works of Aristotle: The Revised Oxford Translation: Edited by Jonathan Barnes*, Princeton, New Jersey: Princeton University Press.

Armstrong, K (2000) *The Battle For God: Fundamentalism in Judaism, Christianity and Islam*, London: Harper Perennial.

The Assessment Reform Group (1999) *Assessment for Learning: Beyond the Black Box*, Cambridge: University of Cambridge School of Education.

Astley, J and Francis, L J (eds) (1996) *Christian Theology & Religious Education: Connections and Contradictions*, London: SPCK.

Auerbach, E (2003) *Mimesis: The Representation of Reality in Western Literature*, Princeton: Princeton University Press.

Bakhtin, M M (1981) *The Dialogic Imagination: Four Essays by M M Bakhtin, edited by Michael Holquist, translated by Caryl Emerson and Michael Holquist*, Austin, Texas: University of Texas Press.

Ball, S J (2003) 'The Teacher's Soul and the Terrors of Performativity', *Journal of Education Policy*, 18:2, pp. 215–28, 2003.

Ball, S J (2007) *Education Plc: Understanding Private Sector Participation in Public Sector Education*, London: Routledge.

Barbour, I (2000) *When Science Meets Religion: Enemies, Strangers, or Partners?* London: SPCK.

Bastiani, J (ed.) (1997) *Home-School Work in Multicultural Settings*, London: Fulton.

Bastiani, J and Wolfendale, S (eds) (1996) *Home-School Work in Britain: Review, Reflection and Development*, London: Fulton.

Baumfield, V, Bowness, C, Cush, D and Miller, J (1994) *A Third Perspective*, privately published.

Benjamin, S (2002) *The Micropolitics of Inclusive Education: An Ethnography*, Buckingham: Open University Press.

Benn, C, and Chitty, C (1996) *Thirty Years On: Is Comprehensive Education Alive and Well or Struggling to Survive?* London: Fulton.

Berger, P L (ed.) (1999) *The Desecularization of the World: The Resurgence of Religion in World Politics*; Grand Rapids, Michigan: William B Eerdmans.

Berkowitz, M W and Bier, M C (2007) 'What Works in Character Education', *Journal of Research in Character Education*, 5:1, pp. 29–48.

Bhindi, N and Duignan, P (1997) 'Leadership for a New Century: Authenticity, Intentionality, Spirituality and Sensibility', *Educational Management and Administration*, 25:2, pp. 117–32.

Billington, T (2000) *Separating, Losing and Excluding Children: Narratives of Difference*; London: RoutledgeFalmer.

Biott, C (1991) *Semi-Detached Teachers: Building Support and Advisory Relationships in Classrooms*; London: Falmer.

Biott, C and Storey, J (eds) (1986) *The Inside Story: Initiating and Sustaining Action Research in Schools With External Support*; Cambridge: Cambridge Institute of Education.

Black, P (1998) *Testing: Friend or Foe? Theory and Practice of Assessment and Testing*; London: RoutledgeFalmer.

Black, P and Wiliam, D (1998a) 'Assessment and Classroom Learning', *Assessment in Education: Principles, Policy & Practice*, Vol 5:1, pp. 7–74, March 1998.

Black, P and Wiliam, D (1998b) 'Inside the Black Box: Raising Standards Through Classroom Assessment', *Phi Delta Kappan*, Vol 89:2, pp. 139–48, October 1998.

Blumberg, S H (2008) 'Face To Face: The Need for Technology-Free Space in Religious Education', *International Seminar for Religious Education and Values Conference; Ankara, Turkey, July-August 2008*.

Boschki, R (2005) 'Re-Reading Martin Buber and Janusz Korczak: Fresh Impulses Toward a Relational Approach To Religious Education', *Religious Education*, 100:2, pp. 114–26, Spring 2005.

Bottery, M (1992) *The Ethics of Educational Management: Personal, Social and Political Perspectives on School Organization*; London: Cassell.

Bottery, M (1997) 'Teacher Professionalism Through Action Research: Possibility or Pipe-Dream?', *Teachers and Teaching: Theory and Practice*, 3:2, pp. 273–92.

Bottery, M (2007) 'Reports from the Front Line: English Headteachers' Work in an Era of Practice Centralization', *Educational Management Administration and Leadership*, 35:1, pp. 89–110, January 2007.

Bowker, J (ed.) (1997) *The Oxford Dictionary of World Religions*; Oxford: Oxford University Press.

Bowring-Carr, C and West-Burnham, J (1997) *Effective Learning in Schools: How to Integrate Learning and Leadership for a Successful School*; London: Pearson.

British Sociological Association (BSA) (2004) *Statement of Ethical Practice for the British Sociological Association*; Belmont, Durham: British Sociological Association (and www.britsoc.co.uk/equality/Statement+Ethical+Practice.htm and www.sociology.org.uk/as4bsoce.pdf, accessed 24 October 2008.

Bryk, A S and Schneider, B (2002) *Trust in Schools*; New York: Russell Sage Foundation.

Buber, M (1958) *I and Thou: Translated by Ronald Gregor Smith: Second Edition with a postscript by the author*, Edinburgh: T&T Clark.

Buber, M (1965) *The Way of Man According to the Teaching of Hasidism*; London: Routledge.

Buber, M (1998) *The Knowledge of Man: Selected Essays*; New York: Humanity Books.

Buber, M (2002a) *Between Man and Man*; London: Routledge.

Buber, M (2002b) *Meetings: Autobiographical Fragments (3rd edition)*; London: Routledge.

Cain, J (2002) 'On the Problem of Hell', *Religious Studies* 38, pp. 355–62.

Cavalli-Sforza, L L, and Feldman, M W (1981) *Cultural Transmission and Evolution*; Princeton: Princeton University Press.

Cherry, F (1995) *The 'Stubborn Particulars' of Social Psychology: Essays on the Research Process*; London: Routledge.

Chichester Diocesan Board of Education (2006) *Educating the Whole Child: Spiritual, Moral, Social and Cultural Development*; Hove: Schools Department, Chichester Diocesan Board of Education.

Chitty, C (2002) *Understanding Schools and Schooling (Key Issues in Teaching and Learning)*; London: RoutledgeFalmer.

Copley, T (2005) *Indoctrination, Education and God: The Struggle for the Mind*; London: SPCK.

Costello, J E (2002) *John Macmurray: A Biography*; Edinburgh: Floris.

Council of Europe (1996) *Children's Rights and Childhood Policies in Europe: New Approaches? Proceedings: Closing Conference of the Childhood Policies Project, Leipzig, May-June 1996*; Strasbourg: Council of Europe Publishing.

Craft, A, Jeffrey, B and Leibling, M (ed.) (2001) *Creativity in Education*; London: Continuum.

Crichton, M (2007) *The Myth of Inclusion?* Hull: Unpublished PhD Thesis, University of Hull.

Dalin, P, with Rolff, H-G, in cooperation with Kleekamp, B (1993) *Changing the School Culture*; London: Cassell.

Dalin, P and Rust, V D (1983) *Can Schools Learn?*; Windsor: NFER-Nelson.

Daniels, H (ed.) (1993) *Charting the Agenda: Educational Activity after Vygotsky*; London: Routledge.

Daniels, H (ed.) (1996) *An Introduction to Vygotsky*; London: Routledge.

Daniels, H (2001) *Vygotsky and Pedagogy*; London: RoutledgeFalmer.

Davie, G (1994) *Religion in Britain since 1945: Believing without Belonging*; Oxford: Blackwell.

Davies, G (1998) 'What is Spiritual Development? Primary Headteachers' Views', *International Journal of Children's Spirituality*, Vol. 3 No. 2, pp. 123–34.

Dearey, H P (2008) *A Report on Spirituality in Education, Health and Social Care: Draft*; Hull: Centre for Spirituality Studies, University of Hull.

Dearing, R (2001) *The Way Ahead: Church of England Schools in the New Millennium (The Dearing Report)*; London: Church House Publishing.

Department for Children, Schools and Families (DCSF) (2007) *The Children's Plan: Building Brighter Futures*; Norwich: HMSO.

Department for Education and Employment (DfEE) (1999) *All Our Futures: the National Advisory Committee for Creativity, Culture and Education*; London: DfEE.

Department for Education and Employment (DfEE) (2001) *Schools: Building on Success: Raising Standards, Promoting Diversity, Achieving Results*; London: Stationery Office.

Department for Education and Skills (DfES) (2003a) *Parental Involvement*; www.standards.dfes.gov.uk/parentalinvolvement (accessed 24 October 2008).

Department for Education and Skills (DfES) (2003b) *Parents' Centre: Learning Support*; www.dfes.gov.uk/parents/support (accessed 24 October 2008).

Department for Education and Skills (DfES) (2004a) *Every Child Matters: Change for Children*; Nottingham: DfES.

Department for Education and Skills (DfES) (2004b) *Every Child Matters: Next Steps*; Nottingham: DfES.

Department for Education and Skills (DfES) (2005) *GCSE and Equivalent Results and Associated Value Added Measures For Young People in England, 2003/04*; London: DfES. Also available from www.dfes.gov.uk/rsgateway/DB/SFR/s000585/SFR25-2005.pdf (accessed 24 October 2008).

Department of Education and Science (DES) (1977) *Curriculum 11–16: Working papers by HM Inspectorate: a contribution to current debate*; London: DES.

Department of Education and Science (DES) (1989) *Discipline in Schools: Report of the Committee of Enquiry chaired by Lord Elton*; London: HMSO.

Department of Health (DoH) (2004) *The Children Act*; London: The Stationery Office.

Descartes, R (1912) *A Discourse on Method, Meditations and Principles*; London, Toronto, New York: Dent Dutton.

Dewey, J (1916) *Democracy and Education: An Introduction to the Philosophy of Education*; New York: The Free Press.

Dryden, W (ed.) (1984) *Individual Therapy in Britain*; Milton Keynes: Open University Press.

Dunne, J (1997) *Back to the Rough Ground: Practical Judgment and the Lure of Technique*; Notre Dame, Indiana: University of Notre Dame Press.

Durkheim, E (1973) *Emile Durkheim on Morality and Society: Selected Writings: Edited and with an Introduction by Robert N Bellah*; Chicago: University of Chicago Press.

East Riding of Yorkshire Council (2005) *Agreed Syllabus for Religious Education*; Beverley: East Riding of Yorkshire Council.

Eco, U (ed.) (2004) *On Beauty*; London: Secker & Warburg.

Edwards, S D (2001) *Philosophy of Nursing: An Introduction*; Basingstoke: Palgrave.

Emoto, M (2004) *The Hidden Messages in Water*; Hillsboro, Oregon: Beyond Words.

Encyclopædia Britannica (2008) *Encyclopædia Britannica Standard Edition [incorporating Merriam-Webster's Dictionary & Thesaurus]*; Chicago: Encyclopædia Britannica.

Encyclopaedia Judaica (editor-in-chief Wigoder, G) (1971) *Encyclopaedia Judaica*; Jerusalem: Keter Publishing House.

Epstein, D (2002) 'Re-Theorising Friendship in Educational Settings', *Discourse: Studies in the Cultural Politics of Education*, 23:2, pp. 149–151, August 2002.

Fajerman, L, Jarrett, M and Sutton, F (2001) *Children as Partners in Planning: A Training Resource to Support Consultation with Children*; Save the Children.

Fergusson, D and Dower, N (eds) (2002) *John Macmurray: Critical Perspectives*; New York: Lang.

Fielding, M (1999) 'Communities of Learners: Myth: Schools Are Communities', pp. 67–87 in O'Hagan, B (ed.) (1999) *Modern Educational Myths*; London: Kogan Page.

Fines, J and Nichol, J (1997) *Teaching Primary History: Nuffield Primary History Project*; Oxford: Heinemann.

Flutter, J and Rudduck, J (2004) *Consulting Pupils: What's In It for Schools?*; London: RoutledgeFalmer.

Forsyth, B (writer, director) (1981) *Gregory's Girl*; Lake Films.

Frazer, J G (1922) *The Golden Bough*; www.forgottenbooks.org (accessed 24 October 2008): Forgotten Books.

Frederickson, N and Cline, T (2002) *Special Educational Needs, Inclusion and Diversity: A Textbook*; Buckingham: Open University Press.

Friedman, M (1999) 'The Interhuman and What is Common to All: Martin Buber and Sociology', *Journal for the Theory of Social Behaviour*, 29:4, pp. 403–17.

Friedman, M S (2002) *Martin Buber: The Life of Dialogue (4th edition)*; London: Routledge.

Furlong, J and Oancea, A (2005) *Assessing Quality in Applied and Practice-based Educational Research: A Framework for Discussion*; Oxford: Oxford University Department of Educational Studies and the ESRC.

Gardner, H (1991) *The Unschooled Mind: How Children Think & How Schools Should Teach*; New York: Basic Books.

Glatzer, N N and Mendes-Flohr, P (eds) (1991) *The Letters of Martin Buber: A Life of Dialogue*; Syracuse, New York: Syracuse University Press.

Gormley, A (1997) *Another Place: Cast Iron 100 Elements, 189 × 53 × 29 cm*; Cuxhaven Germany, Stavanger Norway, De Panne Belgium, Crosby Beach, Merseyside, England (information at the sites, and at www.antonygormley.com, accessed 24 October 2008).

Greenfield, T and Ribbins, P (eds) (1993) *Greenfield on Educational Administration: Towards a Humane Science*; London: Routledge.

Grove, J and Smalley, S (2003) *Diversity and Inclusion and Religious Education: A Good Practice Guide*; AREIAC.

Guignon, C (2004) *On Being Authentic*; Abingdon, Oxon: Routledge.

Hall, J and Taylor, J (ed.) (2005) *Excellence and Distinctiveness: Guidance on RE in Church of England Schools*; London: National Society.

Hartland, I (1999) *Shaping the Spirit: Promoting the Spiritual Development of Young People in Schools: Guidance on Spiritual Education from Kent SACRE 1999*; West Malling, Kent: Kent County Council.

Hatfield, E (2004) *Feeling included? A critical analysis of the impact of pedagogy on inclusion in a primary school*; Hull: MA dissertation, University of Hull.

Hay, D (2002) 'Relational Consciousness in Children: Empirical Support for Macmurray's Perspective', in Fergusson, D and Dower, N (eds) (2002) *John Macmurray: Critical Perspectives*; New York: Lang.

Hay, D (2006) *Something There: The Biology of the Human Spirit*; London: Darton, Longman & Todd.

Hay, D (2007) *Why Spirituality is Difficult for Westerners*; Exeter: Societas Essays in Political & Cultural Criticism.

Hay, D with Nye, R (2006) *The Spirit of the Child: Revised Edition*; London: Jessica Kingsley.

Hayes, D (ed.) (2007) *Joyful Teaching and Learning in the Primary School*; Exeter: Learning Matters.

Hedley, J (2007) *Experts help North Tyneside add spirit to learning*; www.northtyneside.gov.uk/news/newsinfoitem.shtml?p_ID=4908 (accessed 24 October 2008).

Hegel, G W F (1988) *Lectures on the Philosophy of Religion*; Berkeley, Los Angeles: University of California Press.

Held, D (1987) *Models of Democracy*; Cambridge: Polity.

Hey! (2008) 'Photography Donations Wanted For Cancer Centre', *Hey!: Hull and East York-shire Hospitals Newsletter*, 3, 18–31 August 2008.

Hey, V (2002) 'Horizontal Solidarities and Molten Capitalism: the subject, intersubjectivity, self and the other in late modernity', *Discourse: Studies in the Cultural Politics of Education*, 23:2, pp. 227–41, 2002.

Hick, J (ed.) (1974) *Truth and Dialogue: The Relationship Between World Religions*; London: Sheldon.

Higher Education Funding Council for England (Hefce) (2005) *Guidance to panels: January 2005: Ref RAE 01/2005*; Higher Education Funding Council for England, Scottish Higher Education Funding Council, Higher Education Funding Council for Wales, Department for Employment and Learning Northern Ireland, online at www.rae.ac.uk/pubs/2005/01 (linked from www.hefce.ac.uk/research) (accessed 24 October 2008).

Hinnells, J (2007) 'Parsi Zoroastrians', *SHAP: World Religions in Education: 2007/2008: Diversity and Distinctiveness*, pp. 56–8, 2007.

Hogg, J (1978) *The Private Memoirs And Confessions Of A Justified Sinner: Written By Himself: With A Detail Of Curious Traditionary Facts And Other Evidence By The Editor*; London: Folio.

Hopkins, B (2004) *Just Schools: A Whole School Approach to Restorative Justice*; London: Jessica Kingsley.

Hornby, G (2000) *Improving Parental Involvement*; London: Continuum.

Hornby, N (2000) *About A Boy*; London: Penguin.

Houston, G (1998) *Virtual Morality: Christian Ethics in the Computer Age*; Leicester: Apollos.

Houston, P D and Sokolow, S L (2006) *The Spiritual Dimension of Leadership: 8 Key Principles to Leading More Effectively*; Thousand Oaks, CA: Corwin Press.

Howie, G (ed.) (1968) *Aristotle on Education*; London: Collier-Macmillan.

Hoyle, E and Wallace, M (2005) *Educational Leadership: Ambiguity, Professionals & Managerialism*; London: Sage.

Hull, J M (1998) *Utopian Whispers: Moral, Religious and Spiritual Values in Schools*; Norwich: RMEP.

Hutcheson, E (1975) *The Literature of the Piano: A Guide for Amateur and Student: Second Edition Revised by Rudolph Ganz*; London: Hutchinson.

Ipgrave, J (2001) *Pupil-to-Pupil Dialogue in the Classroom as a Tool for Religious Education: Warwick Religions and Education Research Unit Occasional Papers II*; Coventry: WRERU.

Ipgrave, J (2003) *Building E-Bridges: Inter-Faith Dialogue by E-Mail*; Birmingham: REToday Services.

Ipgrave, J (2004) 'Including Pupils' Faith Background in Primary Religious Education', *Support for Learning*, 19:3, pp. 114–18, August 2004.

Kelly, G A (1955) *The Psychology of Personal Constructs*; New York: Norton.

Kim, S C H and Kollontai, P (eds) (2007) *Community Identity: Dynamics of Religion in Context*; London: T&T Clark.

Kirkpatrick, F G (2005) *John Macmurray: Community Beyond Political Philosophy*; Lanham, Maryland: Rowman & Littlefield.

Klass, D (1999) *The Spiritual Lives of Bereaved Parents*; Philadelphia: Brunner/Mazel.

Klass, D, Silverman, P R and Nickman, S L (eds) (1996) *Continuing Bonds: New Understandings of Grief*; Philadelphia: Taylor & Francis.

Lacey, P (2001) *Support Partnerships: Collaboration in Action*; London: Fulton.

Lave, J and Wenger, E (1991) *Situated Learning: Legitimate Peripheral Participation*; Cambridge: Cambridge University Press.

Lawrence-Lightfoot, S (2000) *Respect: An Exploration*; Cambridge, Massachusetts: Perseus.

Lawrence-Lightfoot, S (2003) *The Essential Conversation: What Parents and Teachers Can Learn From Each Other*; New York: Ballantine.

Leavis, F R (1948) *Education & the University: A Sketch for an 'English School'*; London: Chatto & Windus.

Leavis, F R and Leavis, Q D (1969) *Lectures in America*; London: Chatto & Windus.

Levinas, E (1989) *The Levinas Reader, Edited by Seán Hand*; Oxford: Basil Blackwell.

Lindon, J (1999) *Understanding World Religions in Early Year Practice*; London: Hodder & Stoughton.

Lipman, M (2003) *Thinking in Education: Second Edition*; Cambridge: Cambridge University Press.

Lokhorst, G-J (2006) 'Descartes and the Pineal Gland', in *Stanford Encyclopedia of Philosophy*, plato.stanford.edu/entries/pineal-gland/#2.2

Lynch, S (2005) *Philosophy and Friendship*; Edinburgh: Edinburgh University Press.

MacBeath, J, Thomson, B, Arrowsmith, J and Forbes, D (1992) *Using Ethos Indicators in Secondary School Self-Evaluation: Taking Account of the Views of Pupils, Parents, and Teachers: School Development Planning Support Materials*; Edinburgh: Scottish Office Education Department.

McCutcheon, R T (ed.) (1999) *The Insider/Outsider Problem in the Study of Religion: A Reader*; London: Cassell.

McDonald, J P (1989) 'When Outsiders Try to Change Schools From the Inside', in *Phi Delta Kappan*, 71:3, pp. 206–12, November 1989.

McGregor, G P (1991) *A Church College for the 21st Century? 150 Years of Ripon & York St John 1841–1991: A Study of Policy and its Absence*; York: William Sessions for University College of Ripon and York St John.

McIntosh, E (2001) 'The Concept of the Person and the Future of Virtue Theory – Macmurray and MacIntyre', *Quodlibet Journal*, 3:4, www.quodlibet.net/mcintosh-virtue.shtml (accessed 24 October 2008).

Macmurray, J (ed.) (1933) *Some Makers of the Modern Spirit: A Symposium*; Whitefish, Massachusetts: Kessinger.

Macmurray, J (1968) *Lectures/Papers on Education*; Edinburgh: Edinburgh University Library, Special Collections Gen 2162/2.

Macmurray, J (1979) *Ye Are My Friends and To Save From Fear*; London: Quaker Home Service.

Macmurray, J (1991a) *The Self as Agent: Volume 1 of The Form of the Personal: Introduction by Stanley M Harrison*; London: Faber.

Macmurray, J (1991b) *Persons in Relation: Volume 2 of The Form of the Personal: Introduction by Frank G Kirkpatrick*; London: Faber.

Macmurray, J (1992) *Freedom in the Modern World*; New Jersey: Humanities Press.

Macmurray, J (1995) *Reason and Emotion*; London: Faber.

Macmurray, J (1996) *The Personal World: John Macmurray on Self and Society: Selected and Introduced by Philip Conford*; Edinburgh: Floris.

Macmurray, J (2004) *John Macmurray: Selected Philosophical Writings, Edited and Introduced by Esther McIntosh*; Exeter: Imprint Academic.

McNiff, J, accompanied by Whitehead, J (2000) *Action Research in Organisations*; London: Routledge.

Macpherson, C B (1973) *Democratic Theory: Essays in Retrieval*; Oxford: Clarendon.

Maritain, J (1971) *Education at the Crossroads*; New Haven, Connecticut: Yale University Press.

Marks, W E (2004) *The Holy Order of Water: Healing Earth's Waters and Ourselves*; Great Barrington, Massachusetts: Steiner Books.

Marland, M (1993) *The Craft of the Classroom: A Survival Guide;* Oxford: Heinemann Educational.

Marx, K (1973) *Grundrisse: Foundations of the Critique of Political Economy (Rough Draft): Translated with a Foreword by Martin Nicolaus*; Harmondsworth: Penguin.

Marx, K and Engels, F (1970) *The German Ideology: Students Edition*; London: Lawrence & Wishart.

Mason, M (2000) 'Spirituality – What On Earth Is It?', *Paper given at the International Conference of Children's Spirituality at Roehampton Institute, Summer 2000*, available at www.humanism.org.uk/site/cms/contentViewArticle.asp?article=1264 (accessed 24 October 2008).

Messiou, K (2006) 'Conversations With Children: Making Sense of Marginalization in Primary School Settings', *European Journal of Special Needs Education*, 21:1, pp. 39–54, February 2006.

Mitscherlich, A and Mitscherlich, M (1975) *The Inability to Mourn: Principles of Collective Behavior*; New York: Grove Press.

Mosley, J (1993) *Turn Your School Round: A Circle Time Approach to the Development of Self-Esteem and Positive Behaviour in the Primary Staffroom, Classroom and Playground;* Wisbech, Cambridgeshire: Learning Development Aids.

Mosley, J (1996) *Quality Circle Time in the Primary Classroom: Your Essential Guide to Enhancing Self-Esteem, Self-Discipline and Positive Relationships: Volume 1;* Wisbech, Cambridgeshire: Learning Development Aids.

Moustakas, C (1994) *Phenomenological Research Methods;* Beverley Hills, CA: Sage.

Munn, P (ed.) (1993) *Parents and Schools: Customers, Managers or Partners?;* London: Routledge.

Myers, K (2005) *Teachers Behaving Badly: Dilemmas for School Leaders;* London: Routledge-Falmer.

Nesbitt, E (2004) *Intercultural Education: Ethnographic and Religious Approaches;* Brighton: Sussex Academic Press.

Newton, C, and Tarrant, T (1992) *Managing Change in Schools: A Practical Handbook;* London: Routledge.

Noddings, N (1984) *Caring: A Feminine Approach to Ethics and Moral Education;* Berkeley: University of California Press.

Noddings, N (1994) 'Conversation as Moral Education', *Journal of Moral Education*, 23:2, 1994, Vol 23, Issue 2.

Noddings, N (2003a) *Happiness and Education;* Cambridge: Cambridge University Press.

Noddings, N (2003b) 'Is Teaching a Practice?', *Journal of Philosophy of Education*, 37:2, pp. 241–51, 2003.

Nursing Midwifery Council (NMC) (2004) 'The NMC Code of Professional Conduct: Standards for Conduct, Performance and Ethics', *NMC July 2004*, www.nmc-uk.org (accessed 24 October 2008).

Office for Democratic Institutions and Human Rights (ODIHR) (2007) *Toledo Guiding Principles on Teaching About Religions and Beliefs in Public Schools: Prepared by the ODIHR Advisory Council of Experts on Freedom of Religion or Belief;* Warsaw, Poland: ODIHR/OSCE (and at www.osce.org/publications/odihr/2007/11/28314_993_en.pdf, accessed 24 October 2008).

Office for Standards in Education (Ofsted) (1994) *Spiritual, Moral, Social and Cultural Development;* London: HMSO.

O'Hanlon, C (2003) *Educational Inclusion as Action Research: An Interpretive Discourse;* Maidenhead: Open University Press.

Olsen, J and Cooper, P (2000) *Dealing With Disruptive Students in the Classroom;* London: Kogan Page.

Ota, C and Chater, M (eds) (2007) *Spiritual Education in a Divided World: Social, Environmental & Pedagogical Perspectives on the Spirituality of Children and Young People;* Abingdon, Oxfordshire: Routledge.

Owen, N (2007) *Killing Creativity;* The Open University and BBC, www.open2.net/childofourtime/2007/creativity.html (accessed 24 October 2008).

Oxford English Dictionary (OED) (2005) *The Oxford English Dictionary: Third Edition;* Oxford: Oxford University Press (and at www.oed.com and dictionary.oed.com, accessed 24 October 2008).

Plato (1908) *Republic of Plato;* Translated into English by A D Lindsay, 2nd edition; London: Dent.

Pring, R (2000) *Philosophy of Educational Research;* London: Continuum.

Pring, R (2004) *Philosophy of Education: Aims, Theory, Common Sense and Research;* London: Continuum.

Pring, R and Walford, G (eds) (1997) *Affirming the Comprehensive Ideal;* London: Falmer.

Qualifications and Curriculum Authority (QCA) (2008) *Creativity and Critical Thinking;* curriculum.qca.org.uk/key-stages-3-and-4/cross-curriculum-dimensions/creativitycritical thinking/index.aspx.

Ranson, S (2000) 'Recognizing the Pedagogy of Voice in a Learning Community', *Educational Management & Administration*, 28:3, pp. 263–79.

Rawls, J (1972) *A Theory of Justice;* Oxford: Oxford University Press.

Riley, K (2007) 'Reconfiguring Urban Leadership Taking a Perspective on Community', *BERA Conference, London*, 5–8 September 2007.

Roberts, P (2006) *Nurturing Creativity in Young People: A Report to Government to Inform Future Policy*, London: Department for Culture, Media and Sport.

Robinson, S, Kendrick, K and Brown, A (2003) *Spirituality and the Practice of Healthcare*, Basingstoke: Palgrave Macmillan.

Rosen, C (1995) *The Romantic Generation*, Cambridge, Massachusetts: Harvard University Press.

Rosen, C (2002) *Piano Notes: The Hidden World of the Pianist*, London: Penguin.

Roseneil, S (2004) *Towards A More Friendly Society - Work, Care and Play in the 21st Century: Centre for Policy Studies in Education (CPSE) Seminar, University of Leeds*, 3 June 2004.

Royal Ministry of Church, Education and Research (1994) *Core Curriculum for Primary, Secondary and Adult Education in Norway*, Oslo: Akademika a/s.

Rudduck, J and Fielding, M (2006) 'Student voice and the perils of popularity', *Educational Review*, 58:2, pp. 219–31, May 2006.

Rudge, L (1998) '"I Am Nothing: Does It Matter?": A Critique of Current Religious Education Policy and Practice on Behalf of the Silent Majority', *British Journal of Religious Education*, Vol 20:3, pp. 155–65.

Rumi (1995) *The Essential Rumi: Translated by Coleman Barks with John Moyne, A J Arberry and Reynold Nicholson*, Harmondsworth: Penguin.

Rush, C (1994) *Last Lesson of the Afternoon: A Satire*, Edinburgh: Canongate.

Ryan, A (1995) *John Dewey and the High Tide of American Liberalism*, New York: Norton.

Sacks, J (2003) *The Dignity of Difference: How To Avoid the Clash of Civilizations (2nd edition)*, London: Continuum.

Salmon, P (ed.) (1980) *Coming to Know*, London: Routledge.

Salmon, P (1994) 'Grids are all very well, but . . .', *Preston, Lancashire: EPCA (European Personal Construct Association) Newsletter* 1994, 2.

Salmon, P (1995) *Psychology in the Classroom: Reconstructing Teachers and Learners*, London: Cassell.

Salmon, P (1998) *Life at School: Education and Psychology*, London: Constable.

Samier, E A and Bates, R J, with Stanley, A (eds) (2006) *Aesthetic Dimensions of Educational Administration and Leadership*, Abingdon: Routledge.

Schiller, F (1967) *On the Aesthetic Education of Man in a Series of Letters*, Oxford: Clarendon.

Schilpp, P A and Friedman, M (eds) (1967) *The Philosophy of Martin Buber [Library of Living Philosophers]*, London: Cambridge University Press.

Schön, D A (1983) *The Reflective Practitioner*, New York: Basic Books.

Schön, D A (1987) *Educating the Reflective Practitioner: Toward a New Design for Teaching and Learning in the Professions*, San Francisco: Jossey-Bass.

School Curriculum and Assessment Authority (SCAA) (1995) *Spiritual and Moral Development: SCAA Discussion Papers: No. 3*, London: SCAA.

Schreiner, P, Kraft, F and Wright, A (eds) (2007) *Good Practice in Religious Education in Europe: Examples and Perspectives of Primary Schools*, Berlin: Lit for the Comenius-Institut.

Schutz, A (1973) *Collected Papers I: The Problem of Social Reality*, Martinus Nijhoff: The Hague.

Selsam, H and Martel, H (eds) (1963) *Reader in Marxist Philosophy: From the Writings of Marx, Engels, and Lenin*, New York: International Publishers.

Sennett, R (1978) *The Fall of Public Man*, London: Penguin.

Sennett, R (2003) *Respect in a World of Inequality*, London: Norton.

Sennett, R (2008) *The Craftsman*, London: Allen Lane.

Shorter Oxford English Dictionary (SOED) (2007) *Shorter Oxford English Dictionary: Sixth Edition*, Oxford: Oxford University Press.

Silverman, D (ed.) (1997) *Qualitative Research: Theory, Method and Practice*, London: Sage.

Sink, C A, Cleveland, R and Stern, J (2007) 'Spiritual Formation in Christian School Counseling Programs', *Journal of Research on Christian Education*, 16: pp. 35–63.

Smith, G (2005) *Children's Perspectives on Believing and Belonging*, London: National Children's Bureau for the Joseph Rowntree Foundation.

Smith, M K (2000) 'Martin Buber on Education', *The Encyclopedia of Informal Education*, www.infed.org/thinkers/et-buber.htm (accessed 24 October 2008).

Smith, W C (1978) *The Meaning and End of Religion*, London: SPCK.

Spark, M (2000) *The Prime of Miss Jean Brodie*, London: Penguin.

Spender, D (1982) *Invisible Women: The Schooling Scandal*, London: Writers' and Readers' Collective.

Spinoza, B (1955) *The Ethics*, New York: Dover.

Steiner, R (1996) *Rudolf Steiner in the Waldorf School: Lectures and Addresses to Children, Parents, and Teachers – 1919–1924*, Hudson, NY: Anthroposophic Press.

Stern, A (1971) 'Equality', *Proceedings of the XIVth International Congress of Philosophy, Vienna, September 1968*, pp. 520–6.

Stern, L J (1999) *Developing as a Teacher of History*, Cambridge: Chris Kington.

Stern, L J (2001a) *Developing Schools as Learning Communities: Towards a Way of Understanding School Organisation, School Development, and Learning*, London: London University Institute of Education: PhD Thesis.

Stern, L J (2001b) 'John Macmurray, Spirituality, Community and Real Schools', *International Journal of Children's Spirituality*, Vol 6:1, pp. 25–39, April 2001.

Stern, L J (2002) 'EMU Leadership: An Egalitarian Magnanimous Undemocratic Way for Schools', *International Journal of Children's Spirituality*, Vol 7:2, pp. 143–58, August 2002.

Stern, L J (2003a) *Involving Parents*, London: Continuum.

Stern, L J (2003b) 'Above and Beyond: What Does ICT Have to Do With Spiritual Development: Julian Stern Explains', *Teaching Thinking*, 11, pp. 14–18, Summer 2003.

Stern, L J (2004) 'Marking Time: Using Music to Create Inclusive Religious Education and Inclusive Schools', *Support for Learning*, 19:3, pp. 107–13.

Stern, L J (2006a) *Getting the Buggers to Do Their Homework*, London: Continuum.

Stern, L J (2006b) *Teaching Religious Education: Researchers in the Classroom*, London: Continuum.

Stern, L J (2007a) *Schools and Religions: Imagining the Real*, London: Continuum.

Stern, L J (2007b) 'Mattering: What it Means to Matter in School', *Education 3–13*, 35:3, pp. 285–95, August 2007.

Stern, L J (2007c) 'Action Philosophy in Jewish and Christian Traditions', *REsource*, 30:1, pp. 9–12, Autumn 2007.

Stern, L J and James, S (2006) 'Every Person Matters: Enabling Spirituality Education for Nurses', *Journal of Clinical Nursing*, 15:7, pp. 897–904, July 2006.

Stern-Gillet, S (1995) *Aristotle's Philosophy of Friendship*, Albany, NY: SUNY.

Stewart, W (2008) 'Non-faith Schools can be Spiritual', *Times Educational Supplement*, 18 January 2008, p. 10.

Stoll, L and Myers, K (eds) (1998) *No Quick Fixes: Perspectives on Schools in Difficulty*, London: Falmer.

Stone, M (1994) *Eggshells and Thunderbolts*, London: BBC and the Culham College Institute.

Strauss, A L and Corbin, J (1990) *Basics of Qualitative Research: Grounded Theory Procedures and Techniques*, London: Sage.

Swinton, J (2001) *Spirituality and Mental Health Care: Rediscovering a 'Forgotten' Dimension*, London: Jessica Kingsley.

Taylor, C (1989) *Sources of the Self: The Making of the Modern Identity*, Cambridge: Cambridge University Press.

Taylor, C (1991) *The Ethics of Authenticity*, Cambridge: Cambridge University Press.

Times Educational Supplement (TES) (1996) 'Lonely Leaders', *Times Educational Supplement*, 12 July 1996.

Times Educational Supplement (TES) (1998) 'Give Us Our Daily Worship', *Times Educational Supplement*, 14 August 1998.

Times Higher Education (2008) 'Keep Peer Review at REF Core, Chairs Warn', *Times Higher Education*, 28 August 2008, pp. 4–5.

Topping, K J (1986) *Parents as Educators: Training Parents to Teach Their Children*, London: Croom Helm.

Trilling, L (1972) *Sincerity and Authenticity: The Charles Eliot Norton Lectures, 1969–1970*, Cambridge, Massachusetts: Harvard University Press.

United Nations (UN) (1959) *United Nations Declaration of the Rights of the Child*, New York: United Nations General Assembly.

United Nations (UN) (1989) *United Nations Convention on the Rights of the Child*; New York: United Nations General Assembly.

United Nations Children's Fund (UNICEF) (2008) *Your Rights Under the UNCRC*; www.unicef.org.uk/youthvoice (downloaded 8 September 2008).

United Nations Educational, Scientific and Cultural Organisation (UNESCO) (1994) *The Salamanca Statement and Framework for Action on Special Needs Education*; Paris: UNESCO (and www.unesco.org/images/0011/001107/110753eo.pdf).

University of Bristol Graduate School of Education Document Summary Service (University of Bristol) (1998) *Teachers' Legal Liabilities and Responsibilities (DfEE Circular 4/98: QTS Standards): The Bristol Guide*; Bristol: University of Bristol.

Vernon, M (2005) *The Philosophy of Friendship*; Basingstoke, Hampshire: Palgrave Macmillan.

Vincent, C (2000) *Including Parents? Education, Citizenship and Parental Agency*; Buckingham: Open University Press.

Walker, D P (1964) *The Decline of Hell: Seventeenth Century Discussions of Eternal Torment*; Chicago: University of Chicago Press.

Watson, B (2004) 'Spirituality in British State Education: An Alternative Perspective', *Journal of Beliefs & Values*, 25:1, pp. 55–62, April 2004.

Watson, J (2007) 'Spiritual Development: Constructing an Inclusive and Progressive Approach', *Journal of Beliefs and Values*, 28:2, pp. 125–36, August 2007.

Webb, D (2007) *Privacy and Solitude in the Middle Ages*; London: Continuum.

Wegerif, R (2008) 'Dialogic or Dialectic? The Significance of Ontological Assumptions in Research on Educational Dialogue', *British Educational Research Journal*, 34:3, pp. 347–61, June 2008.

Wenger, E (1998) *Communities of Practice: Learning, Meaning, and Identity*; Cambridge: Cambridge University Press.

West-Burnham, J and Huws Jones, V (2007) *Spiritual and Moral Development in Schools*; London: Continuum.

White, J (2007) 'Wellbeing and Education: Issues of Culture and Authority', *Journal of Philosophy of Education*, 41:1, pp. 17–28, February 2007.

Whitehead, J and McNiff, J (2006) *Action Research Living Theory*; London: SAGE.

Wiliam, D (2005) *Formative Assessment: The Research Evidence*; Educational Testing Service (www.ets.org, accessed 24 October 2008).

Willes, M J (1983) *Children into Pupils: A Study of Language in Early Schooling*; London: Routledge & Kegan Paul.

Wittgenstein, L (1958) *Philosophische Untersuchungen: Philosophical Investigations* (2nd edition); Oxford: Blackwell.

Wolfendale, S (ed.) (2002) *Parent Partnership Services for Special Educational Needs: Celebrations and Challenges*; London: David Fulton.

Wolfendale, S and Bastiani, J (eds) (2000) *The Contribution of Parents to School Effectiveness*; London: David Fulton.

Wood, N (1959) 'A Guide to the Classics: The Skepticism of Professor Oakeshott', *The Journal of Politics*, 21:4, pp. 647–62, November 1959.

Woods, G (2007) 'The "Bigger Feeling": The Importance of Spiritual Experience in Educational Leadership', *Educational Management Administration Leadership*, 35:1, pp. 135–55, January 2007.

Wright, A (1999) *Discerning the Spirit: Teaching Spirituality in the Religious Education Classroom*; Abingdon: Culham College Institute.

Yeats, W B (ed.) (1936) *The Oxford Book of Modern Verse: 1892–1935*; Oxford: Oxford University Press.

Yeats, W B (2002) *W. B. Yeats: Selected Poems*; London: Orion.

Yovel, Y (1989a) *Spinoza and Other Heretics: The Marrano of Reason*; Princeton, New Jersey: Princeton University Press.

Yovel, Y (1989b) *Spinoza and Other Heretics: The Adventures of Immanence*; Princeton, New Jersey: Princeton University Press.

Yvenes, M and Madshus, E (eds) (2008) *Architect Sverre Fehn: Intuition – Reflection – Construction*; Oslo: National Museum of Art, Architecture and Design.

Zumthor, P (2006) *Thinking Architecture: Second Edition*; Basel, Switzerland: Birkhäuser.

Index

Abbott, Chris 47
acting, actors (*see* drama)
action philosophy 63
action research (*see* research)
Adam and Eve 7, 153
Alexander, Robin 85
alienation 104–6, 107, 108, 110–12, 144 (*see also* solitude)
Almond, Brenda 8
alone (*see* loneliness, solitude)
Alperson, Philip 25, 26
Anderson, Rob 100
Anglicanism (*see* Christianity)
anomie 104, 106–7, 108, 109–10 (*see also* solitude)
apprenticeship 76–7, 87, 109, 118
architecture xiii–xiv, 91, 156, 162, (*see also* Sverre Fehn, Peter Zumthor)
Aristotle xv, 2–3, 7, 13, 17, 20, 21, 23, 24–5, 27, 28, 29, 31, 33–4, 40, 45, 103, 118, 124, 125–6, 128–9, 132, 133, 155
arithmetic (*see* mathematics)
armed services 115
Armstrong, Karen 5
art, arts 55, 59, 64, 71, 87, 90–1, 104, 127, 162, 184
assembly 99, 119
assessment 172
Astley, Jeff 3, 12, 14
atheism (*see* secular, *see also* humanism)
Auerbach, Erich 145
Augustine, Saint (Saint Augustine of Hippo) 9
authenticity 9, 59, 121

Bach, Johann Sebastian 123
Bacon, Francis 114
Bakhtin, Mikhail 19, 80–1
Ball, Stephen J 110, 119–20, 125
Barbour, Ian 4
Bastiani, John 55
Baszanger, Isabelle 21
Bates, Richard J 86
Baumfield, Vivienne 54
beauty 13, 57–8, 61, 160–1
behaviour (*see* discipline)
behaviourism 141
Benjamin, Shereen 172–3
Benn, Caroline 48
Berger, Peter L 17
Berkowitz, Marvin W 89
Bernard, Saint (Saint Bernard de Clairvaux) 113–14, 115–16
Bernstein, Basil 59, 65, 147
Bhindi, Narottam 101
Bible 88, 129–30 (*see also* Adam and Eve)
Bier, Melinda C 89
Billington, Tom 105
Biott, Colin 153, 154, 155
Black, Paul 172
Blair, Tony 27
Bloom, Allan 9
Blumberg, Sherry 64
boarding (residential) schools 115
Bottery, Mike 101, 116, 153
Bowker, John 54
Bowring-Carr, Christopher 101
Britain (*see* United Kingdom)
Bryk, Anthony S 154

Buber, Martin 1, 8–10, 11, 18, 19, 21, 23, 28, 35–7, 40, 47, 50, 51, 57, 75–7, 78–81, 82–5, 86–91, 100, 105–6, 115, 123–4, 154, 165
Buddhism 69, 146
bullying 31, 175
Bush, George W 101, 102

Cage, John 122–4
Cain, James 54
Calvinism (*see* Christianity)
Cartesian philosophy (*see* Descartes)
Catholicism (*see* Christianity)
Cavalli-Sforza, Luigi Luca 161
character education 89 (*see also* personal, social and health education)
Chater, Mark 2, 10, 12, 90, 105
Chaucer, Geoffrey x–xi
Cherry, Frances E 136
Children's Plan (DCSF 2007) 77, 81
China (*see* Hong Kong)
Chitty, Clyde 48, 105
Christianity 3, 26, 54, 65, 68–9, 102, 125, 129, 145–7
Church of England (*see* Christianity)
circle time 69, 99, 185
Cissna, Kenneth N 100
Cline, Tony 48
commercialisation 161
communes 115
community xv, 1, 18, 21, 23–46, 47, 91, 153, 160–1
computers (*see* Information and Communication Technology)
confidentiality 137
Conford, Philip 5
Cooper, Robin 53
Copley, Terence 15–16
Corbin, Juliet 21
courage 18, 136, 152–5
Craft, Anna 58
creativity 21, 36, 47, 50–1, 56–63,

70–2, 103, 151–2, 160–1
Crichton, Michèle 48

Dahl, Robert A 107
Dalin, Per 21, 143
Daniels, Harry 56, 59, 65–6, 168–9
Dante Alighieri 14, 145
Darwin, Charles 161–2
Darwinism (*see* Charles Darwin)
Davydov, Vasily 56, 59
Davie, Grace 17, 170
Davies, Geraint 14
Dead Sea 89–90
Dearey, Paul 10, 16–17
death 16, 19, 84, 91, 96, 98–9 (*see also* suicide)
Delors, Jacques 13
democracy 20, 103, 107, 155
Descartes, René 3–5, 7
design and technology 61
Dewey, John 87, 90
dialogue xv, 1, 18–19, 21, 34–5, 36, 47, 50, 57, 75–100, 107, 113, 121, 151, 160–1
Diogenes 3
discipline 60–2
Dodier, Nicolas 21
Donovan, Peter 52
Dower, Nigel 8, 25, 57
drama 64 (*see also* performance)
Dryden, Windy 49
dualism 2–5, 11, 133–4, 142
Duignan, Patrick 101,
Dunne, Joseph 2, 13, 17–18
Durkheim, Émile 106

Eco, Umberto 13, 58
Edwards, Stephen D 8
Egan, David 16
Elton Report (DES 1989) 137
emotion 5–6, 8
Emoto, Masaru 3
Engels, Frederick 1, 6, 8, 25, 104
Engeström, Yrjö 56

England (*see* United Kingdom)
English 55, 61, 64, 65, 66, 67, 75, 99, 168, 173, 183
Epstein, Debbie 23, 34
equality 20
Erricker, Clive 7
ethnographic research 20, 149–50
ethos xv, 15–18
Every Child Matters (DfES 2004a) 13, 91
examinations (*see* assessment)

faith 13
Fajerman, Lina 77
family xiv, 1, 12, 23, 28, 30, 32, 37, 43–4, 45, 56, 57, 63, 71–2, 77, 80, 81, 90, 94, 98, 104, 111, 121, 127–8, 132, 133, 134, 154, 171 (*see also in loco parentis*)
fear 13
Fehn, Sverre 81, 91
Feldman, Marcus W 161
Fergusson, David 8, 25, 57
Feuerbach, Ludwig 6, 25, 27
Fielding, Michael 27, 172
Fines, John 100
Flutter, Julia 154
followership 20
food (*see* household, *see also* personal, social and health education)
Forsyth, Bill 113
France 12
Francis, Leslie 3, 12, 14
Frazer, James George 138
Frederickson, Norah 48
Freud, Sigmund 11, 29
Friedman, Maurice 9, 18, 19, 79, 82, 83–4, 86, 87, 88–9
friendship xv, 1, 13, 17, 19, 23–46, 47, 123, 153, 160–1, 166, 170–1
Furlong, John 150

Gadamer, Hans-Georg 7
Gardner, Howard 76

Germany 83, 85, 142
Giraudoux, Jean 135
Glatzer, Nahum N 83
globalisation 17
God, or god 4, 9, 11, 15, 17, 54, 59, 68, 106, 145, 161
Goethe, Johann Wolfgang von 107
golem 8, 85, 123–4
Gormley, Antony 162
governing bodies (of schools) 103, 111, 119, 139, 159
Greece 33, 125, 138
Greenfield, Thomas 101
Grey, Mary 105
grounded theory 20–1
Grove, Julie 48
Gryn, Rabbi Hugo 22
Guignon, Charles 9–10

Hall, John 3, 12, 147
Hanks, William F 49, 147
Hartland, Ian 14
Hatfield, Elizabeth 49, 113, 173–4
Hawkesworth, Mary 25
Hay, David 6, 7, 10, 13, 20, 102
Hayes, Denis 29
health (*see* personal, social and health education)
Hedley, Jeanette 13
Hegel, Georg Wilhelm Friedrich 4, 11, 25, 80–1, 84
Held, David 33
heuristic research (*see* phenomenology in research)
Hey, Valerie 30, 34
Hick, John 21
Hillman, James 91
Hinduism 54, 69, 146
Hinnells, John 44
Hippo (Hippon) 3
history 55, 60, 66
Hobbes, Thomas 5, 7, 102
Hogg, James 102
homework 56, 87

Hong Kong 22, 166
Hopkins, David 16, 94
Hopper, Edward 12
Hornby, Garry 55
Hornby, Nick 29
household 114–7
Houston, Graham 52
Houston, Paul D 101
Howie, Gillian 25
Hoyle, Eric 145
Huws Jones, Vanessa 3, 14, 16, 94, 96
Hull, John 77
humanism 16, 18 (*see also* secular, www.humanism.org.uk)
humility 124, 125–32, 133, 136, 139, 150–2
Hutcheson, Ernest 123

Ibsen, Henrik Johan 122
idealism 4–5
imagination (*see* creativity)
inclusion 9, 13, 21, 39–40, 47–50, 51–6, 65–9, 72, 82–3, 160–1
Information and Communication Technology (ICT, computing and related technologies including television) 55–6, 64, 115 (*see also* Luddism)
in loco parentis (in the place of the parents) 118 (*see also* family)
Ipgrave, Julia 77, 85
ipsative assessment (*see* assessment)
Ireland (Irish Republic) 151

Jackson, Robert 7
James, Sarah 81, 89
Jerusalem 83, 85
Judaism 69, 125, 138, 146
Jung, Hwa Yol 25
justice 18, 94–5

Kant, Immanuel 4, 118
Kaurismäki, Aki 142
Kelly, George 49, 153, 167

kibbutzim 115
Kim, Sebastian 27
Korczak, Janusz 35–7
kindness 49, 136, 155–6
Kipling, Rudyard 151
Kirkpatrick, Frank 27
Klass, Dennis 56–7, 91, 113
Kollontai, Pauline 27

Lacey, Penny 154
languages (*see* modern foreign languages)
Lave, Jean 27, 49, 56, 76, 147
Lawrence-Lightfoot, Sara 23, 36, 55, 81, 132, 154
leadership xv, 20, 21
learning xv, 18, 21
Leavis, Frank Raymond 85–6, 90
Leavis, Queenie Dorothy 86
Levinas, Emmanuel 6, 82
Lewis, Jeff 29
Lindon, Jennie 77
Lipman, Matthew 85
Liszt, Franz (Ferenc) 122–4
literacy (*see* English)
Logan, John 96,
Lokhorst, Gert-Jan 3, 4
loneliness 13, 101, 102–3, 104–13, 160–1 (*see also* alienation, solitude)
Luddism 64 (*see also* Information and Communication Technology)
Lynch, Sandra 23, 29

MacBeath, John 91
McCutcheon, Russell 52, 148, 155
McDonald, Joseph 143, 155
McGregor, Gordon P 162
McIntosh, Esther 8, 27
Macmurray, John 1, 8–10, 13, 19, 21, 23, 26, 27–9, 30–1, 32–7, 40, 45, 55, 57, 60–2, 76, 79, 82, 101, 106, 115, 117, 129, 133, 148, 153, 156, 163, 170, 173
McNiff, Jean 153

Macpherson, Crawford Brough 106–7
Madshus, Eva 81, 91
magnanimity 20, 47, 72–3, 103, 116, 124, 125–32, 133, 151, 160–1
Major, John 105
Maritain, Jacques 30, 36
Marks, William E 3
Marland, Michael 121
Martel, Harry 1, 6
Marx, Karl 1, 6, 7, 8, 11, 12, 25, 60, 84, 104, 105, 106, 110
Mason, Marilyn 5–6, 16
materialism 2, 5–7
mathematics 26, 28, 61, 65, 173, 184
Matoes, Abba 117
Mead, George Herbert 7, 87
megalopsychia, megalopsuchia (*see* magnanimity)
Mendelssohn, Felix (Jakob Ludwig Felix Mendelssohn-Bartholdy) 15
Mendes-Flohr, Paul 83
Messiou, Kyriaki 49
methodology (*see* research)
Mill, James 106
Mill, John Stuart 106–7
mirrors 138, 144–5
Mitscherlich, Alexander 31, 141–2
Mitscherlich, Margarete 31, 141–2
modern foreign languages 55, 75
modesty 136, 150–2
Mosley, Jenny 99 (*see also* circle time)
Moustakas, Clark 20, 148–9
Munn, Pamela 55, 154
Murray, Chic 113
music 55, 60, 64, 91, 100, 118, 120, 122 (*see also* performance)
Myers, Kate 53, 118
mysite.wanadoo-members.co.uk/ friendsfoodfaith/fffindex.htm (*see* Greg Smith)

Nehru, Jawaharlal (Pandit) 54
Nesbitt, Eleanor 2
Newman, Randy 102

Newton, Colin 154
Nichol, Jon 100
Nietzsche, Friedrich 5, 60
Noddings, Nell 8, 23, 34–5, 107
non-religious (*see* secular, *see also* humanism)
Norway 12
numeracy (*see* mathematics)
Nursing and Midwifery Council (NMC) 81–2
Nussbaum, Martha 26
Nye, Rebecca 10, 13, 20

Oakeshott, Michael 85
Oancea, Alice 150
O'Hanlon, Christine 153, 154
Olson, Carl 53
openness to criticism 136, 150–2
originality (*see* creativity)
Ota, Cathy 2, 10, 12, 90, 105
Owen, Nick 58

Paganini, Niccolò 123–4
Palestine 90
parents (*see* family)
peer review 150–2
performance 103
performativity (*see* performance)
personal, social and health education 10–11, 70–1, 89, 96, 98, 154
Pfeutze, Paul E 87
phenomenology in research 148–50
photography 138, 144, 154
physical education 64
Plato 24, 27, 144–5, 162
poetry 144–5
policy 1, 12–14, 47–8, 50–1, 77, 81, 85, 119, 121, 136, 143, 150, 161–2, 172
politics (*see* policy)
Popper, Karl Raimund 141
positivism 141
pride (*see* magnanimity)
Priestley, Jack 2

Pring, Richard   48, 85, 136, 137, 147, 148, 149–50, 154, 155
prison   115
privacy   51, 102 (*see also* solitude)
Protestantism   (*see* Christianity)
psychoanalysis   141–2
psychology   141–2
Quakerism (the Religious Society of Friends)   29

racism and antiracism   (*see* equality)
Ranson, Stuart   48
Rawls, John   26
reading   (*see* English)
registration   95–6
relativism   16
religion   xv, 1, 5, 12, 13, 14, 15–18, 28, 53–4
Religious Education (RE)   55, 68–9, 146–7, 168, 169, 183
Religious Society of Friends   (*see* Quakerism)
research   21–2, 135–63 (*see also* ethnographic research, phenomenology in research)
Research Assessment Exercise (RAE)   20, 150
Research Excellence Framework (REF)   150
respect   136, 152–5
restorative justice   (*see* justice)
Ribbins, Peter   101
Richard of Bury   191
Riley, Kathryn   133
Roberts, Paul   50, 51
Robinson, Ken   50
Robinson, Simon   3, 10–11
Rogers, Carl Ransom   9, 100
Rolff, Hans-Gunter   143
Roman Catholicism   (*see* Christianity)
Rose, Nikolas   32
Rosen, Charles   15–16, 122–3
Roseneil, Sasha   29, 31, 132, 170
Rousseau, Jean-Jacques   9

Royal Opera House, London   51
Rudduck, Jean   154, 172
Rudge, Linda   xiii, 146
Rumi (Jala al-Din al-Rumi)   xiv
Rush, Christopher   120
Russell, Bertrand   54
Rust, Val   21, 143
Ryan, Alan   87

Sacks, Jonathan   7, 162–3
Salamanca Statement   13, 47
Salmon Line   36, 63, 166, 167–8, 182 (*see also* Phillida Salmon)
Salmon, Phillida   105, 152–3 (*see also* Salmon Line)
Samier, Eugenie A   13, 86, 156
Schaeder, Grete   83
Schiller, Friedrich von   13, 104
Schilpp, Paul Arthur   82, 86, 87
Schneider, Barbara   154
Schön, Donald A   87
school management committees   (*see* governing bodies)
Schreiner, Peter   17
Schumpeter, Joseph A   107
Schutz, Alfred   52
science   55, 67, 71, 182
Scotland   138 (*see also* United Kingdom)
secular   5, 8, 15, 17, 54,
Seldon, Anthony   105
Selsam, Howard   1, 6
Sennett, Richard   8, 9, 11, 103, 118, 122–4
sexism   (*see* equality)
sexuality   34, 81, 82, 114, 115, 154
Shakespeare, William   102, 122
siblings   (*see* family)
Silverman, David   21, 148
Simon, Ernst   82
Simpsons, The   52–3
Sinatra, Frank (Francis Albert)   102
sincerity   20, 121, 135–6, 144, 147–50
Sink, Christopher A   12

Skinner, Burrhus Frederic 141,
Smalley, Sarah 48
Smith, Adam 7
Smith, Greg 170–1
Smith, Martin 75, 83
Smith, Wilfred Cantwell 15
social networking (*see* Information
 and Communication Technology)
social studies 55
Socrates 24
Socratic methods (*see* Socrates)
Sokolow, Stephen L 101
solitude 92–3, 102, 113–17, 133,
 160–1 (*see also* privacy)
Spark, Muriel 120
Special Educational Needs (SEN)
 (*see* inclusion)
special needs (*see* inclusion)
Spender, Dale 56
Spender, Stephen 123
Spinoza, Benedictus (Baruch) 4, 11
sport (*see* physical education)
spragging 94–5
Steiner, Rudolf 45–6
Stern, Axel 20
Stern, Julian 1, 8, 19, 20, 27, 28, 48,
 50, 54, 55, 56, 64, 76, 81, 82, 89, 91,
 100, 103, 107, 120, 136, 142–3, 147–8,
 161, 167, 168, 170, 171–2, 173, 174
Stern-Gillet, Suzanne 128
Stewart, William 16
Stirner, Max (Johann Kaspar Schmidt)
 6, 102
Stoll, Louise 53
Stone, Mary 96,
Storey, John 153
Strauss, Anselm L 21
Streisand, Barbra 102
suicide 106, 107 (*see also* death)
Sweden 151
Swinton, John 2

Tarrant, Tony 154
Taylor, Charles 9–10, 11, 12, 19, 20,

54, 59, 86–7, 91, 162
Taylor, Jeremy 3, 147
Teece, Geoff 53–4
Thatcher, Adrian 3, 12, 14
toilets (*see* household, *see also*
 personal, social and health
 education)
Topping, Keith 55
tradition xiii
Trevarthen, Colwyn 57
Trilling, Lionel 104, 105, 107, 120,
 124, 135–6, 144, 147
trust 136, 152–5
truth, truthfulness 14, 17–18, 21, 136,
 155–6
ugliness 13

United Kingdom 3, 10, 12, 13, 20, 22,
 32, 48, 50, 60, 77, 81, 89, 114, 166,
 174
United Nations Convention on the
 Rights of the Child (UNCRC, UN
 1989, UNICEF 2008) 77
United Nations Declaration of the
 Rights of the Child (UN 1959) 77
United Nations Declaration on the
 Elimination of All Forms of Intoler-
 ance and Discrimination Based on
 Religion or Belief (*see*
 www2.ohchr.org/english/law/
 religion.htm)
United Nations Declaration on the
 Rights of Persons Belonging to
 National or Ethnic, Religious and
 Linguistic Minorities (*see*
 www2.ohchr.org/english/law/
 minorities.htm)
USA 12, 77, 89, 97, 158, 166

Vernon, Mark 29, 113–15
Vincent, Carol 55, 154
virtues 136–56 (*see also* courage,
 humility, kindness, modesty,
 openness to criticism, respect,

sincerity, trust, truthfulness)
Vygotsky, Lev 21, 59

Walford, Geoffrey 48
Walker, Daniel Pickering 54
Wallace, Mike 145
Waller, Willard 81
war 105
Watson, Brenda 16
Watson, Jacqueline 90
Webb, Diana 113–15, 115–17, 191
Wegerif, Rupert 80–1
Wenger, Etienne 27, 49, 56, 76, 147
West-Burnham, John 3, 14, 16, 94, 96, 101
White, John 85–6
Whitehead, Jack 153
Wilde, Oscar 120, 135–6, 144, 145
Wiliam, Dylan 172
Willes, Mary 121–2
Winnicot, Donald Woods 9–10
Wittgenstein, Ludwig 2, 7, 148

Wolfendale, Sheila 55, 154
Wong Ping Ho 2, 12
Wood, Neal 102
Woods, Glenys 101
Wright, Andrew 7, 13, 14
www2.ohchr.org/english/law/religion.htm 13
www2.ohchr.org/english/law/minorities.htm 13
www.answers.com/topic/randy-newman?cat=entertainment 102

Yeats, William Butler 106, 123
York Minster 66, 68, 99
Yovel, Yirmiyahu 11
Yvenes, Marianne 81, 91

Zoroastrianism 44
Zumthor, Peter xiii–xiv, 12, 135, 140, 142, 156, 160